Progress in Tourism, Recreation and Hospitality Management
Volume Two

Progress in Tourism, Recreation and Hospitality Management

Published in association with the Department of Management Studies for Tourism and Hotel Industries, University of Surrey, UK.

Progress in Tourism, Recreation and Hospitality Management

Volume 2

Edited by
C. P. Cooper

JOHN WILEY & SONS
Chichester • New York • Brisbane • Toronto • Singapore

First published in Great Britain in 1990 by Belhaven Press

Reprinted in February 1994 by John Wiley & Sons Ltd,
Baffins Lane, Chichester,
West Sussex PO19 1UD, England
National   Chichester (0243) 779777
International   + 44 243 779777

Other Wiley Editorial Offices

John Wiley & Sons, Inc., 605 Third Avenue,
New York, NY 10158-0012, USA

Jacaranda Wiley Ltd, 33 Park Road, Milton,
Queensland 4064, Australia

John Wiley & Sons (Canada) Ltd, 22 Worcester Road,
Rexdale, Ontario M9W 1L1, Canada

John Wiley & Sons (SEA) Pte Ltd, 37 Jalan Pemimpin # 05-04,
Block B, Union Industrial Building, Singapore 2057

Library of Congress Cataloging-in-Publication Data:

A CIP catalog record for this book is available from the
Library of Congress

British Library Cataloguing in Publication Data:

A catalogue record for this book is available from the
British Library

ISBN 0–471–94510–2

Typeset by Joshua Associates Limited, Oxford
Printed and bound in Great Britain by
Antony Rowe Ltd, Chippenham, Wiltshire

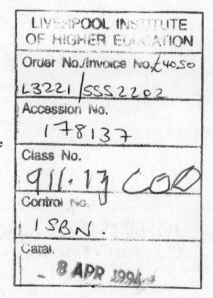

Contents

List of contributors

Professor Brian Archer
Department of Management Studies for Tourism and Hotel Industries
University of Surrey
Guildford GU2 5XH
UK

Brian Archer is a Pro-Vice-Chancellor of the University of Surrey and Head of the Department of Management Studies for Tourism and Hotel Industries. His particular research interest is in planning and development and the economics of tourism.

Mr Francis Buttle
Department of Hotel, Restaurant and Travel Administration
University of Massachusetts
Amherst
Massachusetts 01003
USA

Francis Buttle is a lecturer in marketing and has been involved in marketing research, management and education for more than eighteen years across three continents. He is author of the textbook *Hotel and Foodservice Marketing: A Managerial Approach* and has written some 70 articles.

David Gilbert
Department of Management Studies for Tourism and Hotel Industries
University of Surrey
Guildford GU2 5XH
UK

David Gilbert is marketing lecturer and course tutor for the University of Surrey's Diploma/MSc in Tourism Marketing. His research interests relate to aspects of marketing and he is currently examining the factors of consumer behaviour in tourism.

Dr Frank Go
Faculty of Management
University of Calgary
2500 University Drive N.W.
Calgary
Alberta T2N 1N4
Canada

Frank Go is a consultant, lecturer and author who specializes in business intelligence on 'away-from-home' markets, including travel, lodging, leisure time and foodservice industries.

Dr Yvonne Guerrier
Department of Management Studies for Tourism and Hotel Industries
University of Surrey
Guildford GU2 5XH
UK

Yvonne Guerrier is a lecturer in organizational behaviour. Her research interests include managers' careers and management development and work flexibility, especially in the hospitality industry.

K Michael Haywood
School of Hotel and Food Administration
University of Guelph
Ontario N1G 2W1
Canada

K Michael Haywood is Associate Professor at the University of Guelph. He is a writer, lecturer and adviser on marketing and tourism management.

Mr Alan Jefferson
British Tourist Authority
Thames Tower
Blacks Road
London W6 9EC
UK

Alan Jefferson became marketing manager of the British Tourist Authority in 1975 and director of marketing in 1981. He now has responsibility for the marketing of Britain internationally.

Mr Michael Kipps
Department of Management Studies for Tourism and Hotel Industries
University of Surrey
Guildford GU2 5XH
UK

Michael Kipps teaches in the field of applied science. His research interests focus around the application of scientific method to problems in the food-service industry.

Dr John Latham
Department of Management Studies for Tourism and Hotel Industries
University of Surrey
Guildford GU2 5XH
UK

John Latham is a mathematician. His special interest is tourism statistics, particularly the methodological aspects of data collection.

Mr Andrew Lockwood
Department of Management Studies for Tourism and Hotel Industries
University of Surrey
Guildford GU2 5XH
UK

Andrew Lockwood lectures in the operations management aspects of hotels and catering. His research interests include manpower management and work flexibility in hotels and the definition and measurement of service quality.

Mr Mohit Mehrotta
Department of Hotel, Restaurant and Travel Administration
University of Massachusetts
Amherst
Massachusetts 01003
USA

Mohit Mehrotta is a graduate student and research assistant in the Department of Hotel, Restaurant and Travel Administration, University of Massachusetts, Amherst, Massachusetts, USA. He previously worked in the Indian hotel industry. He has a Bachelor's degree in Commerce and diplomas in Hotel Management and Catering Technology and Advanced Hospitality Management.

Dr Lisle S Mitchell
Department of Geography
University of South Carolina
Columbia
South Carolina 29208
USA

Lisle S Mitchell is Professor of Geography at the University of South Carolina. His geographic interests in tourism research centre on bibliographic surveys, methods of delineating tourism regions and tourism development and planning.

Mr Michael R Nowlis
Institut de Management Hotelier International
Cornell/ESSEC
7 Le Campus
95033 Cergy-Pontoise Cedex
France

Michael Nowlis is currently Deputy Director of the Institut de Management Hotelier International. His research interests include applications of technology in the catering field and the evolution of consumer behaviour in the food service industries.

Dr Paul Reynolds
Department of Hospitality Management
Hong Kong Polytechnic
Hung Hom
Kowloon
Hong Kong

Paul Reynolds is a senior lecturer in the Department of Hospitality Management at Hong Kong Polytechnic. He is currently researching multinational hotel groups and their strategies in China.

Mr Cordell W Riley
Bermuda Department of Tourism
Global House
43 Church Street
Hamilton HM12
Bermuda

Cordell Riley is statistical and research officer for the Bermuda Department of Tourism.

Dr Gareth Shaw
Department of Geography
Exeter University
Amory Building
Rennes Drive
Exeter EX4 4RS
UK

Gareth Shaw is a senior lecturer in geography and joint director of the Tourism Research Group at the University of Exeter.

Dr Pauline J Sheldon
School of Travel Industry Management
University of Hawaii at Manoa,
George Hall
2560 Campus Road
Honolulu
Hawaii 96822
USA

Pauline Sheldon is associate professor of tourism at the School of Travel Industry Management, University of Hawaii. Her research interests include tourism demand modelling and forecasting, tourism information systems and tour packaging.

Ms Julie Sheppard
Department of Management Studies for Tourism and Hotel Industries
University of Surrey
Guildford GU2 5XH
UK

Julie Sheppard is currently working as a consultant to the food and catering industry. She has held posts at Manchester and Bradford Universities, Channel 4 Television and the London Food Commission. She has written widely on food hygiene matters.

Mr Christopher G Smith
Department of Management Studies for Tourism and Hotel Industries
University of Surrey
Guildford GU2 5XH
UK

Christopher G Smith is a lecturer in food and beverage management and a specialist in food production operations. His research interests include developments in catering equipment and the catering industry and the application of computers to catering operations.

Professor Richard V Smith
Department of Geography
Miami University
Oxford
Ohio 45056
USA

Richard V Smith is Professor and Chair of the Department of Geography, Miami University (Ohio). Tourism interests focus on delimiting tourism regions, studying the structure of tourism within identified regions, planning for tourism and consideration of tourism as a factor in an area's economic future.

Mrs Melanie Storey
Department of Management Studies for Tourism and Hotel Industries
University of Surrey
Guildford GU2 5XH
UK

Melanie Storey is a geographer with extensive experience in hotel management and catering.

Dr James Thomson
Department of Management Studies for Tourism and Hotel Industries
University of Surrey
Guildford GU2 5XH
UK

James Thomson has worked in the field of food-related research for many years, and is the author of many papers in this area of study.

Dr Alan Williams
Exeter University
Amory Building
Rennes Drive
Exeter EX4 4RS
UK

Alan Williams is joint director of the Tourism Research Group at the University of Exeter.

Editorial preface

This is the second volume of *Progress in Tourism, Recreation and Hospitality Management*, an annual publication designed to provide an authoritative international review of research and major issues of current concern in the fields of tourism, recreation and hospitality management. The concept of Progress is to divide these fields into subfields of specialization and to publish annually a number of reviews as well as shorter contributions covering particular regional approaches or views of practitioners. For the first two or three issues, contributions have been invited from authors who are internationally recognized in their specialist field, but for later issues contributions to Progress from readers will be welcomed.

It is intended that Progress will provide leadership in research and become the established publication for researchers, students and staff in academic institutions as well as a source of reference and orientation for practitioners in both corporate and public organizations world-wide. In many respects, by basing Progress in the University of Surrey's Department of Management Studies for Tourism and Hotel Industries, the achievement of these aims is facilitated. The Department has a long pedigree in tourism, recreation and hospitality and has been influential in both formulating and contributing to the body of knowledge in these fields, not only by research but also through course development. The complement of experts in the Department have been generous with their advice on the commissioning and reviewing of contributions for Progress.

Progress will provide 'state-of-the-art' reviews of research at the leading edge, while also in the early issues relating recent material to the more historic milestones of the fields' development. It is expected that the pages of Progress will discuss and reflect the emergent issues and developments which will shape the progress of research in tourism, recreation and hospitality in the 1990s.

Progress of research and the dissemination of its findings have been accelerated by a number of recent developments. New courses in tourism, recreation and hospitality are being launched and new academic departments are being formed across the globe. New professional bodies are emerging—in particular the International Academy for the Study of Tourism (Butler and Wall, 1989) and the International Academy for Hospitality Research, supported by a range of new synoptic texts and journals (such as the *Journal of Contemporary Hospitality Management*). Conferences too are being held with tourism, recreation or hospitality as the theme (Var, 1989; Page, 1989), and there is a healthy increase in papers from researchers in these subject areas at other conferences (Teye, 1989). Finally, across all three of these areas information technology continues to transform research opportunities and the exchange of information.

Funding for research is increasingly being sought from the private sector, thereby hastening cooperative research and paving the way for new industrial partnerships with academics and their institutions (Shafer, 1987). However, these arrangements often experience teething problems stemming from stereo-types of the impractical and non-commercial researcher set against the industrialist, who is seen as only interested in short-term applied research and who may raise objections to the dissemination and exchange of information which has been gathered for a commercial sponsor (Beaman and Meis, 1987). Yet these problems are not irreconcilable. After all, industry has a vested interest in the future and in innovation, while the researcher wishes his work to be of value (Shafer, 1987).

The danger, of course, is that research becomes industry dominated rather than industry sensitive and any attempt to draw together a conceptual base or body of knowledge is neglected. In hospitality, for example, some argue that research should be industry driven and that current knowledge is insufficient to build a conceptual or theoretical framework (Littlejohn, 1989). Yet until such a framework is developed research progress will be handicapped and risks becoming a hostage to the rapidly changing priorities of industry. What is needed for the 1990s is a long-term strategic research vision to select, sort and seek support for key research areas (Shafer, 1987). This may well run alongside the predominantly industry-led research; indeed, the two sectors are likely to be complementary.

Littlejohn (1989) suggests that in broad terms these research areas are already emerging: research in the physical and natural sciences applied to hospitality—examples of this can be seen in applied nutrition and hazard analysis; the application and honing of research techniques and thinking from the social sciences applied to tourism, recreation and hospitality (Slattery, 1983; Smith, 1989); and the gradual formation of a body of knowledge in these subject areas (Nailon, 1982).

Through the pages of this new publication we aim to progress these fields 'into a systematic and cumulative body of knowledge' (Goeldner, 1988) by drawing together research material and allowing teachers, researchers and practitioners to keep up to date with research findings, to profit from previous work and, through their contributions to Progress, so to build effectively upon it.

Chris Cooper
University of Surrey
December 1989

References

Beaman, J., Meis, S., 1987, 'Managing the research function for effective policy formulation and decision making', in Ritchie, J. R. B. and Goeldner, C. R. (eds), *Travel, Tourism and Hospitality Research: A Handbook for Managers and Researchers*, Wiley, New York, pp. 34–44.

Butler, R. W., Wall, G., 1989, 'Formation of the international academy for the study of tourism', *Annals of Tourism Research*, 16(4): pp. 572–4.

Goeldner, C. R., 1988, 'The evaluation of tourism as an industry and discipline', paper presented to *Teaching Tourism in the 1990s*, Conference, University of Surrey, proceedings forthcoming.

Littlejohn, D., 1989, 'Hospitality research—philosophies progress', in Teare, R. (ed.), *Current Issues in Services Research*, Dorset Institute of Higher Education, Poole, pp. 132–51.

Nailon, P., 1982, 'Theory in hospitality management', *International Journal of Hospitality Management*, 1(3): pp. 135–43.

Page, S. J., 1989, 'Geographical approach to international tourism', *Tourism Management*, 10(1): pp. 74–5.

Ritchie, J. R. B., 1987, 'Roles of research in tourism management', in Ritchie, J. R. B., Goeldner, C. R. (eds), *Travel, Tourism and Hospitality Research: A Handbook for Managers and Researchers*, Wiley, New York, pp. 13–21.

Shafer, E. L., 1987, 'Technology, tourism and the 21st Century', *Tourism Management*, 8(2): pp. 179–82.

Slattery, P., 1983, 'Social scientific methodology and hospitality management', *International Journal of Hospitality Management*, 2(1): pp. 9–14.

Smith, S. L. J., 1989, *Tourism Analysis: A Handbook*, Longman, London.

Teye, V., 1989, 'Geography and tourism at the AAG meeting', *Annals of Tourism Research*, 16(4): pp. 567–9.

Var, T., 1989, 'Tourism research: expanding boundaries', *Annals of Tourism Research*, 16(4): pp. 569–71.

1 Conceptual issues in the meaning of tourism

D. C. Gilbert

Introduction

Tourism as a domain of study has, in the main, provided descriptive analysis based on the 'world view' of various authors. The task for the future may have to be linked to the principal premise that there is a need to develop a deeper understanding of the consumer of the tourism product. Contemporary tourism theory has to accept that narrow operative views of tourism behaviour may be inappropriate. The scope, content, and role of being a tourist is often misperceived.

The traditional simplistic view of tourist behaviour could be rejected and replaced with a new understanding of the tourist as a consumer who demonstrates particular actions of behaviour. These actions involve the needs, motivation, attitudes, values, personality and perceptions which all lead to specific preferences for tourism-related activities.

To approach the subject in a scientific manner it is not necessary to establish facts, test a hypothesis or construct some *a priori* theory. Initially it is important to identify the peculiar character and concepts of tourism as a particular phenomenon. However, as a phenomenon it has meaning but no substantial property, no real form or ways of changing. It relies on theorists to attribute a particular nature, and to identify component parts. In order to provide a definition of tourism we need to examine the construction of different ideas or meanings emanating from the current practice of industry and the contemporary ideas of theorists.

The work of theorists has to be a filtering out of the unimportant from an array of valid attributes which make up the daily routines of what we currently term tourism. From these attributes we can develop universal statements and explanations. The definitions should therefore emanate from the process of tourism and be grounded in its nature. This chapter recognizes that tourism is concerned with economic, epistemological and social issues and it attempts to provide analysis of the conceptual basis for these perspectives.

Scope, nature and meaning of tourism

The underlying objective of this chapter is to highlight the need for more development of a consumer behaviour approach within tourism. It is believed that extra emphasis must be placed on a social action, activity-based under-standing of tourism behaviour within the wider field of recreation. As a starting point it is necessary to ground this examination of tourism in an understanding of just what it is that we define and label as tourism.

Various definitions, concepts and descriptions of tourism arise from the multidisciplinary nature of the topic. As a relatively new subject area it has drawn on other disciplines in order to develop theoretical and empirical roots applied to tourism as a phenomenon. This has led to a body of knowledge and domain of study which have been formed from the melting-pot of Geography, Economics, Sociology, Psychology, Business Science and Anthropology.

Within these disciplines, some tourism theorists work from the perspective of believing that either supply (those interested in the technical or economic aspects of measurement) or demand (those utilizing social action or a beha-vioural approach of understanding) is the more fruitful basis for academic activity. Modern marketing philosophy emphasizes the need to understand the consumer through demand analysis prior to creating the appropriate supply of the product. In planning, marketing has to collect information from both areas so as to assess consumer needs, trends, market worth, competition etc. When we speak of tourism we need to remember that inherent in the term is a mean-ing which constitutes both tourist and industry. Each of these associations renders the meaning of tourism unclear. This is because neither is discrete, unambiguous or easily identified. Tourism encompasses the act of a tour and of travel, providing meanings of action within the concept of tourism as well as the more normal use of tourism as a noun.

The use of the term tourism has led to a range of complex meanings which have become associated with: the movement of people; a sector of the economy; an identifiable industry; services which need to be provided for travellers. Wahab (1971) views this complex combination as a *system* that relates to the sociosphere and interrelated industries and trades. Much of what we define as tourism has its roots in early economic requirements where income and expenditure figures were gathered in order to carry out economic analysis. This is less straightforward than it seems, as there has to be a distinc-tion made between those services and goods provided solely for tourist consumption as opposed to other types of consumers. If we recognize that retailing, hospitality, transport, attractions etc. supply other markets than just tourists then we can understand why it is difficult to isolate resources, revenues and returns which are attributable solely to tourism. The problem we face with tourism is that in defining its industry we attempt to isolate a particular type of consumer (i.e. the tourist as opposed to the local shopper, local traveller etc.) and we do not focus on the wider aspects of the provider or producer of the service.

The problem in the development of meaning for the word tourism is that it is used as a single term to designate a variety of concepts. The essence of tourism is to be found in a combination of factors conveying ideas of both industry and tourism typologies. The confusion and ignorance relating to the combination of these factors can only be resolved when a clearer exposition is given of the subject area.

The dimension and nature of the tourism industry provides for a complex set of interrelating services for the tourist. Figure 1 indicates the range of inputs required to sustain the necessary set of services for a modern tourism industry. The dimension of the tourism industry includes the core product components of transport, attractions, accommodation and catering. In addition there are the peripheral public and private services which are necessary to facilitate the overall operation of the tourism industry.

Definitions of tourism

There are various definitions of tourism which can be placed in the context of their conceptual basis. The particular concern and perspective of each individual theorist has led to the evolution of a number of different definitions for the phenomenon of tourism.

If we begin our understanding of tourism by reference to *Webster's Dictionary* we find that the term *tourist* is said to be derived from the word 'tour', meaning 'a journey at which one returns to the starting point; a circular trip usually for business, pleasure or education during which various places are visited and for which an itinerary is usually planned'. Such a definition provides for a number of motives for travel, each of which creates different market needs. Many of the definitions, which have been commonly referred to, emphasize the tourist as either an object or a unit of expenditure rather than a reflexive, subject being.

In outlining a number of definitions which have been used to clarify the underlying concepts of tourism it is sensible to identify how other theorists have classified the subject. Burkhart and Medlik (1974) and later Heeley (1980) approached the classification of definitions of tourism from the premise that there are two main groups within which definitions broadly fall. The first area identified is that of conceptual definitions which attempt to elucidate the essential nature of tourism as an activity. The second group comprised technical definitions within which there are a designation of types of tourist and of what constitutes tourism activity. The technical definitions allow various agencies to compile statistical measurements of activity. Buck (1978) followed by Leiper (1979) expanded the typologies of conceptual and technical to include the addition of holistic definitions which embrace *the whole essence* of the subject area and allow for both an interdisciplinary and multidisciplinary approach.

A review of the literature reveals that technical rather than conceptual definitions were utilized in the initial attempts to clarify the phenomenon of tourism. Because of this we find many early definitions of tourism ignore its social nature.

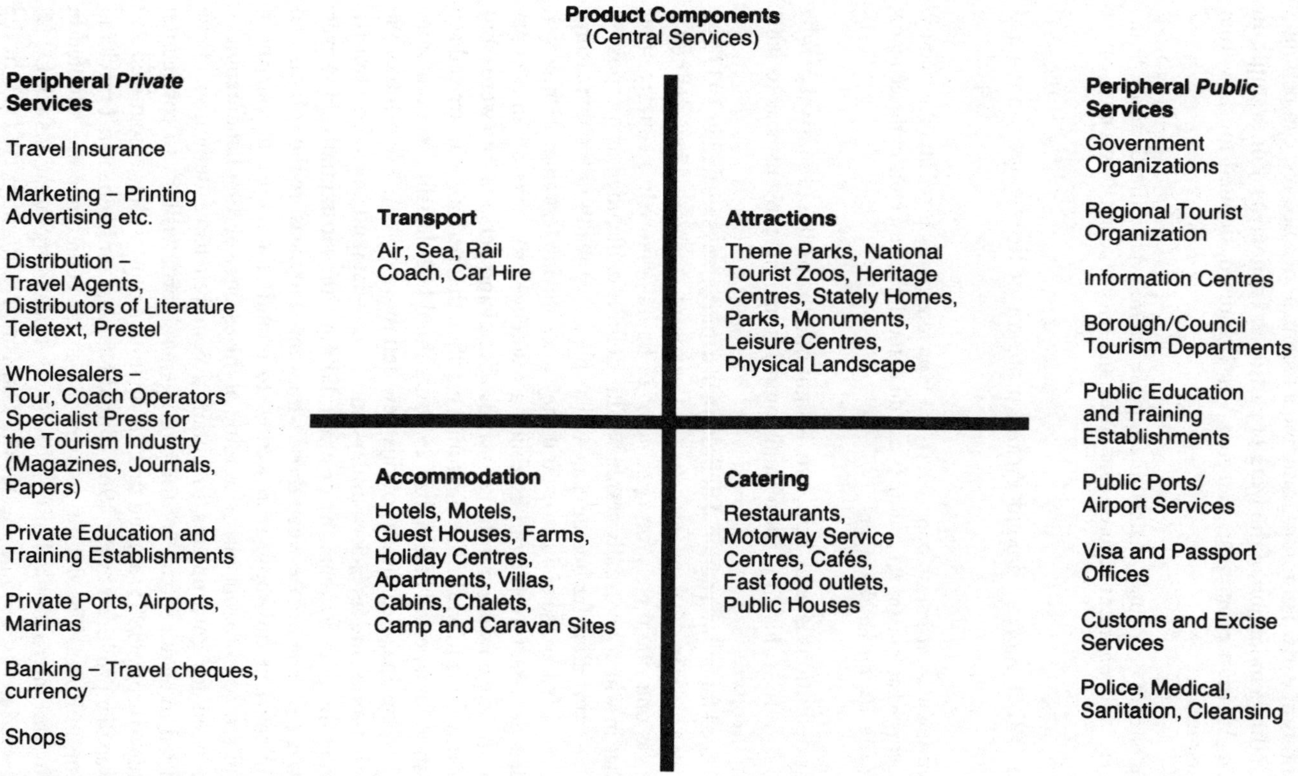

Peripheral *Public* Services

Government Organizations

Regional Tourist Organization

Information Centres

Borough/Council Tourism Departments

Public Education and Training Establishments

Public Ports/ Airport Services

Visa and Passport Offices

Customs and Excise Services

Police, Medical, Sanitation, Cleansing

Product Components (Central Services)

Attractions

Theme Parks, National Tourist Zoos, Heritage Centres, Stately Homes, Parks, Monuments, Leisure Centres, Physical Landscape

Catering

Restaurants, Motorway Service Centres, Cafés, Fast food outlets, Public Houses

Transport

Air, Sea, Rail Coach, Car Hire

Accommodation

Hotels, Motels, Guest Houses, Farms, Holiday Centres, Apartments, Villas, Cabins, Chalets, Camp and Caravan Sites

Peripheral *Private* Services

Travel Insurance

Marketing – Printing Advertising etc.

Distribution – Travel Agents, Distributors of Literature Teletext, Prestel

Wholesalers – Tour, Coach Operators Specialist Press for the Tourism Industry (Magazines, Journals, Papers)

Private Education and Training Establishments

Private Ports, Airports, Marinas

Banking – Travel cheques, currency

Shops

Figure 1.1 *Dimension of the tourism industry*
Source: D. Gilbert, 1989.

Early definitions

Indications of early definitions, utilizing a technical perspective, can be found through the examination of the work of particular economists. For example, in 1910 an Austrian economist, Herman Von Schullard, defined tourism from this perspective:

the sum total of operations, mainly of economic nature, which directly relate to the entry, stay and movement of foreigners inside and outside a certain country, city or region.

Wahab (1971) quotes Edmond Picard, professor of Economics, who stated that:

The function of tourism is to import currency from foreign resources into the country. Its impact is what tourism expenditures can do to the different sectors of the economy and in particular the hotel-keepers.

Early definitions give us very little insight into the nature of tourism or why people travel. At this time individual countries had no consensus as to what tourism involved.

The need for an international definition of a tourist was satisfied in 1937 by a committee of statistical experts at the League of Nations. They defined a tourist: 'as one who travels for a period of 24 hours or more in a country other than that in which he usually resides.' This definition included as 'purpose of visit' those travelling for business as well as pleasure, health or family reasons. It also included cruise visitors even if they were staying less than 24 hours. It excluded persons travelling to establish a residence or to take up an occupation, or those who were travelling to study abroad and persons who were commuters travelling to work. The definition clarified that persons who arrived at a destination for a period of less than 24 hours should be classified as excursionists. The principal weaknesses of this new definition were its exclusion of the domestic tourist and its lack of understanding of what it means to be a tourist.

During the next 30 years the position did not alter substantially. However, there was a divergence between those who wanted to measure the volume and value of tourism and those who wanted to include the nature of tourism in order to create a broader understanding of the essence of the phenomenon.

The need for governments to obtain a comprehensive definition of the tourist led to an acceptance of the more general term 'visitor'. In connection with this Murphy (1985) argued that the definition most widely recognized and used was that produced by the 1963 United Nations Conference on Travel and Tourism in Rome. The definition provided at this conference was adopted in 1968 by the International Union of Official Travel Organizations (IUOTO) which was later to become the World Tourism Organization (WTO). In the adoption of the definition it was recommended that the term *visitor* should be divided into the two categories of *tourists* and *excursionists*. Tourists would be classified as those making overnight stays and excursionists as those who were on day visits.

The definition stated that a visitor was:

any person visiting a country other than that in which he has his usual place of residence, for any reason other than following an occupation remunerated from within the country visited.

Within this definition it can be seen that the emphasis for tourism concerns travellers who made visits to foreign countries whether it was for pleasure, business or a combination of the two. A major feature of the definition was its provision for internationally accepted categories against which expenditure could be attributed. The concept of this approach involved economic comparison between countries and regions, with the emphasis being placed more on the benefits rather than the costs or needs of tourism. The adoption of definitions similar to that of the WTO creates meanings for tourism linked to economic exchange or market activity. This creates object- rather than subject-based associations. As the tourist is part of the subject world, we should search for other definitions which balance out the need for both measurement and tourist identity.

Emergence of a broader concept—the holistic approach

Walter Hunziker and Kurt Krapf, in their general theory of tourism published in 1942, attempted to distil the essence of tourism as both a human and economic activity. Their approach was subsequently developed by Burkart and Medlik (1974). They defined the subject of tourism as:

the totality of relationships and phenomena linked with the stay of foreigners in a locality provided they do not exercise a major, permanent or temporary remunerated activity' (translated from Hunziker and Krapf, 1942).

The work of Hunziker and Krapf is the base upon which several later definitions were built. They viewed tourism as a composite phenomenon embracing a whole range of different relationships between travellers and the host population. Tourists are represented as transitory, embarking on short-term, temporary visits as distinct from those individuals who migrate and arrive for the purpose of long-term visits. It is probably fair to assert that Hunziker and Krapf's ideas of relationships were incorporated into later ideas of tourism, and that therefore they had a partial influence on the modern concept of tourism. However their definition from a technical point of view was weak. While it introduced ideas concerning the social nature of tourism, it relied on the use of accommodation as a necessary component of tourism and it stipulated that only those following a remunerated occupation within the country visited would be excluded from tourism measurements.

Burkart and Medlik (1974), in their endeavours to clarify the situation in the early 1970s, proposed that it would be useful to distinguish between the conceptual and the technical aspects of definitions of tourism.

The basis of their argument revolved around the need to distinguish tourism as a unique domain of study. If they could provide definitions and concepts of tourism which distinguished the subject from other activities and phenomena, it would establish the phenomenon as a separate discipline of study. As both authors were leading figures in the development of a Department of Management Studies for Tourism at Surrey University, they were eager to develop a theoretical framework which would identify and at the same time create boundaries encompassing the particular characteristics of tourism. They stated that whereas the concept of tourism provides a notional theoretical framework which identifies the essential characteristics of the activity, the technical definitions evolved through experience over time, and these definitions provide instruments for particular statistical, legislative and industrial purposes. Each of the different technical definitions is seen to be appropriate for different purposes.

This view of evolutionary definitions grounded in practical application would seem to hold. In 1979 the British Tourism Society adopted a definition of tourism based upon the work of Burkart and Medlik, which in turn was drawn from earlier widely accepted definitions: 'Tourism is deemed to include any activity concerned with the temporary short-term movement of people to destinations outside the places where they normally live and work, and their activities during the stay at these destinations.' Within this definition we can identify the inclusion of those activities which are involved in the stay or visit to the destination. There is also no insistence on overnight stays or foreign visits, and it allows for domestic as well as day visits.

Burkart and Medlik's definition stands in sharp contrast to definitions adopted by others. For example, in certain countries researchers were more concerned about distance travelled away from home than tourist activities. In order to compile figures for day visitors some found it necessary to provide guidelines as to how far 'outside the places where they normally live and work' would constitute the spatial distance of particular types of tourism. In 1979 the Australian Bureau of Industry Economics placed constraints of length of stay and distance travelled on its definition of a tourist: 'A person visiting a location at least 40 kilometres from his usual place of residence, for a period of at least 24 hours and not exceeding twelve months.' Definitions emphasizing the spatial nature of tourism have also been produced in the United States and Canada, where tourist trips are defined as being over 100 miles and 50 miles respectively (Mill and Morrison, 1985).

One further definition which requires some discussion is the one utilized by The International Association of Scientific Experts in Tourism (AIEST) who in 1981 adopted the following definition from a proposal made by Kaspar: 'The entirety of interrelations and phenomena which result from people travelling to, and stopping at places which are neither their main continuous domiciles nor place of work'. This definition includes the spatial and dynamic aspects required for any adequate representation of tourism, but while it captures the concept of tourism it does not allow technical differences to be made by purpose of visit.

Epistemological approaches

There is one other approach which requires exposition. Some authors, such as Jafari (1977), emphasize knowledge-based approaches to the concept of tourism. Jafari creates a holistic definition stressing the concept of a study of man:

Tourism is the study of man away from his usual habitat, of the industry which responds to his needs, and of the impacts that both he and industry have on the host's socio-cultural, economic and physical environments.

Theoretical implications of current tourism definitions

The following fundamentals can be distilled from the various definitions:

1. **Spatial/Dynamic.** Tourism involves the movement of people from one location to another outside of their own community. The movement predominantly corresponds with the use of some form of transportation due to the distances covered. The spatial element, following the work of Gunn (1972); Matley (1976); Dann (1977); and Leiper (1979) can be broken down into three additional elements.

(a) Origin and features of the area from which the tourist travels (normal base) and to which he returns.
(b) Locations which become tourist destinations, regions or host areas due to the attraction of visitors on a temporary basis.
(c) The transit region or route chosen, which connects the origin of travel and final destination through which the visitor will have to travel.

2. **Activity.** People at tourist destinations demand a range of activities, experiences and facilities.

3. **Social.** People enter into a complex system of interacting relationships. The effects of 1 and 2 above and the different needs and motivations of visitors create a social impact which can be both positive and negative.

4. **Economic.** Income is generated by the sector of the economy known as the tourism industry.

A range of implications are associated with these concepts:

1. Due to the importance of day visitors (excursionists) there should be nothing in a definition of tourism which restricts it to only overnight stays.

2. A definition should not restrict the total market to those who travel for leisure and pleasure. There are important market segments where visits away from home for business, religious, health, educational etc. purposes create high levels of demand.
3. While tourism involves the element of travel, we have to be careful not to include commuter or regular local travel to neighbourhood facilities such as schools and shops.
4. Tourism involves the temporary movement of individuals who travel away from their own community and then return.
5. Certain theorists stress that tourism is epistemological in its basis rather than simply economic.

Statistical classifications—the technical approach

The definitions of tourism discussed so far, while providing an indication of what needs to be extracted in relation to the underlying concepts, do not clarify what is included in the classification of measurement. In 1983 the WTO updated its classification by creating a clearer distinction between residents and non-residents. This was required because it is only non-residents who are visitors within international travel.

Residents are those persons returning from a visit abroad (including foreign nationals having their usual place of residence in the country).

International visitors are defined as any people visiting a country other than that in which they have a usual place of residence, for not more than one year, and whose main purpose of visit is other than following an occupation remunerated from within the country visited. The category of International Visitors is subdivided into **International Tourists** and **International Excursionists**.

International Tourists are international visitors staying at least 24 hours but not more than one year in the country visited and the purpose of whose trip may be classified under one of the following headings:

(a) Pleasure, recreation, holiday, sport;
(b) Business, visiting friends and relatives (VFR), mission, meeting, conference, health, studies, religion.

The International Tourist category includes crew members who visit or stop over in the country and use its accommodation facilities.

International Excursionists are international visitors staying less than 24 hours in the country visited. Also treated as a subset within international excursionists are visiting crew members who do not use the country's accommodation facilities.

Domestic travel only became a subject of interest to the international agencies in the late 1970s. The WTO recommended some tentative definitions in its first publication on Domestic Tourism Statistics (1978(b)). These were subsequently updated and approved in 1983, when a definition was produced: 'Domestic visitors are any persons, regardless of nationality, resident of a country and who travel to a place within the same country for not more than one year and whose main purpose of visit is other than following an occupation remunerated from within the place visited.' The category of domestic visitors is sub-divided into domestic tourists and domestic excursionists.

Domestic Tourists are domestic visitors staying at least 24 hours, but not more than one year, in the place visited and the purpose of whose trip can be classified under one of the following headings:

(a) Pleasure, recreation, holiday, sport;
(b) Business, visiting friends and relatives (VFR), mission, meeting, conference, health, studies, religion.

Domestic Excursionists are domestic visitors staying less than 24 hours in the place visited.

The WTO observed that one other element not included in this definition but usually employed in national definitions is a minimum distance criterion. These distance criteria (which have been discussed in more detail earlier) have been incorporated to eliminate local travel or short trips which would not correspond to domestic tourism statistics.

Figure 2 clarifies the WTO classification for tourism.

Measurement issues

The focus of the preceding WTO definition becomes the compilation of statistics from the commercial accommodation sector. It can be argued that this places an emphasis on economic supply analysis whereas more account should be taken of the various consumer features which produce variables in demand.

For example, holiday tourism is paid for out of discretionary income and is therefore sensitive to aggressive pricing. There are features of family life that lead to seasonal demand patterns, differing lengths of stay and resort-based decisions. Age and socio-economic variables produce demand variables based upon short-stay, patterns of visits and destination or number of holidays taken. The VFR market often stays for longer periods and is price sensitive to travel. The VFR market is obviously less likely to use commercial accommodation or be influenced by promotion.

Business tourism, on the other hand, is normally less sensitive to price and more sensitive to service. It is oriented to urban locations and major cities and is influenced by exhibitions, conferences and trade fairs as well as commercial activity. The demand patterns are relatively stable year-round with visits being characterized by short stays.

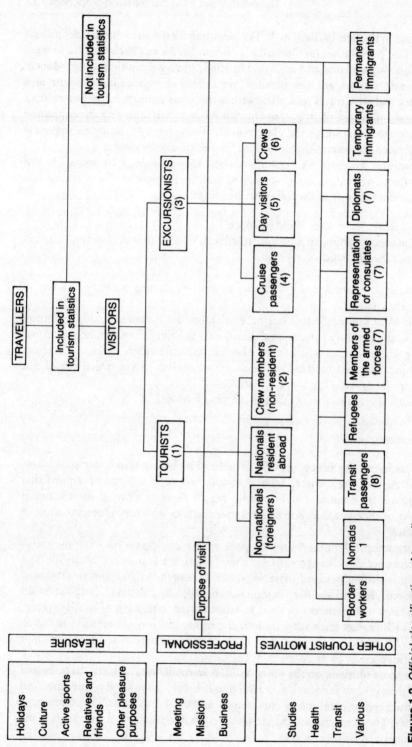

Figure 1.2 *Official classification of travellers*
Source: World Tourism Organization.

TRAVELLERS

Included in tourism statistics

Not included in tourism statistics

VISITORS

TOURISTS (1)

EXCURSIONISTS (3)

Permanent Immigrants

Non-nationals (foreigners)

Nationals resident abroad

Crew members (non-resident) (2)

Cruise passengers (4)

Day visitors (5)

Crews (6)

Temporary Immigrants

Diplomats (7)

Representation of consulates (7)

Members of the armed forces (7)

Refugees

Transit passengers (8)

Nomads 1

Border workers

Purpose of visit

PLEASURE

Holidays
Culture
Active sports
Relatives and friends
Other pleasure purposes

PROFESSIONAL

Meeting
Mission
Business

OTHER TOURIST MOTIVES

Studies
Health
Transit
Various

Current definitions of tourism have been derived for the economist, and are not adequate for marketers. The terminology places an emphasis on the simplistic characterization of demand. It stresses homogeneity: One industry—tourism; One category of consumer—tourist. There are technical definitions of types of tourist, which were examined earlier in this chapter, but these are limited to only five major categories. To date the approach has led to a predominately reductionist perspective of the phenomenon and the mapping out of an area of study which may not be ideal for market-based decision making.

By definition all tourism involves travel yet not all travel is tourism; tourism is part of leisure and recreation yet the majority of this type of activity is home-centred or local to the home. The use of the motor car for shopping allows major distances to be covered on a regular basis; there is no distinction between reasons for the movement of people which restricts the terminology to movement rather than motivation or product needs. The tourism industry is treated as a composite whole, yet it is an amalgam of different service industries providing satisfaction for a wide range of needs. Tourism as a generic term provides a simplistic focal point of activity which may not characterize the overall functions of its definition. An independent tourist will purchase a number of products from different service providers who may also be in the business of transporting goods, catering for local functions or providing public facilities such as toilets and parking for local inhabitants. The tourist's trip may include the experience of a local festival even though it may have been intended purely for local consumption and was not part of an industry structure.

The phenomena of tourism would seem to comprise a range of products formed from the segmented portions of the larger industries. The segmented approach to tourism could then be improved by splitting demand into broader areas. This perspective reclaims overall areas of human activity rather than placing importance on the spatial movement of people. Some segments would consume both local and distant products and there would be no difference between the demand for products based on temporary short-term movements of people to destinations outside the places where they normally live and work and demand from local inhabitants.

The advantage of this point of view is that from a marketing standpoint we can more easily understand the overall objectives and policies of major providers where tourism is not their main market segment. It is more efficient for marketing to focus upon place, transport, accommodation, attractions and organizers within an overall plan for targeting the local and distant consumers. For example, a good health club or restaurant would attract certain segments at varying distances from its premises. Marketing as a philosophy cannot be efficient in aiding the management of peripheral companies in tourism if it provides input solely to the parts, without consideration of the whole.

The heart of the argument is that greater consideration should be given to demand segmentation and activity preferences in the analysis of tourism, whether at an international or domestic level. In addition, if management enterprises in tourism (Figure 1) are to be successful in developing marketing plans then they need to understand the nature and behaviour of each of the segments they attempt to satisfy. This will probably cut across demarcations of tourist, excursionist or recreationalist as these descriptions provide an inadequate basis for management planning. For example, an attraction in a popular resort area will identify those of local origin of visit as potential tourists. The distant target market for these types of attractions will be excursionists living up to two hours' driving time away. The tourist in this instance is treated—from a promotional viewpoint—as part of the local target community.

The real benefit of a social activity or consumer approach to tourism is that it helps overcome the compartmentalization of the areas of leisure, recreation and tourism (LRT). Felder (1987) has argued that definitional problems of LRT have hindered many attempts to clarify and specify theoretical relationships between the three concepts. He argues that leisure and recreation have proceeded as one camp and tourism as another.

The interrelationships between LRT are obvious and therefore progress can only be made if theorists attempt to develop meanings which integrate the function, form and process of tourism as an encompassing social activity, with the consumer as its main focus and perspective. This does not dispense with measurement of expenditure or the monitoring of benefits achieved through movements of visitors. A social activity-based definition for tourism can incorporate methods of economic data collection.

A tourism industry?

One of the benefits of identifying any underlying pattern of consumer behaviour for tourism has to be the improvement which can be gained in marketing within the tourism industry. However, it is necessary to examine whether there is an industry that will be able to benefit from any advance in consumer theory.

Lickorish (1970) describes tourism as '. . . the movement of people, a market rather than an industry . . .' and in 1988 as '. . . a movement of people, a demand force and not a single industry' (Jefferson and Lickorish, 1988).

There will probably be continuous debate over the question of whether tourism constitutes an industry. Industries are made up of firms which produce the same product or groups of products so that the consumer regards these as ideal substitutes for one another even though the products may differ slightly. However, Medlik (1972) argued that 'a firm may consist of more than one establishment and operate in more than one industry'. Clearly we either need to revise our perception of what constitutes tourism or find some incorporation of ideas, first as to how establishments as well as firms make up an industry, and secondly, as to how there can be some overlap between different industries.

Some authors have accepted that tourism is treated as an industry. Wahab (1971) wrote '. . . For the country concerned, tourism is an industry whose "products" are consumed on the spot forming invisible exports . . .'.

In his later work (1975), Wahab proposed that 'any product, whether tangible or intangible, that serves to gratify certain human needs should be considered an industrial product' and that 'if a bond of product unity exists between various firms and organizations in a way that characterized their overall function and determines their place in economic life, they should be considered an industry'. The system which serves tourism is often referred to as a business or industry by other authors (Lundberg, 1976; McIntosh, 1977).

What makes tourism so difficult to define is the very broad nature of both the concept and service inputs. In Figure 1, for example, we can see that tourism envelops various other industries such as the airline, rail, cruise, accommodation and food service industries. It also involves tour wholesalers, retailers and attractions as well as a range of public services. As Young (1973) stated: 'It is a heterogeneous group embracing a large variety of trades and industries which have the supplying of travellers' needs as their common function' and that 'it is wrong to believe that tourism has a recognizable shape with neatly interlocking components'. Rather than examine the structure of the tourism system some authors examine the product or output. Because tourism does not produce a distinct product some economists, such as Chadwick (1981) argue that it cannot exist as an industry. As Papadopolis (1986) has outlined, tourism in the conventional sense is not a market. It does not sell simply one product and there is no single sector involved.

We can also identify the 'free', natural, non-industrial, intangible resource which provides input to the product. Free resources such as climate, beaches, scenic views, host culture and certain other intangibles are inherently non-industrial. It is also difficult to determine what constitutes the tourism industry because some of the services listed in Figure 1 are crucial to tourism while others are only supportive. Furthermore, some services such as catering and transport provide for a whole range of people other than what can be described as a minority of tourists.

Because tourism is difficult to define clearly due to the expansive spread of the activities it covers, there is a problem in determining to what extent it falls within the context of an industry. The problem is that tourism is treated as an holistic concept when in actual fact it is characterized by an extremely fragmented framework of industries, bodies and touristic activity. Mill and Morrison (1985) prefer to think of tourism as an activity rather than an industry. However we need to bear in mind that those activities which go to make up tourism do have a major beneficial effect on many world economies. Within these countries tourism businesses constitute some of the largest single economic groups to be found throughout the world.

In summary, tourism while having no clear boundary delineations or concise conceptual clarification does, due to the overall size and impact of spatial and temporal movements of people with varying service needs for shelter, sustenance, entertainment and travel, produce the basis of an industry. This industry is clearly defined for the 'central services' of airlines, wholesalers, hotels etc. but not for those providing peripheral services. The larger tourism companies providing 'central services' are embarking upon strategies of vertical or horizontal integration which strengthen the idea of tourism as an industry. If major companies create stronger bonds with increased product unity this will ultimately create more need for tourism industry terminology. While it would appear that these changes in industry structure may help future clarification we should be aware that peripheral service industries are becoming increasingly complex, as are many other suppliers in the tertiary service sector. We should not be surprised to find that in the future it may be far more difficult to ascertain the supply characteristics of different types of economic activity. This has led theorists to search for objective methods of measurement by concentrating on sector analysis output.

Smith (1988) implicitly agrees with the notion of a tourism industry and like Medlik (1988), has formulated an operational measurement for tourism industry activity based upon providing a weighting for standard industrial classifications. However, his model, while allowing for a basis of comparison between different industries, requires a number of assumptions to be made in order to calculate final outputs. In his so called *supply-side* view of defining tourism Smith identifies two tiers of tourism business. One is seen to be composed of businesses which serve tourists exclusively while the other is seen to serve a mix of tourists and local residents. He argues for a definition of tourism which will first identify it as an industry and second allow it to conform to existing definitional standards and conventions used in other fields.

This form of theorizing is very much in the tradition of those stressing the technical nature of tourism. Smith assumes that an economic or operational approach to measurement, not applied research into action or activity, will give tourism academics greater status in the eyes of industry and government. He goes so far as to say that defining tourism in terms of tourists' 'actions and activities' or motivations is comparable to defining the health care industry by defining a sick person. It would be a sorry day for medicine when a social or holistic approach did not view the patient as part of the process of health care. Smith's definition for tourism cannot exist without an understanding of what tourists do and consume. The need to measure a fragmented, ill-defined set of services and goods supplied under the umbrella of a tourist industry creates a need to understand a whole range of actions. This means that Smith's definition relies on the other approaches of social-action theorists in order to make his own model operational.

Tourism and travel terminology

In the tourism literature there is an approach whereby various authors use the words *travel and tourism* in combination in the titles of their books as a compromise aimed at those who favour the use of one word over the other, or because they believe in both terms (for example, Foster, 1985; Middleton, 1988). However changes have occurred in the titles of statutory bodies, placing greater emphasis on tourism rather than travel. These include the World Tourism Organization, formerly The International Union of Official Travel Organizations; and The British Tourist Authority, previously (1969) The British Travel Association. In 1981 The United States Travel and Tourism Administration replaced the United States Travel Service, and in 1978 The Travel Industry Association of Canada became the Tourism Industry Association of Canada.

Frechtling (1976) argued that the term tourist has two strikes against it: it is too exclusive and it is perjorative in common parlance. He went on to write that the word 'travel' has one strike against it: it includes extraneous activity. The two strikes of Frechtling are partly if not wholly due to the definitional categories which provide meaning for tourist activities.

Medlik (1988) argued that while Americans seem to prefer the term *travel* this is probably not so in the rest of the world. He cites the example of continental Europe, with German-speaking countries adopting the modern term *tourisimus* rather than the traditional but highly expressive term *fremdenverkehr*. But Wynegar (1984) showed that in the USA 20 states utilized the word travel while 33 states used the word tourism or tourist in the titles of their organization. It would seem that there is widespread and growing use of the word tourism and that this is sufficient reason to accept or adopt it as a comprehensive term.

Public perception of tourism

In understanding the concepts which have been uncovered, it is important to recognize that the lay person's ideas of tourism are different to those of the theorist. The popular notions often contradict the implications and concepts previously discussed.

The findings of many surveys show that tourists are equated with foreign holidaymakers rather than other types of tourist. These findings and other surveys, aimed at identifying the opinion of residents regarding the nature and type of activity associated with the tourist, indicate that tourism is equated with holiday travel. Tourists are viewed as either foreign or domestic visitors on holiday and not as people on business, people visiting friends and relations, people passing through the area, second home owners or day visitors. The typical response to the question 'what is a tourist?' is that it is a person who is visiting the area for leisure purposes. However, while it is increasingly accepted by theorists that tourists should include day visitors, surveys confirm that residents do not see this activity as part of tourism.

The narrow view of the definition of the tourist has been confirmed in surveys such as the Wales Tourist Board survey, 1979; Gilbert's (1988) survey of residents in Newport; and Wanhill's (1988) survey of Surrey councillors, which revealed that 97% defined tourists as holidaymakers staying in the area while only 15% thought those people coming to the area on business were tourists. In addition, 14% felt that those people who were staying in the area, but not working, were tourists. The concept of tourism held by local residents or local politicians would seem to indicate that there is a disparity between official meanings and popular meanings of the term. It is therefore important to indicate to any respondents in tourism surveys, the categories of tourist which relate to questions posed or measurements made regarding the term tourist or tourism.

Tourism as a product

It is important to uncover the characteristics of tourism as a product, as this may have important implications for the nature of consumer behaviour.

Tourism has been repeatedly accepted as a service product by authors of texts related to tourism (Schmoll, 1977; Foster, 1985; Buttle, 1986; Holloway and Plant, 1988; Middleton, 1988). However, not all authors agree that differences exist between goods and services (Wyckham *et al.*, 1975; Bonoma and Mills, 1980; Goodfellow, 1983). Those authors who agree that there are differences stress the characteristics of intangibility, inseparability and perishability as making an important difference to their management. It may not be beneficial to enter the debate over whether tourism products are service products or not, but there is strong support for the rationale of applying service-product theory to tourism. The debate over how products should be defined can be summed up by Blois (1983) who asserts that two knowledgeable observers, presented with the same set of products, would not agree as to which were services.

The other characteristics associated with tourism products include those of amalgam, rigidity of supply, seasonality and substitution effects. Burkart and Medlik (1979) wrote of 'an amalgam of phenomena and relationships', and Wahab *et al.* (1976) of 'an amalgam of various components that complement each other'. Jafari (1974) considered the tourism market basket as the gross amalgam of goods and services. The amalgam creates problems of complementarity where each component part is reliant on each of the other service inputs to create an overall satisfactory product, meaning that each sector and facility involved in trying to satisfy the tourist has a direct effect on demand which can affect the overall industry. This concept was developed at an early stage by Krippendorf (1971).

For the host destination, some aspects of tourism are rigid in supply and impossible to change while others can only be changed in the long term. For example, the natural environment, such as mountains, lakes, seascapes and landscapes; and the culture, heritage and tourist infrastructure are not responsive to the need for change. Some aspects of the tourist industry (Figure 1), such as airline travel, are increasing at such a rate that other services, such as airport facilities, cannot be developed quickly enough to satisfy the growth in demand. There is also a problem of rigidity of supply for most tourism service providers in the high season, when capacity cannot be easily increased.

Patterns of tourist demand indicate fluctuating popularity or seasonality. Consumers of mass-tourism-packaged products will switch demand and substitute one country for another. This substitution can be in response to minor increases or decreases in the relative prices of one country to another, political factors or the perceived risk of physical danger. Wahab *et al*. (1976) writes of high elasticity and flexibility factors creating changes in demand which may even create substitution in the form of the purchase of a car rather than expenditure on tourism. While substitution effects can be reduced by an improvement in product benefit promotion (Gilbert, 1984), they remain an important feature of tourism demand patterns. Medlik and Middleton (1973) and Middleton (1988) define the product as 'based on activity at a destination' and requiring 'a price'. Both of these aspects are inadequate claims because the component of travel, as well as that of free access, are excluded from their meaning of the nature of the tourism product.

If we required a definition of the tourism product, the following could be offered: 'An amalgam of different goods and services offered as an activity experience to the tourist'. This understanding provides for both payment and free access to tourism as well as the combination of a package of components all leading to an experiential state of consumer consumption. This is a social understanding of the tourism product rather than one which emanates from tourism as an industry. However, the service elements of the amalgam inherently incorporate accommodation, transport, attractions etc.

Tourist activity

While any demand for tourism should include some form of activity, this important characteristic is seldom assessed. Nevertheless, it is the experiential activity of tourists which has a bearing on particular types of demand and seasonal variation. In 1977 the National Travel Survey (US Bureau of the Census, 1979) collected, compiled and published information on attendance at six different types of events and attractions and on participation in eleven specific recreational activities. The Canadian Travel Survey (Statistics of Canada, 1984) identified ten different events and attractions and five specific outdoor recreational or sports activities. Research into the activity preferences of the younger age market in the UK was carried out by Gilbert for the English Tourist Board (1986). A number of other surveys have also been reported but only reflect demand patterns and do not provide any insight into how activities serve as indicators of demand criteria. In developing a greater understanding of the role of activities we can draw upon the classification scheme which has been offered by Chadwick (1987).

The classification (Figure 3) reflects the emerging consensus that business and same-day travel are both within the scope of travel and tourism, despite the reservations of some writers. The classification also extends the primary

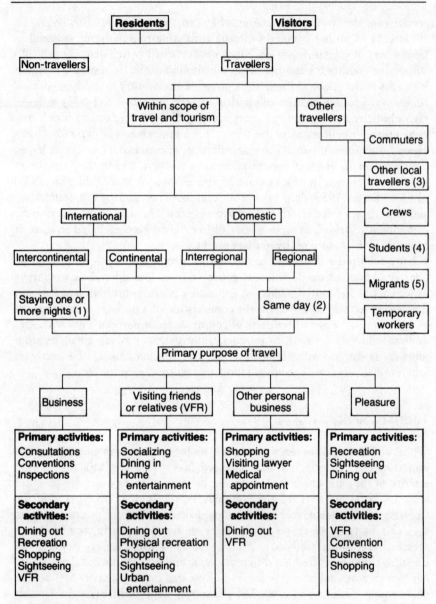

(1) 'Tourists' in international technical definitions.
(2) 'Excursionists' in international technical definitions.
(3) Travellers whose trips are shorter than those which qualify for travel and tourism, e.g. under 50 miles (80 km) from home.
(4) Students travelling between home and school only – other travel of students is within scope of travel and tourism.
(5) All persons moving to a new place of residence including all one-way travellers such as emigrants, immigrants, refugees, domestic migrants and nomads.

Figure 1.3 *Classification of travellers*
Source: Chadwick (1987).

purpose of visit to include activities. It extends the notion that many journeys are undertaken for a combination of reasons yet retains the primary purpose of visit under the headings: business; personal business; VFR and pleasure. Personal business is a welcome addition, because in the future individuals will be more likely to pay visits to specialist service agencies which are not in their local area. For example, a trip to a major city for advice on legal, medical, financial or educational matters could become a feature of the future linked perhaps to a leisure-based activity. If we consider Chadwick's scheme of classification there is no inclusion of education as an activity of tourism, but this could easily be incorporated under the heading of personal business.

The following is an attempt to classify the main types of activity which may represent certain aspects of tourism demand:

(1) *Communing with nature*. Demand for parks, open areas, commons, walking, rambling etc.
(2) *Attractions*. Visiting zoos, safari parks, waxworks, theme parks, *son et lumière* etc.
(3) *Heritage*. Visiting castles, stately homes, museums, ancient monuments, religious sites, galleries, battlefields.
(4) *Sport activity*. Taking part in, or watching, various forms of indoor or outdoor sport including those of a specifically rural or urban nature. These would include ten-pin bowling, fishing, sailing, golf, shooting, swimming, surfboarding, motor racing, football, cricket etc.
(5) *Entertainment*. Other than sport, this would include visits to the cinema, theatre, bars, concerts, discos, restaurants etc.
(6) *Relaxation*. Sunbathing, resting, reading etc.
(7) *Health*. Taking health care treatment, saunas, massage, therapy. Includes moral health such as religion, pilgrimages.
(8) *Shopping*. Browsing, souvenir or antique hunting, special-purchase trips for new outfits, gifts, new high-cost equipment.
(9) *Business activities*. Meetings, conferences, exhibitions etc.

The conceptual framework of tourism

There are many complex, interrelated factors which together characterize the domain of tourism. The main factors which constitute the subject appear to be:

(a) It is a domestic as well as an international movement of people. The movement is spatially far enough to take the person into another community, thus making him a visitor. As visitors, people either become day visitors (excursionists) or tourists. Inherent within the notion of visitor is the role of host or host community, as visits away from home require service provision and consumption. The host community also enters into human relationships as part of product delivery. Both host and visitor will experience either negative or positive feelings as an outcome of the interaction.

The constituent of the phenomenon is the human element as motivator and instigator of travel as an act. This role requires the person as visitor to move across a certain physical distance into unfamiliar communities. The mode of traveller exists within a temporal element which becomes the time elapsed in the round trip between entering the classification of tourist or excursionist and returning home as non-tourist. The role of tourist is only open to those who stay 24 hours, but not longer than one year in a destination, and fulfil WTO criteria of purpose of visit being for pleasure, recreation, sport, business, VFR, meeting, religion, conference, mission, health or studies. The role of excursionist is open to those who fulfil the above WTO criteria but do not stay more than 24 hours.

(b) Tourism is also a fragmented industry of high complexity due to the price-sensitive nature of demand and the intangibility, perishability and inseparability of the product. While it is an industry with no clear boundaries the central rather than peripheral services do offer a more clearly defined group of companies which focus predominantly on the tourist as consumer.

(c) The conceptual basis of current tourism is based on (a) and (b) above; however, other behavioural variables require exposition. Tourism is linked to demand for one or a combination of activities. The choice of these activities will have a direct effect on the type, timing and length of demand. Tourists as subjects enter into problem-solving experiences over which choice to make in order to maximize their satisfaction. The pattern of choice involves decisions as to which activities should be evaluated and included in any travel arrangement. The tourist as human author of his future is provided with choice in the initial stages of the tourism process. Yet this process has to date been ignored in the range and breadth of contemporary tourism theory. Until now, much of what we have taken to mean tourism has been supplied by the economists or geographers. The marketers who are now influencing tourism theory will open up the realm of consumer behaviour.

Conclusion

The nature of tourism is difficult to isolate given the difficulties we face in trying to establish the key concepts from recent practice and theory. However, tourism can be seen to incorporate the travel activity of individuals and it is upon this that a working definition can be constructed. We need to proceed by utilizing the concept of tourism as part of a continuum of activities ranging from local leisure pursuits and home-based activities (non-tourist) to those of travel away from home or work and extended tours (tourist).

It has been established that tourism can be viewed as an industry. However, industries are specifically defined in terms of the goods and services they provide, not the characteristics or motivations of their consumers. To arrive at any true understanding of tourism we can only measure the output of that which we understand. Within tourism the product as an amalgam is not easily identifiable or objectively measured. While definitions exist which try to establish the basis of economic measurement, we must recognize that this only addresses one need within the field of tourism. Different definitions exist which provide for different uses, and it is acceptable to incorporate different definitions in tourism as long as a clear statement is given relating to the use and application of that definition. There may also be a need for a cascade effect of understanding whereby we create a social understanding of tourism prior to carrying out economic assessment. It would follow that this two-stage process requires *two* definitions.

Definitions in tourism can be based upon these statements:

 (i) *Social*: treating tourism as a human, subject-based activity and therefore synonymous with the actions and impacts of tourists.
 (ii) *Epistemological*: dealing with tourism as an academic discipline or body of knowledge related to a field or domain of study.
(iii) *Economic*: assessing the value and output of tourism as an industry involving the measurement of the activities of people, businesses, places and sectors.

The working definition proposed for a *social* understanding of tourism is:

Tourism is one part of recreation which involves travel to a less familiar destination or community, for a short-term period, in order to satisfy a consumer need for one or a combination of activities.

This definition places tourism in the overall context of recreation, retains the need for travel outside of the normal place of work or habitation and more importantly, places the emphasis on the reason for travel, which is to satisfy *consumer need* for a range of activities. The definition emphasizes not only the act of tourism but also the motivational aspect of the reason for being a tourist.

References

Blois, K., 1983, 'Service marketing—assertion or asset?' *Service Industries Journal*, 3(2), July: pp. 113–20.
Bonoma, T. V., Mills, M. K., 1980, 'Services marketing', working papers, Harvard Business School, Cambridge, Massachusetts.
Buck, R. C., 1978, 'Towards a synthesis of tourism theory', *Annals of Tourism Research*, 5(1): pp. 110–11.
Burkart, A. J., Medlik, S., 1974, *Tourism, Past, Present and Future*, Heinemann, London, p. 39.
Buttle, F., 1986, *Hotel and Food Service Marketing*, Holt, Rinehart and Winston, London.
Chadwick, R. A., 1981, 'Some notes on the geography of tourism: a comment', *Canadian Geographer*, 25, summer: pp. 191–97.

Chadwick, R. A., 1987, 'Concepts, definitions and measures used in travel and tourism research', in Ritchie, J. R. B., Gouldner, C. R. (eds), *Travel, Tourism and Hospitality Research*, Wiley, New York, pp. 47–61.

Dann, G., 1977, 'Anomie, Ego enhancement and tourism', *Annals of Tourism Reearch*, 4(4): pp. 184–94.

Felder, A. J., 1987, 'Are leisure, recreation and tourism interrelated?' *Annals of Tourism Research*, 14(3): pp. 311–13.

Foster, D., 1985, *Travel and Tourism Management*. Macmillan Education, London.

Frechtling, D. C., 1976, 'Proposed standard definitions and classifications for travel research', *Marketing Travel and Tourism*, seventh annual conference proceedings, The Travel Research Association, Boca Raton, Florida, pp. 59–64.

Gilbert, D., 1984, 'Tourist product diffrentiation', Tourism, Managing for Results Conference, November, University of Surrey.

Gilbert, D., 1986, '*E.T.B. 18–35 Holiday Preference Report*', internal ETB report, London.

Gilbert, D., 1988, 'Newport visitor survey', carried out by the University of Surrey for Tibbalds Colbourne and Newport Borough Council.

Goodfellow, J. H., 1983, 'The marketing of goods and services as a multidimensional concept', *Quarterly Review of Marketing*, 8(3), April: pp. 19–27.

Gunn, C. A., 1972, *Vacationscape, Designing Tourist Regions*, University of Texas, Austin.

Heeley, J., 1980, 'The definition of tourism in Great Britain: Does terminological confusion have to rule?' *The Tourist Review*, 2(80): pp. 11–14.

Holloway, J. C, Plant, R. V., 1988, *Marketing for Tourism*, Pitman, London.

Hunziker, W., Krapf, K., 1942, *Grundriss der allgemeinen Fremdenverkehrslehre*, Polygraphischer Verlag AG, Zurich.

Jafari, J., 1974, 'The components and nature of tourism: the tourism market basket of goods and services', *Annals of Tourism Research*, 1(3), January: pp. 73–89.

Jafari, J., 1977, 'Editors page', *Annals of Tourism Research*, 6(11): pp. 6–11.

Jefferson, A., Lickorish, L., 1988, *Marketing Tourism—A Practical Guide*, Longman, Harlow.

Jenkins, C. L., 1982, 'The use of investment incentives for tourism projects in developing countries', *Tourism Management*, 3(2): pp. 91–7.

Kaspar, C., 1981, 'Leisure-recreation tourism. An introduction to the general topic of the 31st AIEST congress'. AIEST editions, Berne.

Krippendorf, J., 1971, *Marketing et Tourisme*, Herbert Lang, Berne.

Leiper, N., 1979, 'The framework of tourism. Towards a definition of tourism, tourist and the tourism industry', *Annals of Tourism Research*, 6(4), pp. 390–407.

Lickorish, L. J., 1970, 'Planning for tourism', in Burton, T. L. (ed.), *Recreation Research and Planning*. Allen and Unwin, London, pp. 166–85.

Lundberg, D. E., 1976, *The Tourism Business*, CBI Publishing, Boston.

Matley, I. M., 1976, 'The geography of international tourism', American Association of Geographers, Washington D.C.

McIntosh, R. W., 1977, *Tourism, Principles, Practices, Philosophies*, Grid Inc., Columbus, Ohio.

Medlik, R., 1972, *Profile of the Hotel and Catering Industry*, Heinemann, London.

Medlik, R., 1988, 'What is tourism?', *Teaching Tourism into the 1990s*, International Conference for Tourism Educators, July 1988, University of Surrey, Guildford.

Medlik, R., Middleton, V. T. C., 1973, 'The tourism product and its marketing implications', *International Tourism Quarterly*, 13(3): pp. 28–35.

Middleton, V. T. C., 1988, *Marketing in Travel and Tourism*, Heinemann, Oxford.

Mill, R. C., Morrison, A., 1985, *The Tourism System: An Introductory Text*, Prentice Hall, Englewood Cliffs, New Jersey.

Murphy, P. E., 1985, *Tourism, A Community Approach*, Methuen, London.

Papadopolis, I. S., 1986, 'The tourism phenomenon: an examination of important theories and concepts', *Revue de Tourisme*, No. 3, pp. 2–11.

Schmoll, G. A., 1977, *Tourism Promotion*, Tourism International Press, London.

Statistics Canada, 1984, *Tourism and Recreation*, Statistics Canada, Ottawa.

United Nations, Statistical Office of the, 1971, *Indexes to the International Standard Industrial Classification of All Economic Activities*, United Nations, New York.

United States Bureau of the Census, 1979, *National Travel Survey, Travel during 1977*, U. S. Government Printing Office, Washington D.C.

Wahab, S., 1971, 'An introduction to tourism theory', *Travel Research Journal*, No. 1, pp. 17–30.

Wahab, S., 1975, *Tourism Management*, Tourism International Press, London.

Wahab, S., Crampon, L. J., Rothfield, L. M., 1976, *Tourism Marketing*, Tourism International Press, London, p. 23.

Wanhill, S., 1988, 'UK politics and tourism', *Tourism Management*, 9(1), March: pp. 54–8.

WTO, 1978(a), *Methodological Supplement to World Travel Statistics*, World Tourism Organization, Madrid.

WTO, 1978(b), *Domestic Tourism Statistics*, World Tourism Organization, Madrid.

WTO, 1983, *Definitions Concerning Tourism Statistics*, World Tourism Organization, Madrid.

Wyckham, R. G., Fitzroy, T., Mandry, G. D., 1975, 'Marketing services', *European Journal of Marketing*, 9(1): pp. 59–67.

Wynegar, D., 1984, USTTA research: 'New tools for international tourism marketing', Travel research: The catalyst for worldwide tourism planning, fifteenth annual conference proceedings, Travel and Tourism Research Association, Philadelphia, pp. 183–200.

2 A review of tourism expenditure research
P. J. Sheldon

Introduction

Tourism expenditures represent a major component of the world's economy. Both the International Monetary Fund (IMF) and the World Tourism Organization (WTO) have recommended that tourism receipts and expenditures be included in a country's national accounts. The measurement of tourism expenditures is, however, difficult because the tourism industry consists of many component sub-industries. Whereas expenditures on tangible goods are measured by totalling sales, tourism expenditures are ideally measured by adding up the individual tourist's spending.

This paper reveals that tourism expenditure research falls into two general categories. The first category focuses on **methodologies used to measure and document spending by tourists**. This is most frequently performed by government statisticians to determine the economic significance of tourism in an economy. The other category focuses on the **creation of tourism expenditure models**, both at the micro and macro levels, to better explain and understand the volume and nature of tourist spending. This latter category of research is performed predominantly by academicians. This paper will review both categories, and will focus mainly on international tourism expenditures, as these have the greatest impact on a country's balance of payments. Domestic tourism expenditures will also be discussed to the extent that they are covered in the literature.

Definitions

The term *tourist* must be defined before tourism expenditures can be analysed. Definitions of a tourist can be found in many places (WTO, 1981(b); Gee *et al.*, 1989; McIntosh and Goeldner, 1986). The WTO definition used by most countries includes vacationers, businessmen, excursionists, cruise passengers, students and public officials. Therefore all spending by these travellers should be included in tourism expenditure statistics.

Tourism consumption expenditures are defined as '. . . all payments made by non-resident tourists during their visit to the host country, or any expenses incurred by the said visit' (WTO, 1981(b)). Tourism revenues are defined as

'. . . those revenues obtained by the host country in the form of direct or indirect foreign currency payments made by foreign tourists to cover their costs of goods and services' (WTO, 1981(b)). Typically, these definitions exclude international fares, which are recorded separately. Details of the categories of expenditures generally included in these definitions can be found in WTO (1981(a)).

There is some debate in the literature as to whether these definitions are appropriate. Baretje (1982) suggests that the usual definitional categories do not fully reflect tourism's impact on an economy. He suggests including all expenditures that would not have occurred without tourism, such as all transportation expenditures; all tourism-related investments, dividends, interest and profits; all tourism-induced commodity imports, salaries, training, publicity and promotion expenses; and expenditures on aircraft. A similar argument is made by Gerakis (1965) who suggests that tourism-induced real estate transactions be included. The large volume of foreign investment occurring in real estate in recent years (especially by the Japanese) would, if included, drastically change tourism expenditure figures.

Data collection

Collection of tourism expenditure data is usually the responsibility of the national tourism office, a government statistical agency or the central bank, or is the joint responsibility of more than one of the above. The three most commonly used methods of tourist expenditure data collection are bank records of foreign exchange transactions, surveys of tourists and surveys of tourism establishments (WTO, 1981(a)).

Bank records

Because the central bank of a country typically records all foreign currency transactions, most countries rely on these for estimates of tourist expenditures. The WTO and the IMF provide guidelines on how tourism expenditures and receipts can be accounted for in the Balance of Payments accounts (WTO, 1978; IMF, 1977). According to these two agencies, a model tourism balance would include as **debits** and **credits** the following items:

Debits	*Credits*
a. purchase of goods	a. sale of goods
b. purchase of services	b. sale of services
training of staff	staff training
foreign manpower	salary repatriation
c. transport expenses	c. transport expenses
(non-local)	(local and non-local)
d. investments abroad	d. foreign investment in the country

e. debit expenses   e. credit expenses
   interest   interest
   capital reimbursement   capital reimbursement
f. credit balance   f. debit balance

There are, however, serious limitations associated with relying on this method alone. First, and most importantly, it is not possible accurately to identify all tourism-related foreign exchange transactions. Second, analysis of the data is only possible by country of origin. This is inadequate to fully understand the nature of tourism expenditures. Tourist characteristics such as demographics, and trip characteristics such as length of stay, type of transportation and accommodation type must be also identified, so that spending patterns for these groups can be estimated (Baretje, 1982; WTO, 1981(a)). Because of these limitations, this method is sometimes used in conjunction with other methods such as tourist surveys or tourism establishment surveys.

Tourist surveys

Expenditure surveys of tourists can be performed either at the border, during the vacation or after their return home. Border surveys can be used to estimate expenditures of both returning residents and departing tourists. They require cooperation from government agencies within the country and with the governments of reciprocating countries. For example, Canada and the US survey their own returning residents and then share the results (Bailie, 1985). Border surveys often give the best estimates (White, 1985) and are used by the UK (the British International Passenger Survey), the US, Canada, Ireland and Switzerland (Artus, 1972). A limitation of this method is that tourists on multi-destination trips do not easily recall their expenditures per country, but more readily recall their total expenditures.

Surveys of tourists **during the vacation** require that tourists record their daily spending in a diary. These are used in Hawaii (HVB Expenditure Survey, 1987) and Canada (Bailie, 1985). It may be a more accurate method, as expenditures are recorded as they occur, but it tends to have lower response rates than other tourist surveys. It may also bias spending patterns if each item has to be recorded (Mak *et al.*, 1977). If diaries are distributed to accommodation units, as is often the case, tourists who camp or stay with friends or relatives are excluded, leading to biased results. The US Travel Data Center used a variation of this technique to measure domestic tourism expenditures. Tourists were asked to recall their activities in six categories (transportation, lodging, food, entertainment, gifts and incidental). These activities were then multiplied by previously determined *per unit cost factors* to arrive at aggregate spending. Accuracy of the cost estimates is crucial to the success of this method (Frechtling, 1974).

Mak *et al.* (1977) and Perdue and Botkin (1988) caution against using post-trip surveys **at the traveller's home** because results tend to lack precision due to poor recall. Frechtling (1974) points out that the ubiquitous use of credit cards makes it more difficult for tourists to accurately recall their expenditures, and calls into question all survey results. The British International Passenger Survey, however, does include information on credit card use.

Even though tourist surveys are more accurate than bank records, inaccuracies are still likely when one has to '. . . rely on the memories of a fraction of the people' (Gray, 1966). Sample survey methods also suffer from problems with sample selection and non-response bias. Non-response bias tends to be higher for destination and home surveys than for border surveys, which have the appearance of being more *official*. Often the frequent traveller, who is requested to fill out many surveys, is more likely to contribute to non-response bias than less frequent travellers. Discussions of surveying and sampling issues encountered when estimating tourism expenditures can be found in Pearce (1981) and WTO (1983). Expenditure surveys are also vulnerable to under-reporting because of currency exchange and customs controls limits. They are, however, able to capture tourist characteristics and behaviour, permitting a rich and comprehensive analysis of the data. The results from such analyses are often useful to managers and policy makers.

Surveys of tourism establishments

This method attempts to measure tourism expenditures by totalling the receipts of different firms in the tourism industry. Because it is difficult to identify all establishments in which tourists spend, underestimations occur. Also, the figures may include expenditures by local residents. Lack of inclusion of pre-payments made to tour operators or travel agencies in the home country may also cause underestimation. Analysis of expenditures by area of origin, length of stay and other tourist characteristics is also difficult with this method (Bailie, 1985).

Details of methods used by each major destination country can be found in WTO (1978). A summary of the methods used by countries in various regions of the world is displayed in Table 1.

Bank records are the most commonly used method world-wide, and are also most commonly used in Africa and Europe. Countries in North, South and Central America, however, favour sample surveys of tourists. Table 2 shows the collecting agency and the method used by the top twelve world destinations.

Comprehensive discussions of expenditure data collection in various countries can be found in the tourism literature. For example, Bailie (1985) explains methods used by Canada over the past few decades. Methods used in the United Kingdom and New Zealand are described by Likorish (1975) and Pearce (1981) respectively. Gibbons and Fish (1986) give a good summary of US tourism expenditures and receipts.

Table 2.1 *Tourism receipts data collection methods*
Number of countries using each method by world region

Region	Bank reports on exchange transactions of tourists	Sample surveys	Other[1]
Africa	17	5	6
Americas	8	16	1
Asia/Pacific	5	6	1
Middle East	3	1	1
South Asia	3	3	1
Europe	20	6	2
Total	56	37	12

Note: [1] 'Other' includes: Surveys of tourism establishments, estimations of tourism nights and daily expenditures and information from immigration agencies.
Source: *Methodological Supplement to World Travel Statistics*, WTO, Madrid, 1985.

Table 2.2 *Institutions responsible for collecting data and methods used by the top twelve world destinations*

Country	Source of statistics	Methods used
United States	Bureau of Economic Analysis	Sample surveys of tourists
Spain	Central Bank	Reports on exchange transactions
Italy	Central Bank	Reports on exchange transactions
France	Central Bank	Reports on exchange transactions
United Kingdom	National Tourism Administration	Sample surveys of tourists
Germany (F.R.)	Central Bank	Reports on exchange transactions
Austria	Central Bank	Reports on exchange transactions
Switzerland	Central Bank/Central Statistical Office	Tourist establishment surveys
Canada	Central Statistical Office	Sample surveys of tourists
Mexico	National Tourism Administration	Sample surveys of tourists
Belgium	Central Bank	Reports on exchange transactions
Hong Kong	National Tourism Administration	Sample surveys of tourists

Source: WTO, *Methodological Supplement to World Travel Statistics*, Madrid, Spain, 1985.

Comparisons of methods

Criticisms of data collection methods can be found in White and Walker (1982), Mak *et al.* (1977(a)), and Baretje (1982). Mak *et al.* (1977(a)) found that different survey methodologies produced different expenditure estimates. Two methods were tested on visitors to the Hawaiian Islands: a survey mailed to the tourist's home and the diary method during their stay. Post-trip home surveys were found to underestimate expenditures relative to the diary method. Perdue and Botkin (1988) found two other survey methods (used in Nebraska) also gave significantly different estimates. The two methods tested were tourist surveys conducted at self-selected stops in the destination, and enquiry conversion studies (post-trip home surveys of visitors who had requested information from the state travel office). The post-trip home survey showed significantly higher expenditure estimates than the other method. This contrasts with Mak *et al.*'s study, which concluded that the post-trip home survey underestimated expenditures. Both studies, however, cautioned against the use of post-trip home surveying of visitors, as it appears to be an inferior methodology.

In a disturbing study of data accuracy, White and Walker (1982) demonstrate the extent of inaccuracy of tourism expenditure data collected by major tourist destinations. Tourist expenditures and receipts reported by the governments of 40 countries were analysed. Accurate measurement should have yielded the expenditures in country A by residents of country B to equal country A's measurement of the receipts from tourists from country B. But the study showed that for all but one pair of countries, the figures were drastically different, and that in some instances the errors were 100% or more. In some cases, the two countries could not agree on whether they had a deficit or a surplus with another country. Countries using the same methods tended to have figures that matched more closely, showing the sensitivity of these figures to methodology and the biases created by different collection methods. The authors suggest that incompatible definitions, exchange rate conversions and political influences may explain the glaring differences. This study is an important sign to governments to increase the accuracy of expenditure figures. This is especially important as tourism grows to be the largest sector in so many of the world's economies.

Economic models of tourism expenditures

Tourism researchers, predominantly academicians, have used the data collected by government agencies to model tourism expenditures and to better understand the factors that affect expenditure levels. Most of this research is published either in economic journals such as *Applied Economics* or *International Economics Review* or journals covering economic issues of travel and tourism such as *Journal of Transport Economics and Policy*, *Transportation Research*, *Journal of Travel Research*, *Tourism Management* and *Annals of Tourism Research*. This research is predominantly concerned with constructing aggregate expenditure models of international tourism expenditures using time series macro-economic data. A few models use micro data from tourist surveys (collected either by government agencies or by the authors themselves) to better understand why, how and on what the individual tourist spends his money.

Macro models

The three explanatory variables typically used to explain aggregate international tourism expenditures in macro models are exchange rates, income in the origin country and price levels in the destination compared with those in the country of origin. Many authors have also included price levels in competitive destinations to capture substitution effects. Transportation costs, taste variables, marketing expenditures by the destination, weather and dummy variables to capture significant events also feature in some of the models. Table 3 summarizes the macro models developed by ten authors and shows the variables used and the calculated elasticities. The majority of these studies have modelled tourist expenditures between the US and Europe, leaving future researchers to study the rest of the world. A discussion of the variables used will be followed by a discussion of the model specifications used.

Income

In general, wealthier countries generate more tourists who also spend more than their poorer counterparts. Some studies have used a per capita income variable (Little, 1980; Artus, 1972; Chadee and Mieczkowski, 1987), some an aggregate income variable (Stronge and Redman, 1982; Kwack, 1972) and others have tested both in different model specifications (Gray, 1966; Loeb, 1982). Gray's results showed that elasticity values varied considerably when per capita and aggregate data were used. Even though discretionary or disposable income seem intuitively better to explain tourist spending, most studies have instead used total income.

Kwack (1972) found income to be the major explanatory variable for travel spending. He showed that when estimating US expenditures abroad, the addition of a relative price variable to the regression model (containing an income variable and a dummy variable) added very little to its explanatory power. The addition of the price variable for foreign spending in the US did, however, decrease the residual variance. Little (1980), on the contrary, found income to be less significant than relative price and exchange rates variables.

Knowledge of income elasticities for different countries can assist national tourism agencies in determining target markets for marketing strategies. Research has shown income elasticities to be almost exclusively positive but varying in size depending on the destination and the origin country (see Table 3). Tourism expenditures by foreigners in the US have been shown to be more sensitive to income changes than US spending abroad (Kwack, 1972). Stronge and Redman's study of US tourism spending in Mexico found expenditures in the interior of the country to be income elastic whereas border tourism spending was income inelastic. Border spending at the Canadian and US border has been studied by Kreck (1985).

The magnitude of income elasticities shows whether foreign travel is a normal good (as income increases more is spent on the good), an inferior good (as income increases less is spent on the good) or a luxury good (as income increases, substantially more is spent on the good). Despite rising income levels for US residents and devaluation of the currencies of Canada, France and Italy, US tourism expenditures in those countries have dropped significantly, suggesting that these countries are inferior goods (Little, 1980). Additional evidence that Canada is an inferior good for US tourists can be found in Chadee and Mieczkowski (1987). Countries demonstrating luxury-good characteristics for US tourists are Spain, Portugal, Norway, Sweden, Denmark, Austria, The Netherlands and Switzerland (White, 1985; O'Hagan and Harrison, 1984). Five other groups of European countries had positive income elasticities slightly less than unity, implying they are normal goods.

Income alone, however, does not explain aggregate tourist spending by the residents of a country; proximity to other countries and size of the country are also important determining factors. Small countries bordering many other countries spend a much higher percentage of their private consumption on foreign travel (e.g. Austria 6.7%, Norway 5.3%, The Netherlands 3.9%, Germany 3.8%) than do the US (0.6%) and Japan (0.5%), which are wealthier yet more isolated (Little, 1980).

Exchange rates

Exchange rates have been shown to affect both tourism expenditures and destination choice (Rosensweig, 1986). They have been included in many tourist expenditure models either explicitly or as part of the relative price variable. Gerakis (1965) studied four devaluations (France, Spain, Canada and Yugoslavia) and three revaluations (Finland, Germany and The Netherlands) that all took place in the late 1950s and early 1960s, before floating exchange rates were the norm. He showed that the rate of increase on tourism receipts in the country rose after each devaluation. The percentage increases varied from 15.1% (Canada) to 111.5% (Spain). The devaluations also caused a deceleration in the growth of tourism expenditures in competitive destinations. Revaluation of currencies, on the other hand, were followed by reductions in the country's tourism receipts of about 8%.

Other studies have tested the sensitivity of tourism expenditures to exchange rate fluctuations (Gray, 1966; Artus, 1972; Little, 1980; Loeb, 1982; Chadee and Mieczkowski, 1987) and are summarized in Table 3. When using annual data, the question arises as to which exchange rate should be applied. Gray (1966) dealt with this by using an average of twelve monthly exchange rates and weighted the third quarter (when most travel took place) more heavily. The

Table 2.3 Aggregate models to estimate tourism expenditures[1]

Author and date	Expenditure in	By tourists from	Explanatory variables used and their calculated elasticities				R²
			Income	Exchange rate	Relative prices	Other	
Gray (1966)	US	Canada	1.94 (per capita) 0.84 (aggregate)	−2.14			.90 .83
	Canada	US	2.28 (per capita) 1.12 (aggregate)	−1.22			.95 .98
	Rest of world	US	5.13 (per capita) 2.86 (aggregate)			Travel cost (−0.49)	.94 .97
	Rest of world	Canada	6.60 (per capita) 3.33 (aggregate)	−2.40		Travel cost (−0.21)	.95 .98
Barry and O'Hagan (1971)	Ireland	Great Britain	2.42 (per capita)		1.30		.92
Artus (1972)	12 European countries	US	0.83 to 3.84 (per capita)	−1.19 to −7.63	−1.02 to −5.09 −0.75 to −5.26 (lagged)	Various dummies	.92 to .99
Kwack (1972)	7 destinations	US	1.25		−1.574	Expo (.20)	.97
	US	Seven countries	1.55		−3.02	Expo (−.09)	.98
Little (1980)	10 destinations	US	−0.15 to 4.41 (per capita)	−0.58 to −3.15 (lagged)	−1.08 to −7.29 (lagged)	Political disturbances, Expo, special events, wars	.86 to .97

Study						
Loeb (1982)	US	Japan, Germany, UK, France, Sweden	.9 to 4.8 (per capita)	−0.12 to 4.07	−.5 to −6.4	Expo, Olympic Games .77 to .99
			.9 to 7.1 (aggregate)	−0.19 to 2.64	−.4 to −5.2	None .77 to .99
Stronge & Redman (1982)	Mexico	US	.45		.36 (Mexico to US) −1.20 (Mexico to overseas)	Border income (1.54) .97 Transoceanic fares (−0.26)
	Mexican border	US	Income of border states 2.99		−0.12 (Mexico to overseas)	Transoceanic fares (−0.32) .98
	Mexican interior	US			−0.63 (Mexico to overseas)	Transoceanic fares (−0.25) Overseas travel (0.96)
O'Hagan & Harrison (1984)	15 European countries	US	0.51 to 2.02		Uncompensated −2.56 to 0.35 Compensated −2.52 to 0.50	.19 to .95
White (1985)	Seven groups of countries in Europe	US	0.93 to 1.23		Uncompensated −2.28 to 1.33 Compensated −2.24 to 1.63	Political disturbances .45 to .96 Trend variable to capture tastes
Chadee & Mieczkowski (1987)	Canada	US	1.52 (per capita)	0.52	0.89 (Canadian Travel Price Index)	Seasonal dummies .93 to .95 Population

Note: [1] All authors used the log form of the multiple regression model and estimated it with ordinary squares (OLS) except for Loeb who estimated some models with the Corchrane-Orcutt procedure, and O'Hagan and Harrison (1984) and White (1985) who used the Almost Ideal Demand System (AIDS).

sign (i.e. positive or negative) of the exchange rate elasticity depends on whether it is expressed as the destination currency in terms of the tourist's currency or vice versa. (Elasticities calculated by Loeb (1982) and Chadee and Mieczkowski (1987) are predominantly positive rather than negative, because they defined the variable the opposite way to other authors.) In almost all cases, however, the elasticities showed that a 1% strengthening of the destination currency caused a decline in tourism expenditures to that region of between almost zero and 7.63%. Despite these results, Gerakis (1965) cautions that devaluation alone is not necessarily sufficient to bolster a country's travel account, but that a destination must also be geographically located so that tourism from neighbouring countries can be diverted.

As tourists do not readily know future exchange rates in advance, lagged exchange rates may have better explanatory power. Little (1980) used two-year lags and found them to be statistically significant in almost all cases. Ideally, models should also consider changes in other destinations' exchange rates, which might affect tourism spending.

Relative prices

Tourist expenditures are sensitive to prices in the destination relative to the home country. Ideally, a ratio of the travel price indexes (TPI) in both countries should be used as the relative price variable in tourism expenditure models. Such an index is not always available and so generic consumer price indexes (CPIs) are used by most authors (Chadee and Mieczkowski (1987) used the travel price index). Uysal and Crompton (1985) discuss how to calculate travel price indexes. The ratio of the US CPI to the Mexican CPI (both expressed in dollars) was found to be the best measure of purchasing power for border travellers between the US and Mexico (Gibbons and Fish, 1987). Expenditures by border travellers between the US and Mexico were found to respond more to a combination of price levels and exchange rates than to simply one or the other (Gibbons and Fish, 1987).

While Table 3 shows most price elasticities to be negative, Spain had a positive price elasticity in O'Hagan and Harrison's results (1984). Perhaps this is because US travellers see Spain as an upgraded version of Mexico, with a certain prestige value (Europeans, on the other hand, view Spain as a low-cost vacation). Lower prices in a destination may not only attract more expenditures on tourist related goods, but also cause tourists to purchase goods they would otherwise buy at home and attract residents from neighbouring countries on shopping trips. In these cases, the CPI may be the best measure of prices, because general products are being purchased.

As the availability of price information to tourists planning their trips is limited, lagged price levels may better explain tourist expenditures. Some authors have used lagged data in their studies and found this tends to create multi-collinearity and/or is statistically insignificant (Little, 1980; Stronge and Redman, 1982). The problem may be in lagging annual variables which include a time period long enough for consumers to adjust.

Some authors (Kwack, 1972; Loeb, 1962; Stronge and Redman, 1982) have included a weighted average of competitive destinations' CPIs in their models so that cross-price elasticities can be calculated. The weights ideally represent the proportion of spending by residents in the particular destination and the most frequented competitive destinations (Witt and Martin, 1987). Loeb (1982) also included the CPI of the home country to incorporate the effect of domestic tourism as competition for foreign tourism. A discussion of substitute prices in tourism-demand models can be found in Martin and Witt (1988). Cross-price elasticities measure changes in expenditures in country A in response to price changes in country B, and are able to determine whether countries are substitute destinations. White (1985) found France and UK and France and Germany to have positive price elasticities, implying that they are substitute destinations.

Cross-price elasticities can also measure substitution of one type of vacation for another as the prices of substitute vacations change. Taplin (1980) stressed the need for managers and policy makers to know cross-price elasticities between different vacation modes, such as vacation trips overseas by air, domestic vacation trips by air and domestic vacation trips by automobile. The study's geographical focus was Australia, but because data were not readily available to calculate all cross-price elasticities, Taplin amalgamated elasticity estimates from other studies and inferred the unknown cross-price elasticities. To do this he applied four conditions which each require that summations of certain elasticities equal a pre-determined value. The four conditions applied are (i) homogeneity (own-price, cross-price and income elasticities sum to zero); (ii) symmetry (if one cross-price elasticity, E_{ij}, is known then E_{ji} can be calculated); (iii) Cournot column aggregation (the condition that $\Sigma_i R_i E_{ij} = -R_j$ where R_i and R_j are proportions of total expenditures and E_{ij} is the cross elasticity of demand); and (iv) Engel aggregation (the condition that $\Sigma_i R_i E_{iy} = 1$, where E_{iy} is the income elasticity of demand). The results suggest that a 1% reduction in overseas airfares would increase overseas air trips by 1.8% and decrease domestic trips by 1.7%. A 1% decrease in domestic airfare would increase domestic air travel by 2.1% and decrease overseas travel by 0.4%.

Transportation costs

Transportation costs from the origin to the destination tend to affect tourist expenditures, but are difficult to estimate due to the large number of modes and fares available to most destinations. Many authors have, therefore, not included the variable in their models, either for this reason or because it causes multi-collinearity with the income variable (Fujii and Mak, 1980). Authors who have included it have found it to be statistically insignificant (Little, 1980; Gray, 1966). Stronge and Redman (1982) also found no evidence that increases in transoceanic fares caused US tourists to substitute Mexico for more distant destinations.

Other variables

Political and social events affect aggregate tourism expenditures. Some studies have simply measured the economic impact of such events (Ritchie and Aitken, 1984), and others have included them as dummy variables in models. Examples of dummy variables used in models of tourism expenditures are the 1967 Expo in Montreal (Kwack, 1972; Loeb, 1982), the Olympic Games (Loeb, 1982), and strikes and political disturbances (Barry and O'Hagan, 1971; White, 1985; Little, 1980). Some authors have found that dummy variables add to the explanatory power of the models (O'Hagan and Harrison, 1984; Chadee and Mieczkowski, 1987), while others have found them to be insignificant (Loeb, 1982; Barry and O'Hagan, 1971).

Additional (non-dummy) variables used to explain aggregate tourist expenditures are the weather in the destination (Barry and O'Hagan, 1971), marketing expenditures by the destination (Barry and O'Hagan, 1971), and time-trend variables to capture tastes (Loeb, 1982).

Model specifications

A comprehensive discussion of travel demand model specification can be found in Quandt (1970). The majority of the aggregate tourism expenditure models in the literature use standard multiple regression. There is a consensus that the log-linear form is preferable to the linear form because it better explains the relationships, and because the parameters estimated by the model are the elasticities (Perdue and Botkin, 1988; Loeb, 1982). A typical model specification is as follows:

$$\log \mathrm{EXP}_{ij} = a_0 + a_1 \log Y_j + a_2 \log \mathrm{XR}_{ij} + a_3 \log \mathrm{RP}_{ij} + e_{ij}$$

where EXP_{ij} is the expenditures by tourists from region j in country i, Y_j is the income of country j, XR_{ij} is the exchange rate between the two countries, RP_{ij} is the relative price variable, e_{ij} is the error term and a_0 through a_3 are the parameters (and also the elasticities). The explanatory power of most of the models is high, with adjusted R^2 values often exceeding 0.90 (see Table 3).

Serial correlation (correlated error terms) and multi-collinearity (two or more variables highly correlated) are problems frequently encountered in tourism expenditure regression models. Serial correlation has been overcome by using the Corchrane–Orcutt procedure (Loeb, 1982) and the Dhrymes search method (Kwack, 1972). Multi-collinearity has proven to be a more pervasive problem for many authors, especially between the income and transportation cost variables, between the exchange rate and price variables and between the income variable and trend variable. Fujii and Mak (1980) suggest the use of ridge regression instead of ordinary least squares to estimate models when variables are highly correlated. The estimates produced by ridge regression, even though they may be biased, produce smaller variances of the estimators.

Recently, researchers have looked to more sophisticated models to estimate tourism expenditures. A generic system expenditure model developed by Deaton and Muellbauer (1980) called the **Almost Ideal Demand System**

(AIDS) has been used by White (1984), O'Hagan and Harrison (1980) and O'Hagan and Harrison (1984) to estimate US tourism expenditures in Europe. The model estimates a system of budget-share equations for different groups of commodities. It assumes that the consumer (tourist) makes expenditure decisions in two stages—first in a broad category (region of the world) and then on specific goods (countries) in that category (region). The specification of the model is as follows:

$$s_i = a_i + \sum_{j=1}^{n} b_{ij} \log p_j + c_i \log(x/P^*) + u_i \qquad i = 1 \ldots n$$

where s_i is the percentage share of country i in country j's expenditure in the region, p_j is the price level in country j, x is per capita expenditure in the region, $P^* = \Pi_{pj}^{si}$, n is the number of countries, a_i, b_{ij} and c_i are parameters and u_i is a normal disturbance term. It is estimated using ordinary least squares. An advantage of the model is that it produces both uncompensated and compensated price elasticities. Compensated price elasticities hold total real expenditures constant and estimate how expenditures would be switched from one destination to another.

Another model specification called the linear expenditure system (LES) has been tested using tourism data by Smeral (1988). It is based on the Stone-Geary utility function, and has been shown to be superior to the linear and log-linear regression models in estimating tourism expenditures (Smeral, 1988). A comparison of the accuracy of estimates from the LES model, the AIDS model and the Rotterdam model concluded that elasticity estimates from the LES model are less reliable than those of the other two models (Fujii *et al.*, 1987). The authors suggest that the model is therefore limited in its usefulness for policy formulation, but is acceptable for forecasting purposes.

A comprehensive regional science model called the Tourism Expenditure Model (TEM) has been developed by Fritz *et al.* (1984). Amongst other things, it computes price coefficients for tourism expenditures in five different categories. These coefficients are then combined with tourism flow data to estimate spending generated by tourism in each of the categories.

More research work is needed to test the comparable accuracy of such models. At the same time, researchers should be encouraged to continue to adapt more sophisticated models—especially those using cross-sectional data—from economics and regional science to model tourism expenditure.

No discussion of aggregate tourism expenditures would be complete without mentioning input–output analysis and multipliers. These techniques have been used extensively to analyse the impact of tourism expenditures on the economy of a region, and contribute greatly to the understanding of the overall effect of tourism expenditures. This important topic deserves a review paper of its own, and cannot be given adequate coverage here. The interested reader is therefore referred to major works in this area (Archer, 1976; Archer, 1977; Liu and Var, 1983; Chappelle, 1985; Schaffer, 1985; Liu, 1986; Milne, 1987).

Micro models

This section of the paper will review models which use cross-sectional micro data to analyse tourist characteristics that determine spending patterns, and the distribution of tourist spending amongst different categories of goods.

Tourist characteristics affecting expenditures

The effect of tourist characteristics on expenditures has been analysed by Pizam and Reichel (1979); Mak *et al.* (1977b); O'Leary *et al.* (1987); Sakai (1988); and Tideman (1982). Pizam and Reichel were interested in determining the characteristics that differentiated two groups of US domestic tourists— those spending very large amounts and those spending substantially less than average. They used discriminant analysis on expenditure data collected by the US Bureau of the Census and found 23 characteristics to be significant. Amongst the most important were the education and marital status of tourists, the value of their homes, and the number of cars owned and the size of their communities.

The effect of age on tourist spending patterns has received little research attention. As the mature market continues to grow and constitute a major segment of the travelling public, it deserves more careful analysis. An initial study to determine mature market tourist expenditures on recreation activities has been carried out by O'Leary *et al.* (1987).

In some decision-making situations, the per capita daily spending is more important than the total spending per trip. Mak *et al.* (1977b) tested the notion that the length of stay in a destination determines a tourist's daily per capita expenditures. They used a two-stage least squares model to jointly estimate per capital daily expenditures and length of stay, with both variables being endogenous to the model as follows:

$$ALS_i = f_i (PCDE_i, X_{1i}, \ldots, X_{ni})$$
$$PCDE_i = f_i (ALS_i, X_1i, \ldots, X_{ni})$$

where ALS_i is the average length of stay, $PCDE_i$ is the per capita daily expenditure and X_{ni} represents exogenous variables such as airfare, accommodation type and vacation mode. Their results had low R^2 values, but suggested the following tendencies:

— tourists staying longer at a destination tended to spend less per person per day;
— higher transportation costs to the destination implied higher per capita daily expenditures;
— tourists with higher income and lower education levels tended to spend more per day;
— large travelling groups tended to spend less per person per day;
— repeat visitors and first-time visitors showed no significant difference in their daily spending levels.

Business travellers are typically included in tourism expenditure statistics; however, they have been somewhat overlooked in studies of expenditures. This may be because, in the past, they have constituted a relatively small section of the travelling public. It is now, however, a rapidly growing group as the world becomes a global market-place. Kwack (1972), in his macro study of US expenditures abroad, added variables—import and export figures, direct investment abroad and outflows of US capital—to capture business activity in the model. The only variable associated with business travel found to be significant was direct investment. A more thorough micro-analysis of business travel expenditures has been done by Sakai (1988). The Linear Expenditure System (LES) was used to determine price elasticities for business travellers. Results showed that this group spent more on categories of goods usually sponsored by the traveller's company—namely meals, lodging and transportation. Sakai argues that this is because these goods provide dual benefit— both personal and business. Business travellers also spent less than pleasure travellers on categories of goods such as clothing and recreation.

The expenditure elasticities for each of the five categories of goods (food, lodging, recreation, transport, clothing) showed that the only category differing significantly from unity was lodging (1.10), implying that it is a luxury good. For pleasure travellers, lodging and transportation were determined to be luxury goods (1.13 and 1.12 respectively) and food and recreation were normal goods (0.85 and 0.87 respectively). All categories of goods were price inelastic for business travellers. For pleasure travellers, price elasticities were significantly less than for business travellers in the categories of transportation and clothing. These are important results for travel firms to be aware of when pricing their products. Fundamental to this analysis is the fact that business expenditures create a dual benefit at both the business and the personal level. Sakai (1988) and Clotfelter (1983) both suggest that because personal benefit is obtained from business travel this leads to inefficient allocation of resources, having implications for tax policy relating to business travel.

Conference tourism, which is part of business travel, is growing rapidly and yet has escaped the attention of researchers. Destination cities often expect conference tourists to fill rooms in off-peak seasons and to have higher spending levels than pleasure tourists. A simple cost-benefit analysis of conference tourism in a few cities has been done by Tideman (1982). More work is needed, however, to more fully understand expenditure patterns of conference tourists.

Expenditures on different categories of goods
Other micro studies have analysed the categories of goods that tourists tend to purchase, as well as spending levels in each category. Estimates of tourist expenditures in various categories can be found for British tourist spending in Ireland in Barry and O'Hagan (1971), and for tourist spending in Hawaii in Fujii *et al.* (1985). Fujii *et al.* (1985) used the AIDS model (discussed in the section on macro models) with micro data to estimate a tourist's expenditure in different categories of goods (food, lodging, clothing, transport, entertainment,

other). The dependent variable was budget share spent on a given commodity in a given destination. Cross-price elasticities were found to be very small for all categories of goods except lodging. Increases in lodging prices tended to decrease expenditures on clothing and entertainment but increase food expenditures. Increases in food prices tended to reduce demand for other goods at the destination; not surprising if the tourist has a fixed budget. A further discussion of tourist spending on food can be found in Sheldon and Fox (1988).

Retail shopping in a destination for goods such as souvenirs, gifts and clothing represents a significant proportion of tourist expenditures. It also tends to be more sensitive to changes in relative prices than other categories of goods such as transportation or accommodation. Only a few authors have studied retail spending (Keown, 1989; Keown, *et al*., 1984; Vukonic, 1986).

Parent and Etzel (1976) modelled aggregate retail expenditures in a destination. They used sales tax receipts to estimate total retail expenditures in the region and then subtracted resident spending. Their model is as follows:

$$T_e = R_n - S_r + O_{tx}$$

where T_e is the value of retail expenditures by tourists, R_n are total retail sales, S_r are resident retail expenditures and O_{tx} are retail expenditures by residents outside the region. An advantage of this method is that much of the data required is readily available from tax records.

Different nationalities of tourists have unique expectations and behaviour patterns when shopping on vacation, and retail managers should be aware of this. Keown (1989) studied Japanese tourists' shopping behaviour in Hawaii to identify the types of goods purchased, tourist expectations of the stores and personnel and the information sources used to identify purchase options. The major product categories purchased were liquor, souvenirs and cosmetics. Attributes of the stores such as service, warranties and product knowledge were found to be important for the Japanese tourist. In a comprehensive study of American tourist perception of retail stores in twelve countries, Keown *et al*. (1984) found in-store treatment, the actual purchase, retailers' concern and orientation to the customer and perceived business ethics to be important factors in US tourists' level of satisfaction with the shopping experience. The findings also suggested that price elasticities for retail goods were low.

Some tourist retail shopping is for goods to be consumed on vacation, and some is for goods to take home. Keown suggests that four variables determine tourists' propensity to buy goods for home consumption: the types of products available, the level of domestic tax and import duties, the relative value of goods and the retailers' strategy. In response to low levels of tourist spending in Yugoslavia, Vukonic (1986) surveyed tourists to Yugoslavia to determine why expenditures were so low. He found that one-third of tourists leaving Yugoslavia spent less than they had planned to, and attributes this to a lack of variety of tourist retail products (Keown's first variable).

After retail shopping, spending on entertainment, recreation and visitor attractions is perhaps the most responsive to relative prices. Even though all recreational activities are not necessarily touristic activities, a number of studies shed light on how tourists may spend money on recreational pursuits (Dardis *et al.*, 1981; Thompson and Tinsley, 1979; Fesenmaier and Lieber, 1987; Lieber and Allton, 1983). The more attractions in a region, the more a tourist is likely to spend, both on entry fees and at the concessions in the attraction. Perdue (1986) has investigated how unplanned visits to attractions affect expenditure levels in Nebraska. He uses the diary survey method to show that spontaneous visits increase visitor expenditures by $25 per group per attraction. To increase tourist expenditures in a region, therefore, policy makers may want to encourage tourists to deviate from their itineraries and enjoy attractions *en route*.

Conclusion

The topic of tourism expenditure research is a broad one which includes the basic research issues associated with data collection, in addition to academic research associated with modelling tourism expenditures. This review has shown that the accuracy, compatibility and availability of tourism expenditure data are less than ideal, and require attention from the appropriate governmental agencies in collaboration with academics and economists if their quality is to improve. Academic research has tended to over-emphasize macro models of aggregate tourist expenditures, especially between the US and Europe, and has relied too heavily on standard multiple regression models. To expand the field, researchers should be investigating tourism expenditure patterns in other parts of the world, especially the Asia-Pacific region, and also applying more creative and sophisticated models to explain tourist expenditures in general. The substitution of domestic and foreign tourist expenditures deserves more study, as does the effect of customs and currency controls on international tourist expenditures.

The greatest gap in tourism expenditure research, however, appears to be in the field of micro and behavioural studies. Researchers are encouraged to focus their attention here, even though it may necessitate the collection of their own data. This will provide a more thorough understanding of disaggregate spending patterns of different subgroups such as women, mature travellers and conference tourists. It will also provide insight into why and under what conditions tourists buy goods for home consumption or for vacation consumption. The results of such disaggregate studies should be able to assist managers, marketers and policy makers in their decision-making in ways that aggregate analysis is unable to.

References

Archer, B. H., 1976, 'The anatomy of a multiplier', *Regional Studies*, 10(1): pp. 71–7.

Archer, B. H., 1977, *Tourism Multipliers—the state of the art*, occasional papers in *Economics*, No. 11, University of Wales Press, Bangor.

Artus, J. R., 1972, 'An econometric analysis of international travel', *International Monetary Fund Staff Papers*, 19(4): pp. 579–613.

Bailie, J. G., 1985, 'The evolution of Canadian international travel documentation', *Annals of Tourism Research*, 12(4): pp. 563–79.

Baretje, R., 1982, 'Tourism's external account and the balance of payments', *Annals of Tourism Research*, 9(1): pp. 57–67.

Barry, K., O'Hagan, J. W., 1971, 'An econometric study of British tourist expenditure in Ireland', *Economic and Social Review*, 3(2): pp. 143–61.

Chadee, D., Mieczkowski, Z., 1987, 'An empirical analysis of the effects of exchange rate on Canadian tourism'. *Journal of Travel Research*, 26(1): pp. 13–18.

Chappelle, D. E., 1985, 'Strategies for developing multipliers useful in assessing economic impacts of recreation and tourism', in Dennis B. Propst (ed.), *Assessing the Economic Impacts of Recreation and Tourism*, Southeastern Forest Experiment Station, Asheville, North Carolina, pp. 1–6.

Clotfelter, C. T., 1983, 'Tax-induced distortions and the business-pleasure borderline: the case of travel and entertainment', *The American Economic Review*, 73(5): pp. 1053–65.

Dardis, R., Frederick, D., Lehfeld, A., Wolfe, K. E., 1981, 'Cross-section studies of recreation expenditures in the United States', *Journal of Leisure Research*, 13(3): pp. 181–94.

Deaton, A., Muellbauer, J., 1980, 'An almost ideal demand system', *American Economic Review*, 70(3): pp 312–26.

Fesenmaier, D. R., Lieber, S. R., 1987, 'Outdoor recreation expenditures and the effects of spatial structure', *Leisure Sciences*, 9(1): pp. 27–40.

Fish, M., Gibbons, J. D., 1985/86, 'Target markets for the US international tourism industry', *Mid-Atlantic Journal of Business*, 24, winter 1985/86: pp. 15–30.

Frechtling, D. G., 1974, 'A model for estimating travel expenditures', *Journal of Travel Research*, 12(4): pp. 9–12.

Fritz, R. G., Konecny, M., Stoucas, P. D., 1984, 'Tourism expenditure model—a functional planning and policy-making tool', *Tourism Management*, 5(2): pp. 110–16.

Fujii, E. T., Khaled, M., Mak, J., 1985, 'An almost ideal demand system for visitor expenditures', *Journal of Transport Economics and Policy*, 19(5): pp. 161–71.

Fujii, E. T., Khaled, M., Mak, J., 1987, 'An empirical comparison of systems of demand equations: an application to visitor expenditures in resort destinations', *Philippine Review of Business and Economics*, 24(1&2), pp. 79–102.

Fujii, E. T., Mak, J., 1980, 'Forecasting travel demand when the explanatory variables are highly correlated', *Journal of Travel Research*, 18(4): pp. 31–2.

Gee, C. Y., Makens, J. C., Choy, D. J. L., 1989, *The Travel Industry*, Van Nostrand Reinhold, New York.

Gerakis, A. S., 1965, 'Effects of exchange-rate devaluations and revaluations on receipts from tourism', *IMF Staff Papers*, No. 12, March: pp. 365–84.

Gibbons, J. D., Fish, M., 1985, 'Devaluation and US tourism expenditure in Mexico', *Annals of Tourism Research*, 12(4): pp. 547–62.

Gibbons, J. D., Fish, M., 1986, 'Dynamics of the US international tourism market, 1970–1984', *Journal of Travel Research*, 24(4): pp. 17–24.

Gibbons, J. D., Fish, M., 1987, 'Market sensitivity of US and Mexican border travel', *Journal of Travel Research*, 26(4): pp. 2–6.

Gray, H. P., 1966, 'The demand for international travel by the United States and Canada', *International Economic Review*, 7(1): pp. 83–92.

Hawaii Visitors Bureau, 1987, *Visitor Expenditure Survey*, Honolulu, Hawaii.

International Monetary Fund, 1977, *Balance of Payments Manual*, fourth edition, Washington DC.

Keown, C., Jacobs, L., Worthley, R., 1984, 'American tourists' perception of retail stores in 12 selected countries', *Journal of Travel Research*, 22(3): pp. 26–30.

Keown, C. F., 1989, 'A mode of tourists' propensity to buy: the case of Japanese visitors to Hawaii', *Journal of Travel Research*, 27(3): pp. 31–4.

Kreck, L., 1985, 'The effect of the across-the-border commerce of Canadian tourists on the city of Spokane', *Journal of Travel Research*, 24(1): pp. 27–31.

Kwack, S. Y., 1972, 'Effects of income and prices on travel spending abroad', *International Economic Review*, 13(2): pp. 245–56.

Lickorish, L. J., 1975, 'The statistics of tourism', in W. F. Maunder (ed.), *Review of United Kingdom Statistical Sources*, Heinemann Educational Books, London.

Lieber, S. R., Allton, D., 1983, 'Visitor expenditures and the economic impact of public recreation facilities in Illinois, in Leiber and Fesenmaier (eds), *Recreation Planning and Management*, Venture Publishing, State College, Pennsylvania, pp. 36–54.

Little, J. S., 1980, 'International travel in the US balance of payments', *New England Economic Review*, May, 1980: pp. 42–5.

Liu, J. C., 1986, 'Relative economic contributions of visitor groups in Hawaii', *Journal of Travel Research*, 25(1): pp. 2–9.

Liu, J. C., Var, T., 1983, 'The economic impact of tourism in metropolitan Victoria, B.C.', *Journal of Travel Research*, 22(2): pp. 8–15.

Loeb, P. D., 1982, 'International travel to the United States', *Annals of Tourism Research*, 9(1): pp. 7–20.

Mak, J., Moncur, J., Yonamine, D., 1977(a), 'How or how not to measure visitor expenditures', *Journal of Travel Research*, 16(1): pp. 1–4.

Mak, J., Moncur, J., Yonamine, D., 1977(b), 'Determinants of visitor expenditures and visitor lengths of stay: a cross-section analysis of US visitors to Hawaii', *Journal of Travel Research*, 15(1): pp. 5–8.

Martin, C. A., Witt, S., 1988, 'Substitute prices in models of tourism demand', *Annals of Tourism Research*, 15(2): pp. 255–68.

McIntosh, R. W., Goeldner, C. R., 1986, *Tourism: Principles, Practices, Philosophies*, Wiley, New York.

Milne, S. S., 1987, 'Differential multipliers', *Annals of Tourism Research*, 14(4): pp. 499–515.

O'Hagan, J. W., Harrison, M. J., 1980, 'UK and US visitor expenditure in Ireland', *Economic and Social Review*, 15(3): pp. 195–207.

O'Hagan, J. W., Harrison, M. J., 1984, 'Market shares of US tourist expenditure in Europe: an econometric analysis', *Applied Economics*, 16(6): pp. 919–31.

O'Leary, J. T., Uysal, M., Howell, R., 1987, 'Travel patterns and expenditures of the mature market', *Visions in Leisure and Business*, 6(2): pp. 39–51.

Pearce, D. G., 1981, 'Estimating visitor expenditure: a review and a New Zealand case study', *International Journal of Tourism Management*, 2(4): pp. 240–56.

Perdue, R. R., 1986, 'The influence of unplanned attraction visits on expenditures by travel-through visitors', *Journal of Travel Research*, 25(1): pp. 14–19.

Perdue, R. R., Botkin, M. R., 1988, 'Visitor survey versus conversion study', *Annals of Tourism Research*, 15(1): pp. 76–87.

Pizam, A., Reichel, A., 1979, 'Big spenders and little spenders in US tourism', *Journal of Travel Research*, 18(1): pp. 42–3.

Quandt, R. E., 1970, *The Demand for Travel: Theory and Measurement*, Heath Lexington, Massachusetts.

Ritchie, J. R. B., Aitken, C. A., 1984, 'Assessing the impacts of the 1988 Olympic winter games: the research program and initial results', *Journal of Travel Research*, 22(3): pp. 17–25.

Rosensweig, J. A., 1985, 'The dollar and the US travel deficit', *Economic Review: Federal Reserve Bank of Atlanta*, October 1985: pp. 4–13.

Rosensweig, J. A., 1986, 'Exchange rates and competition for tourists', *New England Economic Review*, July/August 1986: pp. 57–67.

Sakai, M. Y., 1988, 'A micro-analysis of business travel demand', *Applied Economics*, 20(6): pp. 1481–95.

Schaffer, W. A., 1985, 'Using input-output analysis to measure the impact of tourist expenditures: the case of Hawaii', in Dennis B. Propst (ed.), *Assessing the Economic Impacts of Recreation and Tourism*, Southeastern Forest Experiment Station, Asheville, North Carolina, pp. 7–15.

Sheldon, P. J., Fox, M., 1988, 'The role of foodservice in vacation choice and experience: a cross-cultural analysis', *Journal of Travel Research*, 27(2): pp. 9–15.

Smeral, E., 1988, 'Tourism demand, economic theory and econometrics: an integrated approach', *Journal of Travel Research*, 26(4): pp. 38–43.

Stronge, W. B., Redman, M., 1982, 'US tourism in Mexico: an empirical analysis', *Annals of Tourism Research*, 9(1): pp. 21–35.

Taplin, J. H. E., 1980, 'A coherence approach to estimates of price elasticities in the vacation travel market', *Journal of Transport Economics and Policy*, 14(1): pp. 19–35.

Thompson, C. S., Tinsley, A. W., 1979, 'Income expenditure elasticities for recreation: their estimation and relation to demand for recreation', *Journal of Leisure Research*, 11(4): pp. 265–70.

Tideman, M. C., 1982, 'Cost-benefit analysis of congress tourism', *Tourist Review*, 37(4): pp. 22–4.

Uysal, M., Crompton, J. L., 1985, 'Deriving a relative price index for inclusion in international tourism demand estimation models', *Journal of Travel Research*, 24(1): pp. 32–4.

Vukonic, B., 1986, 'Foreign tourist expenditures in Yugoslavia', *Annals of Tourism Research*, 13(1): pp. 59–78.

White, K. J., 1985, 'An international travel demand model: US travel to Western Europe', *Annals of Tourism Research*, 12(4): pp. 529–45.

White, K. H., Walker, M. B., 1982, 'Trouble in the travel account', *Annals of Tourism Research*, 9(1): pp. 37–56.

Witt, S., Martin, C., 1987, 'Deriving a relative price index for inclusion in international travel demand estimation models: comment', *Journal of Travel Research*, 25(3): pp. 38–40.

WTO, 1978, *The Travel Item in the Balance of Payments*, World Tourism Organization, Madrid.

WTO, 1980, *Definitions Concerning Tourism Statistics*, World Tourism Organization, Madrid, pp. 15–16.

WTO, 1981(a), *Guidelines for the Collection and Presentation of International Tourism Statistics*, World Tourism Organization, Madrid.

WTO, 1981(b), *Guidelines on International Tourism Statistics*, World Tourism Organization, Madrid.

WTO, 1982, *Handbook on Sampling Methods Applicable to Tourism Statistics*, World Tourism Organization, Madrid.

WTO, 1983, *Methodologies for Carrying Out Sample Surveys on Tourism*, World Tourism Organization, Madrid.

WTO, 1985, *Methodological Supplement to World Travel Statistics*, World Tourism Organization, Madrid.

3 Geography and tourism: a review of selected literature, 1985–1988

R. V. Smith and L. S. Mitchell

Definitions and concepts

This chapter reports on the recent literature produced on the geography of tourism. The publications reviewed have been selected from the burgeoning volume of work published by English-speaking geographers, mostly from the United States, Canada, New Zealand and Australia. There is substantial literature produced by others, especially from West and Central European countries, as well as growing interest in China and Japan. While a shortage of space prevents us from dealing with developments from these parts of the world, it is hoped that a similar review article covering these contributions can be produced by others.

To set the review that follows into context, perhaps a definition of geography should be offered. There are many definitions of the discipline, but for our purposes the focus is on spatial considerations. More precisely, geographers are concerned with human spatial behaviour and with how people (and groups and organizations and other institutions) organize their use of earth space. Since all of this movement occurs on, just below and just above the earth's surface, geographers are inevitably concerned with the nature and dynamics of that environment within which human activities take place.

It follows then that geographers performing research and writing about tourism (and works accomplished by non-geographers on geographic themes) are concerned with the nature of the places visited and the movements involved in reaching and returning from those places. Tourism accounts for an increasingly large proportion of both our leisure time and our resources. It is dynamic in nature. Therefore, comparative studies of tourism are of increasing importance, as are studies examining countries and places where tourism is becoming more important as an economic and social phenomenon. Paralleling these concerns is an increasing emphasis on developing theory, improving research methodologies and contributing to the growing need for planning on all geographic scales. Tourism, by its very nature, is an activity that focuses on human spatial behaviour and spatial organization. The growing interest of geographers in studying this activity is readily apparent.

North American historical perspective

The roots of research into the geography of tourism have been traced to the 1920s (Carlson, 1980(a)) and are intermingled with the development of the geography of recreation. A number of articles published during that period contained references to recreation and tourism activities and facilities, but the first publication that focused on the theme was by McMurry (1930). Recreation and tourism research increased slowly from 1930 until 1959, but a quantum leap has occurred in the number of publications during the past three decades (Carlson, 1980(a)); Mitchell, 1981). The growing economic and social importance of recreation and tourism and an increase in the number of geographers interested in the topic are the most plausible explanations for this rapid growth.

A fairly large number of articles and manuscripts surveying various aspects of recreation and tourism have been presented over the years. The first was a four-page review included as a portion of a larger chapter on economic geography (McMurry, 1954). Probably the most influential was 'Perspectives on the nature of outdoor recreation: a bibliographical survey' (Wolfe, 1964). Appearing at the very beginning of the rapid increase in publishing activity, this article traced the growth of interest in recreation and predicted the increase in research results.

In 1980 another article, 'Geographical research on international and domestic tourism', and a reference work, 'A bibliography of geographical research on tourism' (Carlson, 1980(a) and (b)) examined the growth of tourism, traced the evolution of geographic research on tourism, discussed research trends of the 1970s and provided a comprehensive bibliography of 349 entries. Another paper, 'Fifty years of recreation geography research: 1930–1979' (Mitchell, 1981), presented results of a survey of eleven geographic and leisure journals and graphically illustrated the growth and classification by topic and region of publications related to recreation, tourism and sport. In addition, the production of theses and dissertations on recreation themes was traced historically and classified by topic. A book chapter entitled 'Geographical research on leisure: reflections and anticipations on Accrington Stanley and fire hydrants' (Butler, 1982) investigated the evolution of geographical research on leisure, emphasized the major concepts of interest during the 1970s, examined the nature of current geographic research on leisure and concluded with a discussion of future research needs and directions.

Another article, 'Reflections on the development of geographic research in recreation: hey buddy, can you s'paradigm?' (Smith, 1983), contained the statement that '. . . recreation geography is as diverse and as eclectic a "specialization" as one can probably imagine'. This article surveyed the field utilizing the concepts of area studies, man–land tradition and spatial analysis, and concluded that the notion of a paradigm is irrelevant to recreation geography, or that recreation geography is at a pre-paradigmatic state. When 'Tourism research in the United States: a geographic perspective' (Mitchell, 1984) appeared, it presented perspectives on the evolution of tourism research, the nature of research, the methods of research and ten research fields and principal findings. This review concluded that the future of tourism research appears bright because of a declining and ageing population, the changing structure of the national economy and the increasing importance of *fitness-wellness* life styles that emphasize positive leisure-time experiences. A later article, 'Recreation geography: inventory and prospect' (Mitchell and Smith, 1985), was a logical extension of earlier reviews by McMurry (1954) and Wolfe (1964). This essay traced the historical development of recreational geography, analysed a selected literature, classified papers presented at meetings of the Association of American Geographers, examined some examples of applied recreational geography and identified departments with strong recreational geography programmes. The conclusion listed six probable trends of the future and stated that '. . . recreational geography is now a major subdivision of the discipline'.

Before this chapter is published, at least three additional reviews of some or all of the major topics of interest to recreational geographers will be added to the literature in the form of book chapters. These will include 'The spatial perspective in recreation and leisure research' by Stephen L. J. Smith; 'Trends in recreation geography', by Lisle S. Mitchell and Richard V. Smith; and 'Applied recreation research' by Robert L. Janiskee and Lisle S. Mitchell.

Four books

Four books published during the recent past are particularly worthy of comment. One is a plea for more scholarly research and writing on tourism, two are textbooks that are really more than conventional texts and one is a handbook on helpful quantitative methods for the tourism geographer.

John Jakle, a professor of geography at the University of Illinois-Champaign, published a provocative book in 1985 entitled *The Tourist: Travel in Twentieth-Century North America*. Jakle's book makes two valuable contributions. First, he focuses on the importance of tourism as a human activity. His argument identifies several aspects of this issue, including the nature of human sociability and the fact that tourism is the activity that permits a large proportion of the population in economically advanced countries to assess the complexity of their world. These and related themes are summarized in his compelling statement that '. . . no widely shared human activity, irrespective of presumed superficialities, should be ignored. The role of tourism as a part of the modern world needs to be fully understood'. The bulk of his book is an intriguing account of tourists and tourism in early twentieth-century North America, offering an ample analysis of trends and options in the years after World War II. After setting the stage with a discussion of tourists in the landscape, he devotes much attention to the rise of the automobile and the expanding range of tourism alternatives. These and other themes lead to an understanding of the fundamental purpose of his book—'to make travel more effective by examining the roots of modern tourism'.

Professor Peter E. Murphy of the University of Victoria published his text, *Tourism: A Community Approach*, in 1985. Murphy's book is both a text that has seen considerable use in university classes and an argument for a new way of looking at and planning for tourism. The geographic focus of the book is Canada, the United States and the United Kingdom. He provides a thorough review of the literature and develops his thesis under the categories of the environment and accessibility, economics and business (economic cycles and benefits and economic response strategies), hospitality and authenticity— along with the related social and cultural strategies for promoting tourism— and planning and management. The latter themes provide Murphy with the vehicle for his contention that tourism should be considered a community industry and that an ecological approach and systems theory should be fully employed in future tourism planning. Murphy clearly believes that communities should control their own destinies and that they have the potential to do so if appropriate planning is undertaken.

The third important book, *Tourism Today: A Geographical Analysis*, was published in 1987. Its author, Douglas Pearce, is a prominent New Zealand geographer who has had much experience in Europe and the United States. Pearce's text follows more conventional lines than does Murphy's, beginning with an introduction to tourism models followed by a discussion of motivations and demand for tourist travel. Patterns of tourism at intra-national and inter-national levels are then reviewed. The remainder of the book focuses on examining the spatial structure of tourism on scales ranging from local to national. Such structures are then examined in the context of special settings such as islands, coastal areas and cities. Pearce provides a conceptual basis for the study of flows and tourist places using well-developed case studies drawn from diverse locales. His book has a broader geographic reach than does that of Murphy. He concludes by arguing for much more research on tourism, especially in Third World areas, now largely ignored in tourism studies. He also cites the need for more systematic and comparative analyses, and finally suggests that many more longitudinal studies must be undertaken to permit a better understanding of developments over time.

The fourth and most recent book of note is Stephen L. J. Smith's *Tourism Analysis: A Handbook* (1989). This book's purpose '. . . is to introduce the reader to a variety of quantitative methods useful for tourism analysis'. Smith has made numerous earlier contributions to the study of both recreation and tourism and is a leader in encouraging a more analytical approach to the study of leisure. He explains relatively complex methods in a clear manner, using contemporary and readily understandable examples. He deals with quantitative methods that help define tourism and explain the tourist, forecast trends, segment markets, select sites, describe tourist regions and estimate economic impacts. In the process of examining and reviewing numerous important methods, he offers an integrated concept of how tourism studies might proceed. This volume is of value to all students of tourism, regardless of the particular discipline they represent or their role in the public or private sectors of tourism.

Bibliographic review of the journal literature

This review is based on a sample of tourism literature taken from ten of the most significant geographic and interdisciplinary journals in the United States and Canada. These journals include: *Annals of the Association of American Geographers, Geographic Review, Economic Geography, Professional Geographer, Journal of Geography, Canadian Geographer, Annals of Tourism Research, Journal of Leisure Research, Leisure Sciences* and *Tourism Management*. A total of 82 articles published between 1985 and 1988, written by geographers and by non-geographers on a geographic theme, were considered for review. Sixty-seven of the articles were subjectively grouped into eleven separate conceptual clusters (Table 1). These clusters will be reviewed in the following order: Spatial patterns, Third World recreation and tourism, Evolution of tourism, Impacts of recreation and tourism, Methods used in recreation and tourism research, Planning and development, Coastal tourism, Tourist accommodation, Resort cycle, Leisure/recreation/tourism concepts and Recreation and tourism destinations.

Spatial patterns

Nine articles in the cluster focus on the spatial patterns of recreation and tourism phenomena (Smith, 1985(a); Perdue and Gustke, 1985; Pearce, 1987(a);

Table 3.1 *The number of articles considered and selected from ten geographic and interdisciplinary journals*

Journal	Considered	Selected
Annals of Tourism Research	54	44
Tourism Management	13	13
Leisure Sciences	5	4
Canadian Geographer	5	3
Journal of Leisure Research	2	1
Professional Geographer	2	1
Geographic Review	1	1
Annals of the Association of American Geographers	0	0
Economic Geography	0	0
Journal of Geography	0	0
Totals	82	67

Pearce, 1987(b); White, 1985; Husbands, 1986; Lawton and Butler, 1987; Fesenmaier and Lieber, 1987; Smith, 1985b). Spatial distributions of tourism phenomena at points of demand and/or supply and along lines of transportation between origins and destinations have long been of interest to geographers. Patterns under scrutiny vary significantly from leisure to vacation travel, from package deals to charters, from domestic to international travel, from activity to tourist space and from cruise ships to restaurants. This extensive range of subjects is an indication of the vitality and variety of the subdiscipline.

Research on the topic of spatial patterns has historically centred on location and travel or the static and dynamic qualities of leisure activities. Only the article on restaurants deals primarily with the distribution of an inanimate object; all the others pertain to the flow of tourists from origins to destinations. It is obvious from the articles reviewed that present research efforts focus on movement rather than on place. Of the manuscripts reviewed, only two provide results that are interconnected—the Pearce articles on charter flights in Europe and in the Mediterranean. The remainder offer findings that are place-specific and unique. These findings make a significant contribution to the study of geographic distributions, but they are scattered across a wide range of research interests.

Third World tourism

A total of nine manuscripts pertaining to some aspect of recreation or tourism in Third World countries are surveyed (Teye, 1986; Teye, 1988(a); Teye, 1988(b); Ferrario, 1986; Ferrario, 1988; Weightman, 1987; Cater, 1987; Burnett and Butler, 1987; Karan and Mather, 1985). Five of the articles are concerned with aspects of leisure activities in Africa. Teye, with three papers, and Ferrario, with two, dominate this cluster with contributions about African tourism. Third World landscapes, in general, are examined in the remaining four studies. All of these are by different authors.

Heterogeneous is the term that best describes the nine manuscripts making up this cluster. Five papers focus on Africa, all with differing emphases. The debilitating effect of liberation wars and coups d'état on the growth of tourism is highlighted. Likewise, the importance of geographic factors such as size, location and climate to the implementation of tourism policy is emphasized. In another vein, we see that the increasing participation of non-white populations in tourist activities in the Republic of South Africa is unappreciated by whites, and that the tourism industry is not making the necessary adjustments. If the political status quo is maintained, this trend will have some interesting effects on the economic, social and political structures of the country.

Two articles with non-African settings consider the importance of natural and cultural adaptations to the presence of tourism in the least developed of the less developed countries. Another suggests that natural, physical factors play a dominant role in the creation of national parks in Third World countries. One essay notes that package tours to India keep tourists from any type of meaningful experience with local peoples and cultures by directing them away from typical environments and creating artificial, cruise-ship-like conditions.

Evolution of tourism

Seven of the eight articles considered in this section were published in a special issue of the *Annals of Tourism Research* entitled 'The evolution of tourism: historical and contemporary perspectives' (Butler and Wall, 1985; VanDoren and Lollar, 1985; Marsh, 1985; Butler, 1985; Weightman and Wall, 1985; Towner, 1985; Hugill, 1985; Bailie, 1985). It should be noted that this cluster would probably not have been included in this review if the special issue had not been published. While geographers use historians' methods as tools to better understand the spatial patterns and processes of recreation and tourism landscapes, the emphasis tends to be placed on the subject matter rather than on history *per se*. In other words, change through time is seen as an important explanatory variable, but chronology in and of itself is not within the direct domain of the geographer.

The eight articles included in this cluster offer an example of the breadth and diversity of interest and method in the examination of recreation and tourism phenomena. Aside from the utilization of time as a frame of reference and the integration of a wide array of concepts in an analytical fashion, there is little similarity among research endeavours. Nevertheless, the approach has done much to elucidate the subject under consideration. The investigation of recreation and tourism processes and patterns over time provides the background information necessary to yield imaginative insights and increase understanding.

Impacts of recreation and tourism

Investigations into the environmental, economic and social impacts of recreation and tourism development have a relatively long history within the discipline of geography (Mathieson and Wall, 1982). A total of seven articles are surveyed here, five taken from another special issue of the *Annals of Tourism Research* (Farrell and McLellan, 1987; Edwards, 1987; Rodriguez, 1987; Gartner, 1987; Liu and Var, 1986; Liu, Sheldon and Var, 1987; Mescon and Vozikis, 1985). One of the coeditors of this number was a geographer, and the title of the issue was 'Tourism and Physical Environment'. The last two papers reviewed were taken from other issues of the *Annals of Tourism Research*.

This cluster of seven articles reveals that concern over tourism impacts is universal, no matter what the country's stage of economic development or technological sophistication. Management of conflicts between differing perceptions, ideologies, philosophies or cultures is considered within a holistic framework of interactive physical and social systems. Individual projects or sites should not be conceived in isolation, but rather planned within a dynamic synergetic network. The role of government in the tourism planning process is seen as important. Perceptions of residents of regions affected by tourism development are positive with regard to economic factors, but tend to be negative about actual or potential environmental influences. In most instances tourism is seen as desirable for economic purposes as long as environmental risks are minimized. Finally, investigations of environmental impacts of tourism from the earth science tradition of geography are conspicuous by their absence.

Methods used in recreation and tourism research

A total of seven manuscripts in this cluster demonstrate the diversity of research methods used in the study of recreation and tourism (Smith, 1987; Taylor, 1986; Milne, 1987; Pearce, 1988; Mieczowski, 1985; Dearden, 1985; Hartmann, 1988). The techniques discussed range from relatively general methods of evaluating large regions to specific ways of measuring tourists' use of leisure time. All of the manuscripts reviewed use statistical techniques as a means to understanding some topic or subject matter end, and not the development or improvement of a methodology as an end in itself.

Methods and methodologies employed in recreation and tourism research are not unique, but are, for the most part, the same techniques used in geography and the social sciences. The articles surveyed here represent a broad cross-section of possible methods. No two of these papers address the same topic although the manuscripts on time budgets and field methods are both related to the collection of research data. The five remaining articles make contributions to a specific, relatively narrow research problem.

Cross-tabulation of tourist travel data and the use of differential multipliers are examples of applying tried-and-true research techniques. The regionalization of tourism resources using principle components analysis is a long overdue application of modern statistical methods that could mark the beginning of a major research agenda. A philosophical statement that integrates the polarized positions of the two leading research thrusts in landscape evaluation research may establish the basis for renewed research efforts. The formulation of a method of mapping tourist climate regions is a truly unique contribution, and should create some interest because of its possible application to tourism regions smaller than the world scale. All in all, the manuscripts surveyed here represent the on-going search for methods of collecting and manipulating data in a dynamic research field in need of philosophical focus.

Planning and development

A total of seven manuscripts constitute this cluster (Getz, 1986; Culpan, 1987; Inskeep, 1987; Murphy, 1988; Pearce, 1988; Romsa and Blenman, 1987; Murphy and Andressen, 1988). Four of the seven articles reviewed deal with planning and development from a holistic perspective, such as models in planning, a model for developing economies, environmental considerations in planning and community-driven planning. Another paper combines a general view with a case study. The final two papers examine planning and development in island environments: one from the perspective of an economic crisis and the other by way of a conceptual approach.

Two elements of planning and development for recreation and tourism are apparent from these manuscripts. One is the need to place all planning efforts in a larger theoretical and practical context. Failure to be comprehensive in the development of tourism projects can result either in the collapse of a leisure enterprise or in negative impacts on the natural, social or political environments. The second commonality is the need for cooperation between government agencies, industry and residents of the community or region being impacted by tourism development. Tourism as an agent to economic diversity and stability, profit or employment opportunity needs to be planned and developed in as democratic and integrative a fashion as possible. All of the essays in this cluster stress these two points in one way or another, highlighting the obvious need for responsibility among all parties in the creation of leisure attractions.

Coastal tourism

This cluster of five papers focuses on tourism activities that occur in three different coastal regions: the Pacific Northwest of the United States, the Caribbean and two separate areas of the Pacific Rim (Miller, 1987; Bacon, 1987; Monk and Alexander, 1986; Chow, 1988; Farrell, 1985). Emphasis on coastal tourism is important because of the ecological significance of the strandline between the land and the water; the concentration of population on the flat, agriculturally productive landform; the natural attractiveness of coastal scenery to tourists; and the agglomeration of tourism facilities near the ocean front.

Coastal tourism research as exemplified by the papers reviewed here deals with four topics: environmental impacts and planning, employment and migration patterns, the importance of tourism markets to development and the importance of tourism to economic growth. Two papers present evidence to support the notion that the potential negative impacts of tourism development in fragile coastal areas need to be anticipated and planned for in a holistic fashion. Likewise, the influence of tourism on the structure and gender of employment needs to be considered. The implementation of an 'open policy' in China has resulted in a rapid expansion of traditional tourism between Hong Kong and the mainland. The best means of continuing tourism development is to place emphasis on this proximate and ethnically similar market and to slowly develop attractions for other, more foreign markets. The climate for economic development of the tourism industry has been found to be positive and improving, first, because of its ability to continue growth through the last recession, and second, because it may be the only economic activity that is viable for many small regions. These five case studies represent the types of research projects that are being conducted in the world coastal zones.

Tourist accommodation

Four papers constitute this cluster (Jeffrey, 1985; Jeffrey and Hubbard, 1985; Nelson and Wall, 1986; Wall, Dudycha and Hutchinson, 1985). Two of the papers deal with hotel characteristics, occupancy trends and temporal and spatial pattern of accommodation in a small region in the United Kingdom. The other articles deal with accommodation in Canada: one examines relationships between accommodation and transportation and another analyses the spatial distribution of hotels in Toronto. Accommodation for the temporary visitor plays a vital role in the tourism industry, and research on this topic cannot be overemphasized.

All of the papers in this cluster note the tendency of concentrating accommodation demand and supply in major business districts and of increasing establishment size. Findings confirm that general spatial and temporal patterns of accommodation are stable, although individual establishments are in a contant state of flux due to unique conditions. Accessibility to transportation modes and potential markets is also revealed as an important factor affecting the industry. Finally, the extensive range of statistical methods used in these papers highlights the need for techniques that provide imaginative insights into research endeavours.

Resort cycle

This cluster consists of four articles (Meyer-Arnedt, 1985; Keller, 1987; Strapp, 1988; Haywood, 1987). Interest in the resort-cycle theory has grown rapidly since it was first proposed by Butler (1980). The manuscripts reviewed are typical examples of the direction in which this type of research is headed. Three are case studies of regions of varying size that are organized around the product life-cycle concept. The other raises an important question: Can the tourist-area life cycle be made operational?

Two of the four papers in this cluster are simple applications of the resort-cycle concept to specific regions. The human–environmental relationships between resort development and physical processes on a barrier island are illustrated. Resort-cycle concepts also provided insights for the formulation of development strategies in a peripheral tourist region. The two remaining articles suggest that the resort-cycle concept is limited in its application. It is noted, in one study, that the model needs to be modified if it is to be used to explain cottage resort development. Suggestions for expanding the theoretical base of the construct are presented in the final essay. These four contributions are evidence that the resort-cycle concept is still important and that the conceptual base of the model is in the process of being extended.

Leisure, recreation and tourism concepts

Data and the concepts that are generated or spawned from them are the driving forces behind tourism research. Without concepts, research would consist of simple descriptions of tourism phenomena. Perspectives and guidelines provided by concepts enable a researcher to produce imaginative insights and gain a more comprehensive understanding of the touristscape. Four articles are included in this conceptual cluster (Smith, 1988; Jansen-Verbeke and Dietvorst, 1987; Lew, 1987; O'Reilly, 1986). The diverse group deals with definitions, disciplinary integrations and research frameworks.

Research on leisure, recreation and tourism is not well grounded in formal theory or in a particular research paradigm, and efforts to clarify rudimentary questions and research designs are continuing. Conceptual issues of tourism, as can be seen from these four articles, are diverse and range from definitions to attempts to integrate complex typologies. An operational *supply-side* definition of tourism narrows the focus of research efforts and neglects the broader perspective. A review of the carrying capacity concept presents a more holistic vision. The last two articles attempt to synthesize either definitions or classification schemes into frameworks that should improve research endeavours. However, the four articles discussed do not constitute a comprehensive sample of the conceptual issues that face the practitioners in the subspeciality.

Recreation and tourism destinations

Destinations, as places of supply, are the terminals of travel and provide the facilities, activities and programmes sought by tourists. Three papers constitute this cluster (Perdue, 1986; Fesenmaier and Lieber, 1988; Haahti, 1986). Destinations as specific places of recreation and tourism attractions are viewed from three different perspectives: accessibility and attractiveness as factors of destination choice, activity as an indicator of destination diversification, and the competitive position of a destination.

Research on the topic of destinations, like that of coastal tourism, is concentrated on relatively small portions of the landscape. Although attractiveness is obviously important to the economic viability of a destination, it is revealed that for recreational boaters, access to a lake is more important than the lake's attractiveness. For most boaters attractiveness and access are of equal importance but, for those who perceive a difference, access is more highly rated. In another setting it is found that there is a direct relationship between the number of recreational activities a household engages in and the number of park destinations visited. This indicates a high degree of activity compatibility at public recreation destinations in Oklahoma. Finland as a tourism destination is perceived by European tourists as presenting a different type of holiday experience. Unfortunately, its similarity to other Scandinavian countries and its relative inaccessibility are cause for some competitive disadvantages. The three articles reviewed here are a representative sample of destination research.

Summary

Between 1985 and 1988, 82 articles by geographers, or on geographic topics by non-geographers, were published. More than 20 manuscripts a year is a large number for a subdiscipline with relatively few active practitioners. Of the total papers surveyed 67 were selected for substantive review because they could be classified into eleven fairly homogeneous clusters. Articles not selected for analysis were ideographic in nature and did not fit into the general themes used for classification. The eleven clusters were not completely discrete and some overlapping of content can be detected. Diversity within and between clusters is an indication of the broad philosophical and methodological approaches adopted by recreation and tourism geographers. Even though the clusters are arbitrary and do not represent all the categories that could have been selected, they do provide a structure for the orderly analysis of manuscripts.

A total of seven geographic and/or interdisciplinary leisure journals contained all of the 67 articles reviewed (Table 1). One journal, *Annals of Tourism Research*, published almost 67% of the manuscripts, and thus is the dominant outlet for recreation and tourism geographers in North America. Interestingly enough, only six papers appeared in the six geographic journals surveyed, and only three of those were selected for review.

Although there is great diversity in subject matter, ideographic position and approach followed, the quality of research here is sound. It is too early to judge whether any of these endeavours will become a classic, or make a significant advance beyond the research frontier, or be the cornerstone of a new research thrust. However, each in its own way makes a contribution to a better understanding of some recreation or tourism theme. Continued research of this magnitude is bound to result in an advancement of knowledge.

One negative aspect of the research reviewed here is the lack of connection between articles and between articles and clusters. Research endeavours are extremely diverse in nature and findings are not accumulated and integrated into the principles or theories necessary to advance knowledge at a rapid rate.

The lack of limits as to research topics is both a blessing and a curse. The blessing is that an extensive range of research topics is investigated, giving free rein to one's imagination. The curse is the lack of a research paradigm in the field. In the long run it is assumed that the blessings will outweigh the curses.

The IGU's Commission on the Geography of Tourism and Leisure

The International Geographical Union's Commission on the Geography of Tourism and Leisure held a pre-congress meeting on 'International Tourism' in Christchurch, New Zealand in August 1988. Thirty-four participants from thirteen countries were present. Paper sessions on international and domestic tourism, transport and travel, hallmark events and tourism in metropolitan areas were included in the programme. Most of the papers will be published in 1989 and 1990 editions of *GeoJournal* and *Tourism Recreation Research*.

Among the issues discussed at the 1988 meeting was a concern over the narrowness of many of the research efforts currently being undertaken. Many, perhaps most, studies focus on accessibility issues, the origin and development of tourism facilities and tourism *places* and the structure of communities that have an economy based on tourism. A number of participants suggested that a substantially broader purview was needed, with a focus on economic, social and environmental impacts of tourism on places and regions. Methodological differences also became apparent. For instance, the approach to tourism studies taken by most European geographers has a distinctly regional orientation. Conversely, the approach of many Americans, Canadians, Australians and New Zealanders is oriented toward behavioural considerations, modelling and the application of research results to real world problems.

A majority of those attending the New Zealand meeting also participated in the 26th Congress of the International Geographical Union in Sydney, Australia later in August. Thirteen papers were presented on tourism-related topics at these meetings under the session headings of impact of tourism, evolution of tourism facilities and planning for tourism. The Commission's life was renewed for another eight years with a slight change in title. Discussions at the Commission's business meeting focused on issues of common concern such as the desirability of standardizing terminology in the recreational and tourism literature.

Conclusion

Notwithstanding the lack of connection between projects, research on the topic of tourism is in a healthy state. The high production rate of scholars in the field is an indication of how dynamic interest is in the study of leisure phenomena and activities. New philosophical and methodological approaches to the subject, as well as more traditional approaches, keep research efforts at a robust level of activity. The interaction and juxtaposition of ideas, techniques and subject matter creates an excellent environment for research, and it is expected that the quantity and quality of recreation and tourism research will continue at a high level in the foreseeable future.

References

Bacon, P. R., 1987, 'Use of wetlands for tourism in the insular Caribbean', *Annals of Tourism Research*, 14(1): pp. 104–17.

Bailie, J. G., 1985, 'The evolution of Canadian international travel documentation', *Annals of Tourism Research*, 12(3): pp. 563–79.

Burnett, G. W., Butler, L. M., 1987, 'National parks in the Third World and associated national characteristics', *Leisure Sciences*, 9(1): pp. 41–51.

Butler, R. W., 1980, 'The concept of a tourism area cycle of evolution: implications for management of resources', *Canadian Geographer*, 24(1): pp. 5–12.

Butler, R. W., 1982, 'Geographical research on leisure: reflections and anticipations on Accrington Stanley and fire hydrants', in Ng, D. and Smith, S. L. J. (eds), *Perspectives on the Nature of Leisure Research*, University of Waterloo Press, Waterloo, Canada.

Butler, R. W., 1985, 'Evolution of tourism in the Scottish Highlands', *Annals of Tourism Research*, 12(3): pp. 371–91.

Butler, R. W., Wall, G., 1985, 'Themes in research on the evolution of tourism', *Annals of Tourism Research*, 12(3): pp. 287–96.

Carlson, A. W., 1980(a), 'Geographical research on international and domestic tourism', *Journal of Cultural Geography*, 1(1): pp. 149–60.

Carlson, A. W., 1980(b), 'A bibliography of geographical research on tourism', *Journal of Cultural Geography*, 1(1): pp. 161–84.

Cater, E. A., 1987, 'Tourism in the least developed countries', *Annals of Tourism Research*, 14(2): pp. 202–26.

Chow, W. S., 1988, 'Open policy and tourism between Guangdong and Hong Kong', *Annals of Tourism Research*, 15(2): pp. 205–14.

Culpan, R., 1987, 'International tourism model for developing economies', *Annals of Tourism Research*, 14(4): pp. 541–52.

Dearden, P., 1985, 'Philosophy, theory, and method in landscape evaluation', *Canadian Geographer*, 29(3): pp. 263–5.

Edwards, J. R., 1987, 'The UK heritage coasts: an assessment of the ecological impacts of tourism', *Annals of Tourism Research*, 14(1): pp. 71–87.

Farrell, B. H., 1985, 'South Pacific tourism in the mid-1980s', *Tourism Management*, 6(1): pp. 55–60.

Farrell, B. H., McLellan, R., 1987, 'Tourism and physical environmental research', *Annals of Tourism Research*, 14(1): pp. 1–16.

Ferrario, R., 1986, 'Black and white holidays: the future of the local tourist industry in South Africa', *Annals of Tourism Research*, 13(3): pp. 331–48.

Ferrario, R., 1988, 'Emerging leisure market among the South African Black population', *Tourism Management*, 9(1): pp. 23–38.

Fesenmaier, D. R., Leiber, S. R., 1987, 'Outdoor recreation expenditures and the effects of spatial structure', *Leisure Sciences*, 9(1): pp. 27–40.

Fesenmaier, D. R., Leiber, S. R., 1988, 'Destination diversification as an indicator of activity compatibility: an exploratory analysis', *Leisure Sciences*, 10(3): pp. 167–78.

Gartner, W. C., 1987, 'Environmental impacts of recreational home developments', *Annals of Tourism Research*, 14(1): pp. 38–57.

Getz, D., 1986, 'Models in tourism planning', *Tourism Management*, 7(1): pp. 21–32.

Haahti, A. J., 1986, 'Finland's competitive position as a destination', *Annals of Tourism Research*, 13(1): pp. 11–35.

Haywood, K. M., 1986, 'Can the tourist-area life cycle be made operational?' *Tourism Management*, 7(3): pp. 154–67.

Hartmann, R., 1988, 'Combining field methods in tourism research', *Annals of Tourism Research*, 15(1): pp. 88–105.

Hugill, P. J., 1985, 'The rediscovery of America: elite automobile touring', *Annals of Tourism Research*, 12(3): pp. 435–47.

Husbands, W. C., 1986, 'Leisure activity resources and activity space formation in peripheral resorts: the response of tourists and residents in Barbados', *Canadian Geographer*, 30(3): pp. 243–9.

Inskeep, E., 1987, 'Environmental planning for tourism', *Annals of Tourism Research*, 14(1): pp. 118–35.

Jakle, J. A., 1985, *The Tourist: Travel in Twentieth-Century North America*, University of Nebraska Press, Lincoln and London.

Jansen-Verbeke, M., Dietvorst, A., 1987, 'Leisure, recreation, tourism: a geographic view on integration', *Annals of Tourism Research*, 14(3): pp. 361–75.

Jeffrey, D., 1985, 'Spatial and temporal patterns of demand for hotel accommodation—time series analysis in Yorkshire and Humberside, UK', *Tourism Management*, 6(1): pp. 8–22.

Jeffrey, D., Hubbard, N. J., 1985, 'Hotel characteristic and occupancy trends—Yorkshire and Humberside hotels, UK, April 1982–March 1984', *Tourism Management*, 6(3): pp. 280–7.

Karan, P. P., Mather, C., 1985, 'Tourism and environment in the Mt. Everest region', *Geographical Review*, 75(10): pp. 93–5.

Keller, C. P., 1987, 'Stages of peripheral development—Canada's Northwest Territories', *Tourism Management*, 8(1): pp. 20–32.

Lawton, L. J., Butler, R. W., 1987, 'Cruise ship industry—patterns in the Caribbean, 1880–1986', *Tourism Management*, 8(4): pp. 329–43.

Lew, A. A., 1987, 'A framework of tourist attraction research', *Annals of Tourism Research*, 14(2): pp. 553–75.

Liu, J. C., Var, T., 1986, 'Resident attitudes toward tourism impacts in Hawaii', *Annals of Tourism Research*, 13(2): pp. 193–214.

Liu, J. C., Var, T., 1987, 'Resident perception of the environmental impacts of tourism', *Annals of Tourism Research*, 14(1): pp. 17–37.

Marsh, J., 1985, 'The Rocky and Selkirk Mountains and the Swiss connection', *Annals of Tourism Research*, 12(3): pp. 417–34.

McMurry, K. G., 1930, 'The use of land for recreation', *Annals of the Association of American Geographers*, 20(1): pp. 7–20.

McMurry, K. C., 1954, 'Recreational geography', in James, P. E. and C. F. (eds), *American Geography: Inventory and Prospect*, Syracuse University Press, Syracuse, New York, pp. 251–5.

Mescon, T. S., Vozikis, G. S., 1985, 'The economic impact of tourism at the port of Miami', *Annals of Tourism Research*, 12(4): pp. 515–28.

Meyer-Arendt, K. J., 1985, 'The Grand Isle, Louisiana resort cycle', *Annals of Tourism Research*, 12(3): pp. 449–65.

Mieczowski, Z., 1985, 'The tourism climate index: a method of evaluating world climates for tourism', *Canadian Geographer*, 29(3): pp. 220–33.

Miller, M. L., 1987, 'Tourism in Washington's coastal zone', *Annals of Tourism Research*, 14(1): pp. 58–70.

Milne, S. S., 1987, 'Differential multipliers', *Annals of Tourism Research*, 14(4): pp. 499–515.

Mitchell, L. S., 1981, 'Fifty years of recreational geography research: 1930–1979', paper presented at the Association of American Geographers in Los Angeles.

Mitchell, L. S., 1984, 'Tourism research in the United States: a geographic perspective', *GeoJournal*, 9(1): pp. 5–15.

Mitchell, L. S., Smith, R. V., 1985, 'Recreational geography: inventory and prospect', *Professional Geographer*, 37(1): pp. 6–14.

Monk, J., Alexander, C. S., 1986, 'Free port fallout: gender, employment, and migration on Margarita Island', *Annals of Tourism Research*, 13(3): pp. 393–414.

Murphy, P. E., 1985, *Tourism: A Community Approach*, Methuen, New York and London.

Murphy, P. E., 1988, 'Community-driven tourism planning', *Tourism Management*, 9(2): pp. 96–104.

Murphy, P. E., Andressen, B., 1988, 'Tourism development on Vancouver Island: an assessment of the core-periphery', *Professional Geographer*, 40(1): pp. 32–42.

Nelson, R., Wall, G., 1986, 'Transportation and accommodation: changing inter-relationships on Vancouver Island', *Annals of Tourism Research*, 13(3): pp. 239–50.

O'Reilly, A. M., 1986, 'Tourism carrying capacity', *Tourism Management*, 7(4): pp. 254–8.

Pearce, D. G., 1987(a), 'Spatial patterns of package tourism in Europe', *Annals of Tourism Research*, 14(2): pp. 184–201.

Pearce, D. G., 1987(b), 'Mediterranean charters—a comparative geographic perspective', *Tourism Management*, 8(4), pp. 291–305.

Pearce, D. G., 1987(c), *Tourism Today: A Geographical Analysis*, Longman, Harlow.

Pearce, D. G., 1988(a), 'Tourist time budgets', *Annals of Tourism Research*, 15(1): pp. 106–21.

Pearce, D. G., 1988(b), 'Tourism and regional development in the European Community', *Tourism Management*, 9(1): pp. 13–22.

Perdue, R. R., 1986, 'Traders and nontraders in recreational destination choice', *Journal of Leisure Research*, 18(1): pp. 12–25.

Perdue, R. R., Gustke, L. D., 1985, 'Spatial patterns of leisure travel by trip purpose', *Annals of Tourism Research*, 12(2): pp. 167–80.

Rodriguez, S., 1987, 'Impact of the ski industry on the Rio Hondo watershed', *Annals of Tourism Research*, 14(1): pp. 88–103.

Romsa, G. H., Blenman, E. H. M., 1987, 'The Prime Minister's dilemma', *Annals of Tourism Research*, 14(2): pp. 240–53.

Smith, S. L. J., 1982, 'Reflections on the development of geographic research in recreation: hey buddy can you s'paradigm', *Ontario Geography*, 9(1): pp. 5–24.

Smith, S. L. J., 1985(a), 'US vacation travel patterns: correlated of distance decay and the willingness to travel', *Leisure Sciences*, 7(2): pp. 151–74.

Smith, S. L. J., 1985(b), 'Location patterns of urban restaurants', *Annals of Tourism Research*, 12(4): pp. 581–602.

Smith, S. L. J., 1987, 'Regional analysis of tourism resources', *Annals of Tourism Research*, 14(2): pp. 254–73.

Smith, S. L. J., 1988, 'Defining tourism: a supply-side view', *Annals of Tourism Research*, 15(2): pp. 179–90.

Smith, S. L. J., 1989, *Tourism Analysis: A Handbook*, Longman, Harlow.

Strapp, J. D., 1988, 'The resort cycle and second homes', *Annals of Tourism Research*, 15(4): pp. 504–16.

Taylor, G. D., 1986, 'Multi-dimensional segmentation of the Canadian pleasure travel market', *Tourism Management*, 7(3): pp. 146–53.

Teye, V. B., 1986, 'Liberation wars and tourism development in Africa: the case of Zambia', *Annals of Tourism Research*, 13(4): pp. 589–608.

Teye, V. B., 1988, 'Coup d'état and African tourism: a study of Ghana', *Annals of Tourism Research*, 15(3): pp. 329–58.

Teye, V. B., 1988, 'Geographic factors affecting tourism in Zambia', *Annals of Tourism Research*, 15(4): pp. 487–503.

Towner, J., 1985, 'The grand tour: a key phase in the history of tourism', *Annals of Tourism Research*, 12(3): pp. 297–333.

VanDoren, C. S., Lollar, S. A., 1985, 'The consequences of forty years of tourism growth', *Annals of Tourism Research*, 12(3): pp. 487–9.

Wall, G., Dudycha, D., Hutchinson, J., 1985, 'Point pattern analyses of accommodation in Toronto', *Annals of Tourism Research*, 12(4): pp. 603–18.

Weightman, B. A., 1987, 'Third World tour landscapes', *Annals of Tourism Research*, 14(2): pp. 227–39.

Weightman, D., Wall, G., 1985, 'The spa experience at Radium Hot Springs', *Annals of Tourism Research*, 12(3): pp. 393–416.

White, K. J., 1985, 'An international travel demand model: US travel to Western Europe', *Annals of Tourism Research*, 12(4): pp. 529–46.

Wolfe, R. I., 1964, 'Perspectives on the nature of outdoor recreation: a bibliographical survey', *Geographical Review*, 54(2): pp. 203–38.

4 Tourism, economic development and the role of entrepreneurial activity

G. Shaw and A. M. Williams

Introduction

Tourism is now one of the largest industries in the world, with tourists spending an estimated $127.8 billion (US) in 1986 on trips outside their own countries (World Tourism Organization, 1987). It is moreover a growth industry at a world level, with tourist arrivals increasing by 5.4% per annum between 1976 and 1986. Inevitably such a large-scale activity has an impact on a wide variety of economies, in both the developed and the developing world. There is growing awareness of this importance, but relatively little appreciation of the specific operating characteristics of tourism firms, and especially of tourism entrepreneurship.

The continual growth of tourism, even in the face of economic restructuring in many mature economies, has enhanced its importance for a number of governments. Indeed, the development of national tourism policies since 1945 clearly highlights the significance that different governments attach to the industry (Williams and Shaw, 1988(a)). In many West European economies, for example, there has been long-standing government involvement with the tourism sector, dating in some cases from the 1920s and 1930s. It was during this time (1925) that the first major transnational agency, the International Union of Official Tourist Publicity Organizations, was established (European Travel Commission, 1988). During the 1980s there has been an increased awareness of the economic importance of tourism within developed economies, generating a range of government policies (OECD, 1986). This renewed interest is due not only to the increased size of the tourism industry but also to a growing appreciation that long-term structural changes have led to an expansion of the service economy. Furthermore, large-scale unemployment has led to governments assessing the role of tourism in a new light, not least because of its employment-generating potential (Williams and Shaw, 1988(b)).

The growth of the tourist industry and its potential for stimulating economic development has formed an important point in much of the literature on tourism. However, despite considerable debate on the subject (for example, Young, 1973; de Kadt, 1979; Mathieson and Wall, 1982) there is still little agreement as to tourism's role in economic development. The overall picture is somewhat clouded, not only by the different assessments of economic development, but also by its socio-cultural and environmental implications (Murphy, 1985).

This chapter does not seek to address all of these issues, but rather to explore the importance of entrepreneurship in relation to the potential for tourism to develop as an industry. This topic remains a relatively neglected research focus in the literature on tourism and economic development, and yet it holds an important key to understanding tourism's impact on local economies (Kilby, 1971).

Approaches to the study of tourism and economic development

The literature on tourism and economic development has mainly focused on two major themes: the economic cost-benefits of tourism and the measurement of tourism's economic impact. The first approach embraces a considerable range of studies, but most are grounded in political economy perspectives of tourism and development. Early work was stimulated by the research of Young (1973), Bryden's (1973) study of the Caribbean and various conferences on tourism's role in developing countries (see, for example, Shivji, 1973). Particular attention has been given to the structure of the tourist industry in developing economies, especially the role played by transnational companies (UN Centre on Transnational Corporations, 1980). The implications of transnational activities for developing countries are considerable: a loss of control by the host country over its national tourist industry, a loss of foreign earnings (since only 22% to 50% of the gross tour revenue remains in the destination country) and the development of isolated tourist enclaves separated from the local population (Lea, 1988). Some of these problems have been confirmed in a recent survey of 22 developing countries by the World Tourism Organization (1985). This research inquired into the countries' attitudes towards transnational tourism, and found that most nations still experienced more disadvantages than benefits (see Table 4.1).

In this context, reliance on international tourism as a strategy for economic development has been criticized because it is so often associated with a dependency upon external sources of growth (de Kadt, 1979). Such sources tend to be fickle in nature. Choices of tourist destinations are susceptible to large fluctuations, particularly because of economic conditions in the tourist's country of origin or the political situation in the holiday destination. There are also significant socio-economic and geographical dimensions of tourism dependency, as shown in Figure 4.1 (Britton, 1981; Pearce, 1987). In this view the major tourist flows and controls emanate from the developed economies and serve to create small resort enclaves within developing countries. It is through such spatial networks that transnational tourism organizations operate and, unless strongly regulated by governments, only limited economic benefits may accrue to the host communities.

Debates over external control and levels of dependency are not limited to developing countries. They have also formed the basis of recent research and

Table 4.1 *Perception of selected developing countries towards transnational tourism*

Question	True %	Partly true %	Untrue %
1. Transnational Corporations (TNCs) have to some extent influenced the type of tourism activity attracted to developing countries	36	55	9
2. Lack of bargaining power is the main problem of developing countries in dealing with TNCs	50	41	9
3. Developing countries are insufficiently informed about the various transnational corporations and forms of their involvement in tourism development	50	27	23
4. TNCs appear at times reluctant to employ local managers and senior staff	59	32	9
5. The most significant benefit of TNC involvement is in speeding up the pace of tourism development	45	32	23
6. The most significant lasting contribution made by TNCs to the developing countries is the transfer of skills, product knowledge, technology and product techniques	27	64	9
7. The working methods and training schemes of TNCs are not always adapted to the stage of development of the receiving country[1]	45	45	9
8. Often, TNCs give less emphasis to training local personnel than to meeting production targets and deadlines	59	32	9

[1] Row adds to 99 due to rounding.
Source: WTO (1985).

discussion on the role of tourism in the mature economies. Within Western Europe a diverse range of countries have tourism industries that are heavily dependent on the international market. In Austria, for example, foreign tourists account for 76% of all overnight stays, while the equivalent proportion in Spain is 66% (Williams and Shaw, 1988(a)). Within the Mediterranean countries, foreign investment is another dimension of the relationship between tourism

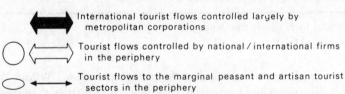

Figure 4.1 *Tourism development in a peripheral economy*
Source: Modified from Lea (1988) and Britton (1981).

and economic dependency, and in this there are at least superficial parallels with the developing economies. In Greece, for example, the relative import- ance of foreign investment peaked in 1968, when it accounted for just over 66% of all investment in tourism (Leontidou, 1988). Most of this foreign capital went into hotel complexes in prime coastal locations, creating a phase of speculative development with all the related environmental and socio-political problems of tourist enclaves (Spanoudis, 1982).

Within the political economy approach only scant attention has been paid to the role of entrepreneurs in the tourist industry. Beyond some general discus- sions about the impact of transnational organizations, the literature is remark- ably uninformative on the influence of small or medium-sized businesses (Harper, 1984). One major exception is the early work of Lundgren (1973), which examined the characteristics of entrepreneurial activity associated with different forms of hotel developments in the Caribbean. Lundgren suggested a three-stage model of entrepreneurial development could be recognized, based on demand and supply linkages with hotels. Even this work, however, neglected to examine the characteristics of entrepreneurs in the tourist industry itself. Instead, it focused on the development of a locally-controlled supply system.

In addition, as Mathieson and Wall (1982) argue, 'although it is attractive to think of a sequence of developmental stages, the exact pattern of entre- preneurial activity is likely to vary from place to place . . .'. Such geographical variations in the development of entrepreneurial activity—which can be con- ceptualized as local contingencies in their formation and operation—have unfortunately been little researched. The exception has been the general recognition that linkages between tourism and local businesses depend on: the types of suppliers and producers in operation, the historical development of tourism within the area (vaguely conceptualized) and the type of tourist devel- opment under consideration. At a more specific level, little is known about the economic behavioural characteristics of entrepreneurs within tourism economies or, more importantly, the impact of these entrepreneurs on economic development.

The importance of such considerations, particularly those associated with linkages, have been central to the second major area of study, that concerned with assessing tourism's economic impact. Much of this literature has focused on tracing and quantifying the ways in which tourism expenditure moves through the economy, a process usually assessed by the use of tourism multipliers (Archer, 1976). When multiplier effects are taken into account, income generated by tourism can be considerable. Thus, in the European Community it has been estimated that direct income from tourism accounted directly for 4% of GDP in 1979, but for 10% when multiplier effects were considered (Commission of the European Communities, 1987).

While such techniques have been used at a national level, more frequent applications have concerned the measurement of tourism impact on a regional or local scale (Murphy, 1985). Arguably, local multiplier effects are scale-specific, being stronger in the larger or more specialized tourist economies. These have greater capacity to support related specialized services and manufacturing activity—an effect which is reinforced by the potential for agglomeration economies. In Austria, one of Europe's more specialized economies, it has been estimated that the investments carried out by tourist enterprises have mainly benefited firms within the immediate local area. More precisely, it is calculated that 57% of these enterprises' capital expenditure is located within 20 kilometres, giving a highly localized multiplier (Zimmermann, 1988). Research on these scales of analysis has led to a refinement of the earlier models of multipliers, thereby building on Archer's (1977) important work which distinguishes between income, employment and output multipliers.

More recent work by Vaughan (1986) has further refined and broadened the scope for using tourism multipliers to investigate tourism's role in the UK economy. In part, the continued interest in tourism multipliers has been stimulated by the increasing attention being paid to tourism as a source of employment growth (Goodall, 1987). Furthermore, Vaughan has argued that tourism multipliers provide valuable information for political decision-makers seeking to influence the national or local allocation of resources or the priority given to tourism (see also Archer, 1982).

While the results obtained from the use of various multipliers can be useful in certain areas of decision-making, the technique itself suffers from a number of technical and conceptual shortcomings. For example, there are difficulties associated with the availability and reliability of data inputs into the model, especially if the studies are based on published secondary information. In addition, the extent of any multiplier effect depends on the size and structure of the economy under consideration and, as a consequence, case studies must be viewed in their full economic and geographical context (Shaw, Williams and Greenwood, 1987(a)).

Multiplier analysis also fails to address many key issues relating to the economic impact of tourism—issues that should form part of the agenda of decision-making bodies. Of particular importance is the study of firm dynamics and the operating characteristics of firms within the tourism industry. These features are all related to entrepreneurial activity which, in itself, is reduced to a largely mechanical response or linkage in multiplier studies. The remainder of this chapter will review the work on firm development within tourism by drawing on case studies from the United Kingdom.

Entrepreneurial activity: a neglected factor in UK tourism

Much of the official analysis of the tourism industry is set within aggregate studies of supply and demand. In the UK, for example, the British Tourist Authority (BTA) produces statistics on national tourism trends that focus on tourist demand in terms of expenditure, purpose of trip, destination and length of stay. Similarly, many of the regional tourist boards are preoccupied with such data in the formulation of regional tourism strategies. In contrast, very little information is available on the operating characteristics of tourism firms, even though they constitute a substantial part of the product which is being marketed by tourist authorities (Brown, 1988).

At a national level, data on the operating characteristics and performance of tourism firms are restricted to occupancy rates, provided by the British Tourist Authority, and *ad hoc* information on the development of new hotels (British Tourist Authority, 1985). This information is supplemented by commercial surveys that present statistics on the economic performance of hotels by size and location (for example, Pannell Kerr Forster, 1986). Such surveys aim to present a national picture but, of necessity, are restricted to rather small samples, usually of less than 200 hotels. While these reports provide a valuable indication of the performance of hotels, they reveal little about the decision-making processes operating within each tourist firm or, indeed, the potential for further development.

At a more detailed level of analysis, research has been undertaken on the changing structure of the UK hotel industry, through the work of Littlejohn (1982) and Slattery (1985). Particular attention has been drawn to the tendency toward increasing concentration in the hotel sector, together with the growth of hotel consortia. According to Littlejohn (1982) these consortia were boosted after the mid-1960s by the need to compensate for the decentralized structure of capital and the difficulties this created for cost cutting and price competitiveness. These organizations were initially concerned with solving marketing problems through developing a brand image, but since the early 1980s they have diversified the services offered to their members. Of particular significance has been the increasing number of consortia offering bulk-purchasing economies of scale to members.

The growth of hotel consortia has been especially rapid in the 1970s and early 1980s in response to changes in demand and levels of competition. Indeed, Slattery (1985) argues that the growth of such consortia is also a direct response to the recession in parts of the industry during the early 1980s. Many medium-sized hotels found that these organizations offered new ways of reducing operating costs and securing various types of economies of scale. Undoubtedly, these changes in operating methods have not only had an impact on concentration trends in the hotel sector, but have also produced a new growth stimulus in the tourism industry, resulting from the more efficient use of resources. Unfortunately, the full impact of this has yet to be assessed. Little is known, for example, about the regional effects of the development of hotel consortia on economic growth, or about any resultant modifications to entre-preneurial activity.

Membership of a voluntary hotel association is not a viable option for many of the smaller establishments that make up the bulk of the tourism accom-modation sector. In these firms there is almost total reliance on the entre-preneurial skills of the owner-manager. Given that close to 90% of hotels are relatively small and owner-managed independents (Stallibrass, 1980), it is surprising how little attention has been paid to small businesses in tourism. As the expansion of the service sector (including tourism) has been identified as one of the major reasons for the growth of small and medium-sized businesses in Europe (Commission of the European Communities, 1987), this neglect is all the more conspicuous. Furthermore, the lack of research on small businesses in tourism stands in marked contrast to studies in other economic sectors, especially manufacturing (for example, Storey, 1983).

There have been only a few case studies of firm formation and entrepreneurial skills in the field of tourism research. Thus, Stallibrass's (1980) study of Scarborough identified the importance of diverse business motivations in the dynamics of the hotel industry, and also found that only one-third of hotel owners had previous experience in tourism. Brown's (1987) research on hoteliers in South-East Dorset has confirmed this pattern, with few owners having had any relevant experience or qualifications; he also found that almost two-thirds of the businesses had turnovers of less than £22,000 in 1985. Two other main features emerge from these studies. The first is that many of the owner-managers had non-economic motives for entering the business. Second, sources of business capital used to establish the firm were extremely varied. This highlights the need to critically re-evaluate many of the conventional economic models used in the analysis of the tourism sector.

One important lead concerning non-economic decision-making is provided by Goffee and Scase's (1983) work on entrepreneurship. This has drawn attention to the importance of capital structures in understanding managerial and entrepreneurial skills. As Table 4.2 shows, they suggest that four main types of 'firm' can be identified, ranging from the highly marginalized, self-employed category through to owner-director companies, where management and

Table 4.2 *Organizational structures and entrepreneurial characteristics*

Category	Entrepreneurial characteristics
Self-employed	Use of family labour, little market stability, low levels of capital investment, tendency toward weakly developed management skills
Small employer	Use of family and non-family labour; less economically marginalized but shares other characteristics of self-employed group
Owner-controllers	Use of non-family labour, higher levels of capital investment, often formal system of management control, but no separation of ownership and control
Owner-directors	Separation of ownership and management functions, highest levels of capital investment

Source: Modified from Goffee and Scase (1983).

ownership are clearly divorced. The studies by both Brown and Stallibrass suggest that many hotel businesses in the UK would fall into either the first or second categories of Table 4.2 (self-employed and small employers) and that many of the units have low levels of capital investment with no formalized management system (Bagguley, 1987).

Recent studies in Cornwall and the Isles of Scilly have investigated more closely the operating characteristics of tourism businesses and have introduced a wider range of empirical information into the debate (Shaw, Williams and Greenwood, 1987(b); Williams, Greenwood and Shaw, 1989). This research has been based on detailed firm-level studies involving 483 interviews in Cornwall and 72 in the Isles of Scilly. Unlike previous studies, most major sectors representing those activities most directly or indirectly dependent on tourism were covered, including accommodation (serviced and non-serviced), attractions, retailing, restaurants, public houses and manufacturing. Within Cornwall 70% of the businesses were in the private ownership of a single individual, while in the Isles of Scilly the figure rose to almost 85%. Furthermore, in Cornwall 48% of all businesses had no full-time employees except the owner and a further 10% had only one full-time worker other than the owner-manager. Again, most of these firms conform to Goffee and Scase's notions of self-employed and small-employer entrepreneurs (see Table 4.2).

Given such background characteristics, these areas provide ideal environments within which to examine the business operations of small tourist-related firms. In addition, Cornwall's tourism industry is going through a difficult period as the market for long-stay holidays in Britain continues to decline (West Country Tourist Board, 1989). Faced with such changes in demand, public and private sector interests within the county are trying to implement new tourism strategies. This led to the establishment of a Tourism Development Action Programme in 1988, which is committed to assisting the development and restructuring of the tourism industry (Cornwall Tourism Development Action Programme, 1988). The success of any such plans aimed at revitalizing tourism depends to a considerable extent on the skills of owners/managers and the flexibility of the local product. This in turn highlights the importance of understanding both the characteristics and the entrepreneurial skills of the small and medium-sized businesses which make up the bulk of Cornwall's tourism industry. Policy objectives are not automatically translated into enterprise responses; implementation depends on entrepreneurship.

The impact of these management factors on the development of the local economy has been explored in a series of papers based on the research findings of the Cornwall study (Shaw and Williams, 1987; Shaw, Williams and Greenwood, 1987(a)). From this work three significant features relating to entrepreneurial behaviour emerge, all of which can be highlighted by reference to the tourism accommodation sector.

The first concerns the **levels of experience and the expertise of the entrepreneurs**. As Table 4.3 shows, the dominant route to entrepreneurship is as an ex-employee without directly relevant job experience. As ex-employees have

Table 4.3 *Characteristics of business within Cornwall's holiday accommodation sectors (% of respondents)*

	Hotels & guesthouses	Self-catering
Ownership		
Individual	85.6	79.7
Group	6.0	4.1
Limited company	2.4	8.1
PLC	1.2	0.0
Partner	4.8	8.1
Total	100	100
Age of owner		
20–30	8.6	2.8
31–40	27.2	15.2
41–50	32.1	28.4
51–60	17.3	37.5
61+	13.6	18.1
Non-response	1.2	0.0
Total	100	100
Birthplace (first five regions)		
Cornwall	16.9	33.8
South West	8.4	9.5
South East	34.9	25.7
Midlands	7.2	8.1
North West	7.2	12.2
Main previous occupations (only top 4 listed)		
Professional	27.3	23.5
Farming		17.6
Secretarial/clerical	16.9	
Retailing	13.0	13.2
Tourist industry	10.4	11.8
Sources of capital (principal sources)		
Personal savings	37.1	37.8
Family savings	15.7	18.0
Bank loan	21.4	19.7
Personal savings and bank loan	11.3	9.8

Source: Modified from Shaw and Williams (1987) and Shaw, Williams and Greenwood (1987a).

no obvious access either to skills or to capital, this is the group who would be expected to encounter the greatest obstacles to entrepreneurship. However, this is the most important route to entrepreneurship in all the subsectors within the tourism industry. Only in manufacturing does it account for less than one-half of the responses. In contrast, in the self-catering and restaurants, cafés and public house sectors, less than 6% had relevant employment experience. This differs significantly from the results of Chivers' survey (1973), which revealed that many ex-chefs succeed in becoming owners or managers of businesses. Another variation to note is the exceptionally large proportion of entrepreneurs in the hotel accommodation sector who had previously been employees in other sectors. Accommodation would seem to be the sector with the lowest entrance barriers (which, of course, supports the notion that the minimum requirement is the provision of bed-and-breakfast services from the family home). In such cases investment in personal consumption (the home) is used to underwrite the costs of producing accommodation services. However, most of the establishments surveyed were considerably larger than this and 60% had more than five bedrooms available. Hence, the findings have general application to the sector as a whole.

The second factor concerns **business motivations**. This is usually a complex combination of motives, aspirations and constraints, but here it is measured simply by responses to the question of why people established their firms. In the Cornish study, economic motives were matched by the importance given to non-economic reasons, such as 'to live in Cornwall'. These environmental factors were especially important in the accommodation sectors, where they accounted for almost a third of the responses. Related to this desire for a better way of life is the fact that a large proportion of the entrepreneurs (55%) were in-migrants, with two-thirds of those in self-catering and over 80% in hotels coming from outside Cornwall.

The third major element identified in the work on Cornwall relates to **sources of capital to finance businesses**. Personal and family savings were the main source of capital and were used exclusively by more than 50% of the entrepreneurs. Even higher figures were recorded in the Isles of Scilly study, with over 70% of the firms in the sample relying on non-commercial sources (Williams, Greenwood and Shaw, 1989). Both studies also found strong links between sources of capital and the age of the entrepreneur, with, for example, older people relying more on personal capital. The predominance of informal sources of capital is strongly suggestive of businesses controlled by entrepreneurs who may have only a limited conception of the need to draw up management strategies or business plans (Schwaninger, 1986).

All these variables relating to the characteristics of owner-managers will have an impact on the economic health of the tourism industry and of particular local economies. As O'Farrell (1986) writes, 'although economic theory has little to say on these matters, there is evidence to suggest that there is a relationship between the personal qualities of the entrepreneur and the economic success of the firm, as measured by its growth and profitability'. Within

Cornwall, for example, relationships have been identified between age of entrepreneur, access to capital and improvements in tourism accommodation establishments. While the relationships between motivation and socio-economic characteristics are often complex, the attraction of middle-aged and elderly in-migrants is likely to have important implications for new investment and innovation.

Attitudes to future investment are a matter of particular concern. One of the key areas is the perception of 'seasonality' (an advantage or a problem) and the capacity to respond to business implications. Entrepreneurs participating in the Cornwall survey were asked two questions in this context: first, how they viewed seasonality problems and, second, what attempts they were making to overcome them. Both sets of responses raised some important issues for the future of Cornwall's tourism industry.

Less than 3% of respondents within the accommodation sectors thought that the short summer season was a major problem for their businesses; instead most cited 'bad weather' as a major difficulty. That so few businesses remarked on the seasonality problem is significant in an industry with such profound seasonal cycles of business activity. This may indicate a passive acceptance of seasonality as being largely fixed and constant. The emphasis is placed on exploiting the short season as much as possible, rather than attempting to lengthen it. Indeed, this possibility is given further support when attention is focused on the attempts by individual firms to counter seasonality problems. The Cornwall survey found that very few accommodation units had marketing strategies aimed at developing off-peak holidays. Thus, only 18% of the sample offered weekend breaks, with 15% (often the same firms) marketing winter weekend breaks.

Conclusions

Obviously, the studies of Cornwall and the Isles of Scilly are very specific projects, in which particular problems are being researched. Nevertheless, this work does highlight the need to take a closer look at entrepreneurial behaviour and, in particular, the activities of small firms in tourism. Within the UK such research is made all the more urgent given the increasing interest paid to tourism as a source for development in many urban and rural environments (English Tourist Board, 1988 and 1989).

In newer areas of tourism development, as well as in more traditional regions, there is a need to understand the potential of local businesses to expand or to respond to change. If, for example, too much attention is paid to the development of large tourist facilities, many local economies may find that tourism does little to stimulate local activities, and much revenue may then be lost to the local area. In this respect tourist regions in developed countries share common problems with tourist enclaves in the developing world. More-over, there has been a tendency in both types of economy to concentrate research on the impact of large national or transnational firms, at the expense of considering the role of smaller businesses. Future research on tourism and economic development will need to examine more closely the relationships between the nature of entrepreneurship, the structural characteristics of the tourism industry and its impact on economic change. The current research on the South West of England may contribute to the development of a more realistic view of tourism's role in economic growth. However, these studies need replicating in a variety of locations and there is also a need to pursue a number of questions in greater detail.

Further research is only the first stage, however. It needs to lead to the development of effective policies. Thus, the work in Cornwall highlights the importance of changing (and sometimes static) entrepreneurial attitudes within parts of the tourism industry and points to an overwhelming need for improved levels of training for managers and owners. The generally low level of previous experience amongst tourist entrepreneurs suggests the need for specific counselling on the requirements of tourists. There is also a need to improve access to formal sources of capital, requiring action both from financial institutions and the tourism firms themselves. For example, one possibility discussed in the Cornish study was the use of an independent broker to act as an intermediary between the firm and the lending agency. Within the context of tourism in developed economies, these ideas clearly require further discussion.

On a wider scale, the performance of local entrepreneurs also holds the key to developing stronger benefits from tourism in Third World areas. In Lundgren's (1973) original discussion of hotel developments within Caribbean countries, it was in part the capacity of local suppliers that determined the extent of local linkages with transnational hotels. Such linkages are vital if benefits from tourism are to flow into and be retained within the host community. It can therefore be argued that a major advance in the understanding of tourism's role in economic development in many different environments can be achieved through research on entrepreneurial activity.

Until now we have used the term 'entrepreneurial' very loosely and often as a substitute for management or decision-making. Yet, as O'Farrell (1986) has shown, there are several different but precise theoretical conceptions of entrepreneurship. These emphasize responding to uncertainty, having a key role in innovation, perceiving and adjusting to disequilibrium and organizing or gap-filling. It is clear that tourism faces considerable problems of uncertainty and disequilibrium, requiring appropriate responses, organization and innovation. Yet these are precisely the qualities which appear to be poorly developed amongst small tourist firms. Therefore, the opening question for any research agenda must be 'why is entrepreneurship so poorly developed in the tourism industry as a whole, and so unevenly (by space and sector) within it?'. Once these questions have been addressed, it may be possible to consider what types of policies are appropriate for the long-term development of tourism.

References

Archer, B. H., 1976, 'Uses and abuses of multipliers', in Gearing, G. E., Swart, W. W., Var, T. (eds), *Planning for Tourism Development: Quantitative Approaches*, Praegar, New York.

Archer, B. H., 1977, 'Tourism multipliers: the state of the art', occasional papers in *Economics*, No. 11, University of Wales, Cardiff.

Archer, B. H., 1982, 'The value of multipliers and their policy implications', *Tourism Management*, 4: pp. 236–41.

Bagguley, P., 1987, 'Flexibility, restructuring and gender: changing employment in Britain's hotels', Lancaster Regionalism Group, working paper No. 24, University of Lancaster.

British Tourist Authority, 1985, *Hotel Development in the UK*, BTA, London.

Britton, S. G., 1981, 'Tourism, dependency and development: a mode of analysis', occasional paper No. 23, Development Studies, Australian National University, Canberra.

Brown, B., 1987, 'Recent tourism research in South East Dorset', in Shaw, G., Williams, A. (eds), *Tourism and Development: Overviews and Case Studies of the UK and the S.W. Region*, Working Paper No. 4, Dept. of Geography, University of Exeter.

Brown, B., 1988, 'Developments in the promotion of major seaside resorts: how to effect a transition by really making an effort', in Goodall, B., Ashworth, G. (eds), *Marketing in the Tourism Industry*, Croom Helm, London.

Bryden, J., 1973, *Tourism and Development: A Case Study of the Commonwealth Caribbean*, Cambridge University Press, Cambridge.

Chivers, T. S., 1973, 'The proletarianisation of a service worker', *Sociological Review*, 21: pp. 633–56.

Commission of the European Communities, 1987, *Job Creation in Small and Medium-sized Enterprises: Summary Report Vol. 1*, Luxembourg.

Cornwall Tourism Development Action Programme, 1988, *Strategy 1988–1991*, Truro.

ETB, 1988, *Tourism and the Inner City*, Planning Advisory Note No. 3, English Tourist Board, London.

ETB, 1989, *Visitors in the Countryside—Rural Tourism, a Development Strategy*, English Tourist Board, London.

ETC, 1988, *40 Years of Joint Action 1948–1988*, European Travel Commission, Paris.

Goffee, R., Scase, R., 1983, 'Class entrepreneurship and the service sector: towards a conceptual clarification', *Service Industries Journal*, 3: pp. 146–60.

Goodall, B., 1987, 'Tourism policy and jobs in the UK', *Built Environment*, 13: pp. 109–23.

Harper, M., 1984, *Small Businesses in the Third World: Guidelines for Practical Assistance*, Wiley, Chichester.

de Kadt, E. (ed.), 1979, *Tourism, Passport to Development*, Oxford University Press, Oxford.

Kilby, P. (ed.) 1971, *Entrepreneurship and Economic Development*, The Free Press, New York.

Lea, J., 1988, *Tourism and Development in the Third World*, Routledge, London.

Leontidou, L., 1988, 'Greece: prospects and contradictions of tourism in the 1980s', in Williams, A. M., Shaw, G. (eds), *Tourism and Economic Development: Western European Experiences*, Belhaven Press, London.

Littlejohn, D., 1982, 'The role of hotel consortia in Great Britain', *Service Industries Review*, 2: pp. 79–91.

Lundgen, J. O. S., 1973, 'Tourist impact/island entrepreneurship in the Caribbean', quoted in Mathieson and Wall (1982).

Mathieson, A., Wall, G., 1982, *Tourism: Economic, Physical and Social Impact*, Longman, London, p. 85.

Murphy, P. E., 1985, *Tourism: A Community Approach*, Methuen, New York.

OECD, 1986, *Tourism Policy and International Tourism in OECD Countries*, OECD, Paris.

O'Farrell, P. K., 1986, 'Entrepreneurship and regional development: some conceptual issues', *Regional Studies*, 20(6): pp. 565–74.

Pannell Kerr Forster Associates, 1986, *Outlook in the Hotel and Tourism Industries*, London.

Pearce, D., 1987, *Tourism To-day: A Geographical Analysis*, Longman, London.

Schwaninger, M., 1986, 'Strategic business management in tourism', *Tourism Management*, 7(2): pp. 74–85.

Shaw, G., Williams, A. M., 1987, 'Firm formation and operating characteristics in the Cornish Tourism Industry', *Tourism Management*, 8(4): pp. 344–8.

Shaw, G., Williams, A. M., Greenwood, J., 1987(a), 'Comparative studies in local economies: the Cornish case', *Built Environment*, 13: pp. 73–84.

Shaw, G., Williams, A. M., Greenwood, J., 1987(b), *Tourism and the Economy of Cornwall*, Tourism Research Group, University of Exeter.

Shivji, J. G. (ed.), 1973, *Tourism and Socialist Development*, Tanzania Publishing House, Dar-es-Salaam.

Slattery, P., 1985, 'Hotel consortia: their activities, structure and growth', *Service Industries Journal*, 5: pp. 192–9.

Spanoudis, C., 1982, 'Trends in tourism planning and development', *Tourism Management*, 3(4): pp. 314–18.

Stallibrass, C., 1980, 'Seaside resorts and the hotel accommodation industry', *Progress in Planning*, 13: pp. 103–74.

Storey, D. J. (ed.), 1983, *The Small Firm: An International Survey*, Croom Helm, Andover.

United Nations, 1980, *Transnational Corporations in International Tourism*, UN, New York.

Vaughan, D. R., 1986, *Estimating the Level of Tourism-Related Employment: An Assessment of Two Non-Survey Techniques*, E.T.B., London.

West Country Tourist Board, 1989, *Towards a Strategy for the 1990s and Beyond*, Exeter.

Williams, A., Shaw, G. (eds), 1988(a), 'West European tourism in perspective', in Williams, A., Shaw, G. (eds), *Tourism and Economic Development: West European Experiences*, Belhaven Press, London.

Williams, A., Shaw, G., 1988(b), 'Tourism: candyfloss industry or job generator', *Town Planning Review*, 59(1): pp. 81–104.

Williams, A. M., Greenwood, J., Shaw, G., 1989, *Tourism in the Isles of Scilly: A Study of Small Firms on Small Islands*, Tourism Research Group, University of Exeter.

WTO, 1985, *The Role of Transnational Tourism Enterprises in the Development of Tourism*, World Tourism Organization, Madrid.

WTO, 1987, *Compendium of Tourism Statistics*, World Tourism Organization, Madrid.

Young, G., 1973, *Tourism: Blessing or Blight?*, Penguin, Harmondsworth.

Zimmermann, F., 1988, 'Austria: contrasting tourist seasons and contrasting regions', in Williams, A. M., Shaw, G. (eds), *Tourism and Economic Development: Western European Experiences*, Belhaven Press, London.

5 Marketing in National Tourist Offices

A. Jefferson

The job of Marketing Director in National Tourist Offices (NTOs) can be likened to walking a political tightrope while juggling five balls marked National Government, Regions, Local Authorities, Trade and, not least, Consumer. Yet the marketer is bound to fail unless he recognizes one fundamental and basic truth—the consumer is king.

The need for a national tourist office

Tourism creates wealth and is an important contributor to foreign currency earnings. It also sustains a great number of jobs and can be used to vivify regions, cities and towns with poor physical resources or declining industries. Tourism is arguably, even now, the world's biggest market. The competition in the market-place is increasingly fierce as more and more countries see tourism as the panacea for their economic problems and unemployment. For example, there are about 100 NTOs in Frankfurt and New York and more than 70 in Tokyo. So, the task to be accomplished by an NTO is the effective and efficient defence of a country's stake in this enormous market with its massive implications for foreign currency, earnings and employment.

Tourism is a market, not a single industry, a trade in people and thus a complex phenomenon with important social as well as economic consequences. Governments, central and local, represent the destination and play a key role in tourism development, not least by ensuring a focal point for co-ordination and, where appropriate, collective action with the large range of interests providing the services, facilities and attractions which make up the whole tourism product (Jefferson and Likorish, 1988).

The NTO has the prime responsibility to act as the inviting host on behalf of the resident population and its visitor resources, which are many and varied. As far back as 1966 the OECD in *Tourism Development and Economic Growth*, set out the ground rules for an NTO. They are as relevant today as they were then:

All countries have an official tourism organization, which plays a leading role in both the formulation and implementation of the government's tourism programme. The functions of this body, however, vary considerably according broadly to the level of tourism development in the country concerned and the degree of direct intervention that the government wishes to exercise.

These differences of function are reflected in the organization's structure and constitutional status. Thus in some countries the national tourism office is part of the central machinery of government through which the government operates directly in the tourism sector. In others it has a semi-autonomous status and functions not as an organ of government but rather as a professional body outside it. As a general rule it may be said that this latter conception of the role of the national tourism office is more appropriate to countries where tourism is already fairly advanced and where the private sector is active in it (OECD, 1966).

In Britain, where tourism is already *fairly advanced*, the number of people employed in tourism-related industries in December 1988 amounted to 1,370,400. An additional 183,000 self-employed people work in the hotel and catering industry in Britain. It is estimated that for every one direct job in the tourist industry, one-half indirect job is created elsewhere in the economy.

In 1988, Britain's overseas earnings from tourism—including fares paid to British carriers—amounted to £7,535 million. Domestic tourism accounted for a further £7,850 million. Tourism represented more than a quarter of exports of all services.

Britain's NTO, the British Tourist Authority (BTA), is the statutory agency of government responsible for discharging the tourism function in overseas markets in so far as marketing is concerned. Thus the BTA is the agency with the unique and indispensable role of destination marketing authority. But it is more than this. The BTA has an advisory role to Government and key interests in providing options for development based on market research and intelligence, and conversely, liaises with Government and key interests in the development and elaboration of the Government's tourism policy. The BTA has responsibility for preparing the marketing strategy which will implement agreed Government tourism policy in consultation with the industry. Most importantly, it provides a cooperative marketing base—the focal point for consultation and operation of the marketing programmes promoting Britain as a tourist destination in selected markets overseas.

It is pertinent at this point to look back to the origins of BTA. It was set up in 1929 as the Travel Association of Great Britain and Ireland and it survived in various forms of voluntary membership association for the next 40 years. The 1969 Development of Tourism Act established the BTA alongside the English Tourist Board (ETB), Scottish Tourist Board and Wales Tourist Board. These organizations (or national boards, as they are generally known) are responsible for marketing in the domestic market—the United Kingdom. Subsequently the Scottish Tourist Board was given statutory powers to market Scotland overseas so long as its policies are complementary to the marketing activities of the BTA by the Tourism (Overseas Promotion) (Scotland) Act 1984.

When the Trade and Industry Select Committee examined the tourist industry in 1985, it reported

... the present legislative framework, creating as it does three independent and separately funded tourist boards in Great Britain, means that there is no overall policy applied to developing tourism in the UK as a whole. There is no co-ordination of funding, so relative priorities are not assessed, nor is there any cohesion between strategies pursued by the boards (HMSO, 1985).

It was in 1985, too, that the Enterprise Unit of the Cabinet Office then headed by Lord Young published *Pleasure, Leisure and Jobs*. 'It may be asked why the Government should involve itself directly in this topic, which is primarily a matter for private enterprise', the report stated. 'Indeed, the Government believes the best way it can help any sector of business flourish is not by intervening but by providing a general economic framework which encourages growth and at the same time removing unnecessary restrictions or burdens.'

Some time later the Secretary of State for Employment, the Rt. Hon. Norman Fowler MP, instituted a review of the BTA and the English Tourist Board. In July 1989 he concluded 'that Government financial support for the promotion of tourism should continue . . .' but looked to the BTA and the ETB '. . . to improve cost-effectiveness and to extend partnerships with the industry'. Specifically, he asked the BTA '. . . to ensure that greater authority is devolved to its overseas regions . . . to work even more closely with the industry in overseas markets and to move some of its operations into the private sector'. He also asked for the ETB to '. . . direct substantially more of its funding to the Regional Tourist Boards under a form of contract . . .' which would enable the regions to '. . . increase their marketing activities and their direct involvement in encouraging the development of tourism locally . . .' but in turn expected '. . . the regional boards to use such funds as a lever to achieve private sector participation . . .' The ETB would, however, continue '. . . to play an important co-ordinating role'. Finally, having suspended the development grant scheme administered by the ETB, Fowler announced that no further offers of financial assistance would be made because '. . . the future growth of tourism no longer depends on this scheme.'[1]

The NTO's marketing resources represent seed money which not only extends promotion of the destination but provides essential support for the marketing arms of the suppliers, many of which are small businesses which could not otherwise enter the international market-place. The essence of the tourism product is the destination and visitor satisfaction with the destination. It follows that the NTO is the only organization which can link the destination with the tourist trades and service interests. Only the Government, custodians of the product by the authority of the people, is empowered to promote the destination either directly or through its appointed agency. That agency must be adequately funded to discharge its responsibility for marketing the destination in a form undiluted by third-party interests, where this is an essential need, working in partnership with third-party interests wherever this is possible and providing the strategic guidelines as well as the cooperative

[1] Written answer to David Gilroy Bevan MP on Tourism Review. *Hansard*, 6 July 1989.

marketing base for the tourist trades. This ensures that the tourist trades are able to pursue the essential collective task as well as their own competitive trading.

Marketing a destination—the constraints

There is an important difference between the anticipation and the consumption of the tourist product. It is not always easy to *sample* the product and there are consequently a number of important marketing implications. To an extent, the promotion is the product. Furthermore, there are some fundamental differences between marketing a tourist destination and marketing consumer goods and services. These differences need to be recognized and addressed in different ways. A national tourist office is in many ways not able to embrace the marketing concept totally.

The marketer in a NTO has no control over the brand name. The brand name of the British Tourist Authority's product is Britain. It cannot be changed or dropped when the going gets rough, though the brand image can. A key role for any NTO therefore is that of guardian of the image. The NTO marketer must be ever vigilant in ensuring that the brand image is the best possible and that damage to the image, if it should occur, is quickly mitigated.

The product is, to a very large extent, inherited. The tourism marketer can never research the market and develop a product from scratch. The climate, geography, topography, history, culture and traditions are all inherited. The product can be modified and appropriate new infrastructure developed. But even here the NTO marketer can only identify opportunities and encourage developments. Rarely is he given the opportunity of bringing the development about. He can present the destination in an appealing way, he can make it easier to buy and he can provide the cooperative marketing base.

The major strategy areas are product, price, promotion and market-place. Yet the NTO has little control over product and in most countries no control over prices charged, either. But the NTO can have an influential role in product presentation and to a much lesser extent in pricing policies. While the organization must work through its advisory committee structure and has only minimal control over channels of distribution, its cooperative marketing programme enables it to play an important role in market analysis and planning without entering the selling arena. Where the NTO is government funded, however, budgets are not ultimately determined by the agency, and this can result in changes of direction and enforced cuts which are not in the long-term interests of the country.

Given these constraints, what can and should the NTO's role be in marketing the destination?

The five roles of the National Tourist Office

Burkart and Medlik (1981) suggested that the NTO's marketing function is twofold: '... in the first place the tourist organization can formulate and develop the tourist product or products of the destination: secondly it can promote them in appropriate markets' (p. 256). It can also be thought of as five-fold, though each role, chameleon-like, spills over into the others, colouring and shading their performance. The five roles are:

(a) guardian of the image;
(b) scene setter;
(c) trail blazer;
(d) marketing co-ordinator;
(e) monitor of visitor satisfaction.

Guardian of the image

It has already been suggested that the unique and indispensable role of the NTO is that of the destination marketing authority. One of its principal tasks is to be the guardian of the image. Transporters often forget the very basic fact that people fly on an aeroplane, sail on a ship or ride in a car or bus to get from A to B. Hoteliers do not always remember that people stay in a hotel at B because there is something they want to see or do there. There has to be a reason for going to B—the destination. It is the job of the NTO marketers (based on research, analysis and segmentation) to determine the images, to create awareness of the destination and position it accurately in the market-place. But that is not enough. Images can become tarnished and sullied; they need constant attention to maintain their glitter and glamour. The marketer must use a number of marketing tools to achieve this.

In tourism, public relations can be the most cost-effective of all the weapons in the marketer's armoury:

At the consumer level the public relations programme must be closely geared to the marketing plan and in line with marketing policy and objectives. Essentially it should be designed to create and maintain an image for the destination which is at once appetizing and appealing. It must make the consumer think 'I would like to go or be there'. The objective of the PR campaign will differ from market to market. Where a currency is weak against that of the destination it will be necessary to make the consumer aware of the best buys, how to make his budget go further, where to find value for money. Reassure him with actual examples that the destination is affordable. On the other hand, in an area of special interest travel, it will be necessary to communicate the unique appeals of the destination *vis-à-vis* the consumer's hobby or avocation. The PR machine will be used to communicate new developments—hotels, events, facilities, to promote themes or anniversaries and it uses a number of techniques to achieve the desired results (Jefferson and Likorish, 1988, p. 143).

The techniques used include press releases, press news bulletins, features, picture stories, press facility visits and new conferences.

Advertising is a more precisely targeted marketing weapon and performs most effectively when it is projected on a backcloth of receptivity created through a good public relations campaign. Strategically, it is one of the image makers, designed to make the destination seem appealing. At the tactical level it can also provide a message of reassurance.

Promotional print is used by the marketer in an effort to persuade the reader to select a particular destination. It is the representation of the product or destination and consequently an important image maker.

Scene setter

According to Middleton (1988),

As in all marketing, the process begins with researching the external environment. Since only larger operators, such as airlines and hotel chains, will have the resources to undertake large-scale marketing research, especially into international markets, a NTO has a unique role to play in the travel and tourism industry in gathering and communicating market analysis and trend data, not only for its own marketing purposes but for the industry as a whole (p. 217).

While marketing should be research-driven, the marketer, not the researcher, should be in the driving seat. The marketer should devise the research programmes' objectives, the researcher should carry out the technical work and help to interpret the findings and finally, the marketer should implement those findings.

One of the vehicles for communicating market analysis and trend data to the industry is the strategy document. The BTA publishes guidelines for tourism planning and marketing on a biennial basis. *Strategy for Growth 1989–1993* was published in late 1988 and sets out key objectives, an analysis of product strengths and weaknesses, factors influencing tourism growth in the next five years and forecasts of potential visits and earnings (BTA, 1988). These sections are followed by guidelines for tourism development in both marketing and product areas. In addition to setting the scene for the British tourism industry for the next five years, the publication looks back to its predecessors, reviewing previous strategies and, especially, previously identified product weaknesses, in order to assess what has been achieved.

In tourism the dictates of the market are often overshadowed by external factors which can set the parameters within which marketing and development takes places. Cleverdon (1983) identifies these forces under six major headings:

1. Society's attitudes and expectations;
2. Socio-demographic changes;

3. Time and money;
4. Cost of travel;
5. Legal and political developments;
6. Technological developments.

The NTO's analysis of these external factors will point the way for both public and private interests in identifying favourable growth markets as well as gaps in the product range—not only segments which offer future potential, but those which need remedial action to mitigate damage. While external factors can be very powerful forces for good, they can also have adverse effects. Nevertheless, effects can be modified or influenced by marketing activity.

The BTA's strategy documents produced in 1984 and 1986 highlighted the need for investment in new hotels, particularly in the budget sector. Five years later the investment in this sector is substantial and looks as if it will continue at a high level. The increase in lead-free petrol is another example.

The BTA warned in 1986 that the availability of lead-free petrol would deter an increasing number of overseas motorists from bringing their cars to Britain from Europe. Since 1987, petrol companies have been increasing the number of outlets . . . already there are over 2,200 outlets through Britain selling lead-free petrol. This means that no European motorist need be deterred from bringing a car requiring lead-free petrol to Britain (BTA, 1988, p. 9).

Product analysis is the key to market segmentation and communications strategy and the pointer of product presentation. The marketer must be scrupulously objective in analysing the product and this analysis should extend to perceptions of the destination in terms of its product strengths and weaknesses. In the minds of consumers perceptions are real enough. Market analysis enables the marketer to understand the characteristics of individual markets and this in turn leads to identification of marketing opportunities. All markets are capable of segmentation and even the simplest can help in the scene-setting task.

Britain's International Passenger Survey divides each market into the following broad segments: holiday independent, holiday inclusive, business travel, visits to friends and relatives, study and miscellaneous. This is a helpful segmentation analysis in determining trends, the strength or weakness of a particular product sector and indicative of changes in perception. For example a decline in the number of students attending English language schools, which might point to increased competition from other destinations, price resistance or in some cases a change in government policy in an important source market. When the pound is strong against a major currency such as the American dollar or the Canadian dollar it is often reflected in a move from the holiday independent category to the visiting friends and relatives category (Jefferson and Likorish, 1988, p. 73).

Tourism marketing needs to be selective in terms of target, medium and message. The BTA publishes a great deal of research data—some free, some saleable—and through its various advisory publications interprets much of this research for the industry as a whole. It helps the industry to develop the right product for the right market and the right segment within that market. It also helps the industry to target messages more precisely against the backcloth of destination-awareness-creating campaigns of the NTO. BTA publishes, for example, a market guide for each market in which it operates. These are available at nominal cost and include not just a distillation of the available research data, but guidance on how to do business in that particular market. BTA also operates through a number of committees and working parties. Many of these committees include representatives of trade associations who can in turn communicate research findings and guidance on particular markets to their membership.

Examples of BTA research and advisory publications range from comprehensive surveys of the British tourism market and the UK exhibition industry to *Visits to Tourist Attractions*, *Holiday Motivations* and *The Economic Significance of Tourism Within the European Community*. Regional fact sheets providing concise key facts of tourism in each of England's twelve regions are available, as well as market guides for overseas markets.

BTA's marketing plan for the financial year 1989/90 was developed to address eight key tasks:

1. To maintain Britain's broad spread of markets to mitigate any sudden drop in traffic from individual markets as a result of external factors.
2. To emphasize value-for-money products in Britain in light of the continued strength of sterling against the currencies of our major markets.
3. To arrest declining share of market from North America and increase traffic from European markets. In European markets there will need to be an emphasis on regional spread and gateways, but not neglecting the promotion of London and the South East as our principal international gateways—marketing will be increasingly geared to the opportunities offered by the opening of the Channel Tunnel in 1993.
4. To maintain pioneering work in new markets which show above-average growth potential in the next five to ten years.
5. To continue to address seasonality, seeking to fill troughs wherever and whenever they occur; to encourage better utilization of tourism infrastructure and so greater full-time employment.
6. To promote tourism especially to the regions with above-average unemployment, namely Scotland, Wales, the North of England, the East Midlands and the West Country.
7. To participate fully in European Tourism Year 1990, placing particular emphasis on the continued raising of standards and welcome and the encouraging of Europeans from other Community countries to explore aspects of our common heritage in the United Kingdom.
8. To increase non-Government funding in support of BTA activity.

In seeking to fulfil these tasks, specific segments offering the greatest potential will be identified for each market. Markets are generally senior citizens, youth, 'special interest' and business travel.

With respect to the fivefold marketing role of the NTO which has been suggested earlier, each of the eight tasks above can be seen in the context of the five roles, though they do spill over into one another:

Guardian of the image	— 1, 2, 3, 4;
Scene setter	— 1, 3, 4;
Trail blazer	— 3, 4, 5, 6;
Marketing coordinator	— 1, 2, 3, 4, 5, 6, 7, 8;
Monitor of visitor satisfaction	— 2, 5.

The marketing plan is developed by BTA's marketing division as the tactical plan for the year ahead—the communications plan of the organization. It is set in the context of the long-term strategy and objectives but has specific tasks and targets for the year ahead. It is from this plan that the catalogue of co-operative marketing opportunities derives. This catalogue is offered to the public and private sectors which are invited to cooperate with the BTA in fulfilling the marketing programmes set out in the plan. This leads to a further NTO role—that of marketing coordinator. But in fact the BTA plays another role, invariably on a solo basis. This role is that of a missionary undertaking the essential pioneering work which has to be done ahead of trade partnerships.

Trail blazer

One of the principal roles of any NTO is to develop new markets, new segments and new techniques. In a commercial organization marketing appropriations are more likely to be required to secure an immediate return on investment. The trade will very often follow only when the missionary work has been done. The return on investment is in the longer term and marketing in these conditions becomes an act of faith.

When India relaxed the fiscal controls of foreign travel, the BTA appointed an executive in London with responsibility for that vast market. Visits to the market-place were very much on a solo basis, nurturing the Indian travel trade and the media, building on what was already there, encouraging operators to include Britain in their programmes and very often helping to devise those programmes. It was a long, lonely adventure. The British trade were invited to participate in BTA organized sales missions. Some took the first tentative steps and were rewarded with business. Now India is among the top 20 markets for travel to Britain.

Now the BTA is engaged in developing the Korean market where, until very recently, outbound travel was strictly controlled. There was no travel so there were no travel writers, and the first group of journalists invited to see the

British product were generalists. Korea will very quickly develop travel writers. Those incoming handling agents who were in at the early stage of market development are reaping the rewards, but there are very few of them. Thus the BTA continues its missionary role.

The development of new market segments is one where the NTO has a key role to play. While incentive travel was a large business in the USA in the 1970s, it was virtually unknown in Asia and little used even in European markets. While the BTA provided substantial resources in developing the incentive travel segment in the USA over many years, it has recently switched to the development of incentive travel from other markets. 'The NTO should never attempt to do other interests' jobs. It should not hold on to successful ventures, a very hard but essential rule to follow. The *missionary task is endless*' (Jefferson and Lickorish, 1988). The BTA is active in developing other segments, notably youth, senior citizens and special-interest travel. Almost 70% of all leisure travellers to Britain are repeat visitors, so it is important to influence tourists when they are young—to think of them as consumer trainees. English language learning is a powerful product area in this context.

At the other end of the age spectrum is an increasingly important segment— the mature traveller. The market offers vast potential, yet it was only a comparatively short time ago that the travel industry first recognized it. By the end of this century there will be 35 million people over 65 in the USA and this pattern is repeated in most developed countries. It is forecast that nearly 20% of the total population of the top seven OECD countries, which are big traffic generators, will be 65 or over. The BTA is still encouraging the trade to develop more products and programmes to meet the needs of this vast market, which is not one segment but several sub-segments.

Another very important segment is special-interest travel. Self-fulfilment and self-expression are increasingly powerful motivators in travel and while some special-interest packages can be developed without recourse to an existing product base—flower arranging, painting, music appreciation—others can only be developed with difficulty. It will almost certainly fall to the NTO to present very fragmented products in an appealing and structured way. The time which needs to be invested in careful and thorough product analysis is often too great for the operator. Once it is developed and the sales potential is demonstrated, the trade will usually take over.

Seasonality is a perennial problem facing tourism marketers and the segments identified above present a viable solution to the problem. BTA launched **Operation Off Peak** in 1985 and it continues to gather momentum. It has been promoted at a number of levels—advisory and educational (publications and seminars), marketing under the **Britain for All Seasons** slogan (advertising, PR and print), and not least, product presentation, especially through special events which can be successfully exploited to fill the troughs.

Trail blazing can be a direct result of governmental guidelines. In November 1974 the then Secretary of State asked the tourist boards to promote economically fragile areas of the country (BTA, 1975); more recently Lord Young, when he was Secretary of State for Employment, advised that extra funds should be spent on the promotion of 'areas of high unemployment with tourism potential' (BTA, 1987). Many of these areas were not known touristically, and it was up to the BTA and the national boards to start image-making programmes, which still continue.

The tourism product is an amalgam of many fragmented products, each independent yet inter-dependent. Increasingly the need is to make it easy for the consumer to buy, so the producers need to have rapid access through the channels of distribution to the ultimate consumer. Every sale made by international airlines is made through computerized reservation systems (CRS), and a number of systems are in operation. The BTA was the first NTO to have space on SABRE, the American Airlines system, which is now in about 10,000 agency outlets in the USA. Comprehensive research into this area led to the realization that there was an increasing need for a *switch* to link the central reservation offices of the major vendors with the international distribution systems, such as SABRE. The BTA is now developing just such a distribution mechanism for British producers through the BRAVO project.

Marketing coordinator

As the destination marketing authority, the BTA offers an opportunity for suppliers (many of whom are small businesses) to enter the international market-place. This cooperative base greatly strengthens the total promotion through a collective destination message. The BTA publishes annually *Promoting Tourism to Britain: How BTA Can Help*, a catalogue of cooperative marketing opportunities embracing all of the marketing tools.

Advertising is invariably undertaken with the air and sea carriers but occasionally with car hire companies, hoteliers and the major tour operators. Direct mail is being used increasingly as the BTA builds up mailing lists of previous enquirers to its offices around the world. The new technology enables the BTA to categorize, replenish and update as well as print out labels.

Brochure production is expensive, but in the case of destination marketing it is the representation of the product. Advertising in the NTO's print provides the essential commercial and price information needed to make it easy to buy the product. Research undertaken into BTA's main guide suggests that 90% of those who obtain it have already decided to visit Britain. It thus represents a very cost-effective way for advertisers to reach a precisely targeted audience, the more so because 80% of leisure travellers to Britain do not buy a fully inclusive package, allowing their pattern of visit to be influenced by marketing. The main guide is very often the potential visitor's principal planning tool.

An exhibition can be an excellent showcase for the destination, and the BTA takes space in a number of holiday exhibitions and trade shows, which provide a focal point for transporters and destination interests to pool resources. The coordinated national presence is much more impactful than a solo position.

Apart from trade shows, the BTA offers sales missions which enable the producer of services to meet with the potential buyer in the market-place. The sales missions organized by the BTA are usually to only one or two places, while roadshows can cover as many as 20 cities over the space of several weeks. The workshop was invented and developed for the travel trade and is a forum where buyers meet sellers. The BTA organizes workshops which are product-specific, such as the English Language Schools Workshop, or general, such as those offered at the time of the World Travel Market. They can be in Britain or in the market-place. These are offered in the shopping lists of cooperative marketing opportunities which BTA produces annually for the private and public sectors.

Distribution of commercial literature to the BTA's overseas offices or direct to the trade, sales of shell folders and maps, as well as film and video production are offered. Joint marketing schemes can be undertaken which can embrace any or all of the marketing tools. BTA targets to raise at least two-thirds of its total marketing spend in the form of non-government funding. An iron test of any NTO's marketing effectiveness is the willingness of the trade to put its money into that NTO's marketing activity.

This unique and important function of representing and coordinating all destination interests in a powerful way through appealing to the visitor is often underestimated. Yet there is one other important field in which BTA engages—that of product presentation. This ranges from the development of umbrella themes to the creation of consortia and marketing cooperatives.

Heritage '84 is a good example of how an umbrella theme was used to provide an opportunity for a re-presentation of the attractions of Britain—a sharper focusing of the many facets of Britain's heritage. It also sought to provide a creative platform for all the organizations concerned with the incoming business to cooperate in marketing the theme. A great number of new and varied heritage products and events were brought on stream, many of which still exist today. From the point of arrival—both British Airports Authority and Sealink had *Heritage '84* banners in the baggage halls—overseas visitors were made aware that 1984 offered a special welcome. Special promotions in duty-free and souvenir shops at airports and seaports ensured that the *Heritage '84* theme carried through to the time they left. The BTA's marketing programmes in 1984 were totally committed to the heritage theme—advertising, public relations, print (including much specialist print), exhibitions, trade shows and sales missions. A regular broadsheet, *Heritage Herald*, was launched to encourage local authorities and industry in Britain to play their part and a logo was developed which continued long after the heritage campaign had run its course.

Many new initiatives need a collective of interests, and schemes such as **Commended Country Hotels, Guest Houses and Restaurants** were devised not only to meet the regional spread objective but to provide the overseas visitor with guidance on good value establishments offering excellent food and a special welcome. The **Great British Heritage Pass** provides entry to 600 stately homes, castles and gardens throughout Britain and is valid for either fifteen days or a month. These are just two examples of product presentation. The BTA has also encouraged marketing consortia such as Wolsey Lodges (a consortium of up-market B&B establishments), UK Waterways Holidays (narrow boats on canals) and B&B (GB), which offers a computerized booking service for bed-and-breakfast accommodation. The BTA in the role of marketing co-ordinator also develops special-interest themed trails which may be linked to an anniversary such as the tercentenary of William and Mary or the novocentenary of the Tower of London, the American bicentennial of 1976 or the Australian bicentennial of 1988.

At one end of the spectrum the BTA's role as marketing coordinator is to provide the cooperative marketing base—the opportunity for a fragmented industry to reach the market-place cost-effectively. At the other end of the spectrum it is concerned with presenting the product in an appealing way and making it easy for the visitor to buy.

The British Travel Centre in central London brings together BTA, British Rail and American Express to offer the most comprehensive tourist information and booking service in London under one roof. There visitors can book coach, rail, air and car travel, accommodation and sightseeing tours, buy theatre tickets, change foreign currency and buy books and souvenirs. The British Travel Centre straddles the twin roles of marketing coordinator and monitor of visitor satisfaction. Close to a million visitors a year stop off there, providing a useful barometer of the way the product is perceived and sold.

Monitor of visitor satisfaction

Visitor satisfaction is researched in a much more structured way through regular annual surveys such as the Overseas Visitor Survey, which samples visitors in a number of centres throughout the country and throughout the year. This not only provides useful information on behaviour, such as where the visitors go, where they stay, how they travel and what they do, but gives an indication of satisfaction and attitudes to price and perceived value for money. The London Visitor Survey polls the huge visitor influx to London in the summer months.

In 1985 the BTA, through its Reception of Overseas Visitors Enquiry, examined visitor reception at ports and transport terminals. This covered welcome, information, passenger handling arrangements, baggage handling, restaurants, toilet facilities, signing and so on.

The NTO has an important responsibility in ensuring the promised quality of service, checking for defects and bottlenecks and, through more formal research, monitoring visitor satisfaction. This in turn provides a good basis for initiatives to improve product presentation, standards of service and initiation of new services and facilities. This may take the form of representation to public or private sector bodies suggesting improvements or changes. The

NTO is the most powerful motivator for the destination, and as such has a vital representational and educational role as well as a promotional one.

Conclusion

In summary, the NTO is at once initiator, motivator and adviser. Its marketing function must be concerned with the product—the foundation of all marketing programmes—the product image and the visitor's satisfaction with the product. While protection of the image is a key role for the NTO, the organization must also be the *patron* of the product and is thus directly concerned with product development and product presentation. Standards, strategies for growth, product initiation and innovation, the establishment of partnerships and new enterprise are all part of the destination tourist organization's job. Much of the NTO's marketing activity is on a cooperative basis, but there are times when essential missionary work is needed in the development of new markets, new segments and new techniques. The NTO must provide a focal point for the doers to pursue the necessary cooperative partnership as well as their own competitive trading. Marketing concerns itself with what consumers want and are prepared to buy. This is as vital to a tourist office as it is to a commercial organization.

References

BTA, 1975, *Annual Report for the year ended March 1975*, BTA, London.
BTA, 1987, *Annual Report for the year ended March 1987*, BTA, London.
BTA, 1988, *Strategy for Growth 1989—1993*, BTA, London.
BTA/ETB, 1989, Tourism Intelligence Quarterly, BTA/ETB 11(1): p. 23.
Burkart, A. J., Medlik, R., 1981, *Tourism Past, Present and Future*, 2nd edition. Heinemann, London.
Cleverdon, R., 1983, *The USA and UK on Holiday*, EIU Special Report.
HMSO, 1985, Trade and Industry Committee, *Tourism in the U.K.*, HMSO, London, Vol. 1.
HMSO, 1985, *Pleasure, Leisure and Jobs*. Cabinet Office, London.
Jefferson, A., Lickorish, L., 1988, *Marketing Tourism*, Longman, London.
Middleton, V. T. C., 1988, *Marketing in Travel and Tourism*. Heinemann, London, p. 217.
OECD, 1966, *Tourism Development and Economic Growth*, OECD, Paris.

6 Bermuda: the role of tourism research

B. H. Archer and C. W. Riley

The purpose of this chapter is to describe the nature of the research undertaken by and on behalf of the Bermuda Department of Tourism and to discuss
the part which this research plays in marketing the island and improving the
product.

Tourism in Bermuda

In the years before World War II, Bermuda was principally a winter destination resort for wealthy North Americans and, to a lesser extent, Europeans.
The rapid expansion of international tourism from the 1950s onwards, however, shifted the emphasis to the summer months, in line with the holiday
habits of the middle and upper income American markets. Over the last 30
years, the number of tourists and cruise passengers has increased fourfold from
142,330 in 1959 to 584,987 in 1988 (see Table 6.1 and Figure 6.1).

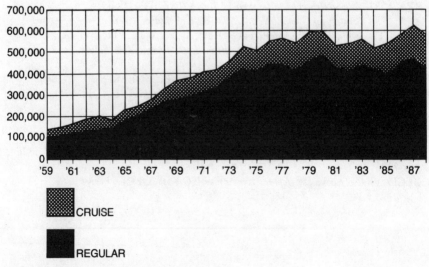

Figure 6.1 *Tourist arrivals to Bermuda*
Source: Bermuda Department of Tourism.

Table 6.1 *Tourist arrivals to Bermuda (1959–1988)*

Year	Regular	Cruise	Total
1959	109,515	32,815	142,330
1960	111,287	40,119	151,406
1961	123,651	46,971	170,622
1962	133,271	59,531	192,802
1963	141,643	62,538	204,181
1964	145,107	43,885	188,992
1965	187,265	50,517	237,782
1966	210,598	46,174	256,772
1967	237,163	44,004	281,167
1968	267,442	63,937	331,379
1969	280,987	89,933	370,920
1970	302,776	86,138	388,914
1971	319,310	93,637	412,947
1972	339,782	81,168	420,950
1973	385,241	82,015	467,256
1974	421,221	110,347	531,568
1975	411,783	99,602	511,385
1976	450,037	108,837	558,874
1977	441,025	131,830	572,855
1978	419,784	131,682	551,466
1979	458,781	140,350	599,131
1980	491,640	117,916	609,556
1981	429,801	104,721	534,522
1982	420,288	124,178	544,466
1983	446,864	120,846	567,710
1984	417,461	111,410	528,871
1985	406,687	142,903	549,590
1986	459,666	132,202	591,868
1987	477,877	153,437	631,314
1988	426,619	158,368	584,987

Source: Bermuda Department of Tourism.

This expansion has been achieved under a policy of demand management combined with control of the available supply of accommodation. A moratorium on major hotel expansion was initiated in the 1960s and strict planning regulations continue to govern new hotel developments. At the same time, to avoid visitor congestion in the country, the number of cruise ships at any one time is strictly controlled. From 1990, for example, the number of regular cruise ships visiting Bermuda will be limited to four per week, particularly during the May to October period. The overall aim is to enhance visitors' enjoyment of the island and to maintain the quality of life for Bermudian residents.

The principal tourist season now runs from April through October with August as the peak month. The Bermuda Department of Tourism has been very active in developing the off-season and smoothing out seasonal effects. The promotion of special-interest group sales is one example. The Department is also very conscious of the need to maintain the highest possible standards of tourism in order to preserve Bermuda's position as a major up-market destination.

The Bermuda Department of Tourism

The Bermuda Department of Tourism is a public sector body financed primarily from an annual government grant which is supplemented marginally by hotel licence fees, sales of some publications and by entry charges to some of the attractions which it controls. Government policy is implemented directly by a Minister of Tourism. Professional control is exercised by a director supported by experienced professional staff. Advice from industry is obtained formally from a statutory Tourist Board appointed by the Premier after consultation with the Minister of Tourism. Informal advice is provided through regular contacts between officials of the Department and operators in the industry. In addition, there is a non-political Tourism Industry Council drawn from a wider cross-section of the industry, which includes union representation as well as representatives from the Ministry of Education and the Bermuda College Department of Hotel Technology. Overseas offices are maintained in New York, Atlanta, Boston, Chicago and Toronto, with representation in Los Angeles. In Europe, a marketing presence is maintained in London, Frankfurt and Gothenburg.

The role of the Department is to promote the development of Bermuda's tourist industry in order to maximize the long-term benefits of the industry to the citizens of the country. In a country of only 22 square miles, *quality* rather than quantity is the primary consideration. While the island offers a wide range of accommodation at different prices, the Department concentrates its efforts primarily upon attracting high-income-group visitors from North America and Europe, and internally upon maintaining a high-quality product. To broaden the island's appeal and encourage future demand, additional efforts are directed towards attracting younger visitors and honeymoon couples in the less crowded *shoulder* seasons.

While the North American market currently provides more than 90% of all visitors, the Department is also attempting to strengthen its European markets. In the last three years successful efforts have been made to attract more visitors from Europe, particularly the United Kingdom and West Germany. As the European market continues to grow, the Department is well aware of the need to effect marginal changes in the product, for example, by the production of brochures and other literature in various languages.

The nature of the research

Although the Department maintains only a small statistical and research section, a considerable amount of in-house research is carried out to monitor international and national trends. The majority of the Department's research, however, is commissioned from agencies. The latter work involves both regular on-going studies and other *ad hoc* surveys carried out either for specific purposes or for strategic reasons.

In-house research

International trends are monitored regularly through principal tourism publications such as WTO reports, the *Economist Intelligence Unit* reports and *Annals of Tourism Research*, in addition to others in the travel press. Members of staff also attend major tourism conferences. Particular attention is paid to trends in the North American market because of its large share of visitors to Bermuda. Trends within Bermuda itself are monitored from data collected from public and private sources in the country. A major source of such data is the information processed from immigration cards (completed by all travellers on entry to Bermuda) about visitors' nationalities, areas of residence, reason for travel to Bermuda, length of stay, intended address while in Bermuda and the travel agent booking the reservation. In addition, studies are conducted on an as-needed basis, such as the one on Rendezvous Entertainment (Rendezvous is the off-season which runs from November 15 to March 31) and ongoing surveys on College Weeks (the annual spring programme for college students). This information is supplemented by the very detailed results of the Airport Exit Survey and Cruise Ship Survey, described below. The immigration data are compiled into a monthly monitoring report which is distributed to the general public (Bermuda Department of Tourism, monthly). Additional information about short-term trends is available from a regular industry survey of hotel occupancy rates and forward bookings.

Apart from the very valuable statistical base provided by this research, the work identifies warning signs of possible short-term difficulties, such as downturns in specific sub-sectors of the market. These trends may require some immediate remedial action and also additional research, such as that described above, to discover the underlying causes. In most such cases further research is commissioned from outside agencies.

On-going commissioned research

Three major on-going studies are carried out by agencies on behalf of the Department. The principal one, carried out continually since 1973, is an Airport Exit Survey (Bermuda Department of Tourism, monthly), the primary objective of which is to monitor tourists' reactions to their visit. A carefully structured questionnaire is being used by trained interviewers in the departure lounge of the airport. The sample is weighted to take account of the frequency and destination of outgoing flights and to ensure that the sample size (3,800 in 1988) is large enough to permit considerable disaggregation of the data. The completed forms are first edited in the Department and then processed by an agency in the USA. The results are available monthly, seasonally and for the whole year.

The information provided by this study covers not only accommodation use and estimates of visitors' expenditure, but very detailed analyses of tourists' use of attractions, shopping, transportation and, perhaps most important of all, their detailed reaction to each of these facilities—the extent to which they are perceived as providing 'value for money' and how they compare with those in other countries which the tourists have visited. In 1988, however, the emphasis shifted to focus on what visitors were *unable* to do while they were on the island and the reasons for this. The wealth of information available from these surveys is a key element in helping the Department to monitor changes and maintain the quality aspect of the country.

A second important on-going survey with the same objectives is the **Cruise Passenger Study** (Bermuda Department of Tourism, monthly). This study has been carried out since 1969 with some years omitted. Trained interviewers administer a shorter questionnaire to a weighted sample of cruise visitors. Again the results are sub-edited in the Department and processed by an agency in the USA. An annual report is presented which covers visitors' expenditures and their use of and reactions to various facilities on the island. As in the case of the Airport Exit Survey, the results are used by the Department to monitor changes.

The third on-going survey is an **annual economic impact analysis** undertaken by another consultant to measure the volume of tourist expenditure on the island and to assess the primary and secondary effects of this expenditure on incomes, government revenue and the balance of payments. Every four years a major update (Archer, 1987) is carried out to rework the basic economic model of the country and to provide a wider and more detailed range of statistical data. The results of these studies are used by the Department and by other ministries to monitor changes in the economic effects of tourism on the country and its citizens.

Ad hoc commissioned research

This group of studies can be divided loosely into two principal categories: those carried out for specific purposes and those with a longer term strategic aim.

Specific-purpose studies are usually carried out to obtain answers to particular problems or to analyse an individual situation. Such studies are normally concerned either with the product and its image or with perceived market difficulties. Occasionally such studies may be carried out to analyze the potential of specific sub-sectors of the market.

Among the former, for example, was a study carried out in February 1985 to assess visitors' attitudes to the government-owned Bermuda Aquarium, Natural History Museum and Zoo complex as an attraction. The objective was to gather more information prior to reaching decisions about its further development. A second study concerned with the product and its image was an Overcrowdedness Study carried out in 1988. The objective here was to assess the extent to which tourists perceived Bermuda to be overcrowded and the effect which this perception had on their vacation experience. The results of this study provided valuable input to policy-making in relation both to the number of cruise liners permitted to visit the island at any one time and also to long-term strategy regarding the provision of additional tourist accommodation.

Although the majority of commissioned research work is concerned with longer-term strategic marketing, some important studies have been carried out to analyse specific market difficulties and to examine the potential of specific events. Early in 1988, for example, an analysis was carried out of the implications of financial concerns (following the Stock Exchange slump in October 1987) with respect to travel to Bermuda. The results of this study provided additional impetus to the Department's decision to develop still further the potential of the European market in order to widen the tourist base of Bermuda.

Another specific problem in Bermuda is marketing the winter season when temperatures—although still very warm compared with the eastern seaboard of North America—are too low for bathing and many potential North American visitors travel instead to the Caribbean and the resorts of Florida. In 1988 a survey of travel agents was carried out to discover the factors which affected tourist bookings in this season. The results of this study provided useful pointers as to the types of product and image development which could enhance tourist bookings for this period.

Among the other specific-purpose studies carried out in recent years was an analysis to assess the merits of the Department participating in bridal expositions. This is an important consideration in view of the importance of the honeymoon market to Bermuda. Other specific studies are undertaken by the overseas offices and by agencies employed by the Department to examine attitudes to Bermuda and local trends.

Strategic studies are concerned with market potential and with local impact. Both are key elements in planning and policy-making. Studies have been carried out in recent years to assess new markets and growth markets, to monitor long-term changes and to examine local opinion in Bermuda about tourism.

A recent study in the first category, for example, was designed to identify the factors which attract or deter British travellers from choosing Bermuda as a vacation destination. Similar studies have been carried out on behalf of Bermuda by local agencies in other countries. Monitoring and tracking studies include detailed investigations of the US and Canadian markets to assess people's attitudes towards Bermuda as a vacation destination and to identify ways and means of increasing the size of these markets for Bermuda.

In the same period, studies have been carried out to monitor travellers' awareness of and attitudes to Bermuda as a travel destination, to monitor travel agents' attitudes towards Bermuda and their experiences with the Bermuda Department of Tourism, to assess travel agents' influence on tourists' choice of destination and travel agents' attitudes towards Bermuda and to assess how airline management and travel wholesalers view Bermuda as a vacation destination. The effectiveness of advertising is also monitored regularly, particularly for its role in creating a positive inclination to travel to Bermuda.

Local impact is also monitored at frequent intervals. If tourism is to provide maximum benefits to the local population, it is essential that the Department of Tourism be fully aware of the impact of tourism and of local opinion. In addition to the economic impact analyses mentioned above, which provide a factual framework, the Department has commissioned four studies in the last three years to assess local viewpoints. Two of these studies were directed towards the population in general to discover how Bermudians view the tourist industry. The other two were designed to obtain the views of 'on-island opinion leaders' about the state of the tourist industry in Bermuda.

Conclusions

To achieve its aim of promoting the development of tourism to the maximum benefit of the citizens of Bermuda, the Bermuda Department of Tourism vigilantly monitors changes in the market-place and is keenly aware of changes in the impact of tourism on the country. Such vigilance and sensitivity are possible only if up-to-date information is available on a regular basis to identify the existence of and to monitor the direction of such changes. Such information is the product of dedicated and rigorous research. In the case of a small country such as Bermuda, most of the research has to be commissioned from agencies and interpreted and supplemented within the Department itself. The Department is, however, currently investigating the possibility of carrying out more of its research in-house. Research so far has helped to provide Bermuda with a high-quality, up-market tourism industry and an ever-widening market base.

References

Archer, B. H., 1987, *The Bermudian Economy: An Impact Study*, Ministry of Finance, Government of Bermuda.

Bermuda Department of Tourism, *Bermuda in Perspective*, a monthly statistical publication of tourist arrivals.

Unpublished research reports mentioned in the text

Archer, B. H., *The Economic Impact of Tourism in Bermuda*, an annual report for the Bermuda Department of Tourism.

Foote, Cone, and Belding, 1985, *Airport Survey of Bermuda Aquarium, Natural History Museum and Zoo*.

Foote, Cone, and Belding, 1985, *A Study of Airline Management and Wholesalers*.

Foote, Cone, and Belding, 1985, *A Study of Travel Agents*.

Foote, Cone, and Belding, 1985, *A Study of Travellers in the United Kingdom*.

Foote, Cone, and Belding, 1985, *A Study of the North American Travel Market (U.S.A. & Canada)*.

Foote, Cone, and Belding/Leber Katz Partners, 1987, *Bridal Exposition Study*.

Foote, Cone, and Belding/Leber Katz Partners, 1987, *Tracking of Travel Agents' Experience and Attitudes Towards Bermuda*.

Foote, Cone, and Belding/Leber Katz Partners, 1987, *Tracking of Travellers' Experience and Attitudes Towards Bermuda*.

Foote, Cone, and Belding/Leber Katz Partners, 1988, *Overcrowdedness Study*.

Foote, Cone, and Belding/Leber Katz Partners, 1988, *Travel Agent (American Society of Travel Agents' Convention) Study*.

Foote, Cone, and Belding/Leber Katz Partners, 1988, *Travel Decline Study*.

Foote, Cone, and Belding/Leber Katz Partners, *Bermuda Airport Study*, an annual report for the Bermuda Department of Tourism including seasonal and monthly reports.

Foote, Cone, and Belding/Leber Katz Partners, *Bermuda Cruise Study*, an annual report for the Bermuda Department of Tourism.

Lieberman Research East, 1985, 1987, *Bermuda On-Island Population Study*.

Lieberman, Research East, 1985, 1987, *On-Island Opinion Leaders' Study*.

Riley, C. W., 1988, *Bermuda Department of Tourism Rendezvous 1987/88 Study*.

Riley, C. W., 1988, *Bermuda Department of Tourism College Weeks' Survey Results 1988*.

7 Tourism in China: is the honeymoon over?

P. Reynolds

Introduction

Although tourism in China is barely into its teens experienced foreign hotel operators are already looking back with fond memories to the halcyon days of the early and mid-1980s. When the Jianguo Hotel, then managed by the Peninsula group, opened in Beijing in 1982, it set the standard for international-class service in China, and was a resounding financial success. Its early followers, such as the Lido Holiday Inn, the Sheraton Great Wall and a few other foreign-managed hotels in Shanghai and Canton, also did well for both joint-venture owners and the management companies. Occupancy rates often ranged above 80%, while room costs were high in view of the level of service provided by inexperienced, if enthusiastic, hotel staff.

Rapidly rising tourist arrivals during those years seemed to point to a rosy future. From 1982 to 1987, the number of foreign tourists to China more than doubled, rising from 764,000 to 1.72 million (Table 7.1), and tourism officials were confident that the country's serious infrastructural difficulties—airport

Table 7.1 *International tourist arrivals, 1978–1988*

Year	Total	%*	Foreigners	%*	Overseas Chinese	%*	Compatriots	%*
1978	1,809,221	–	229,646	–	18,092	–	1,561,483	–
1979	4,203,901	132.4	362,389	57.8	20,910	15.6	3,820,602	144.7
1980	5,702,536	35.6	529,124	46.0	34,413	64.6	5,138,999	34.5
1981	7,767,096	36.2	675,153	27.6	38,853	12.9	7,053,087	37.2
1982	7,924,261	2.1	764,497	13.2	42,745	10.0	7,117,019	1.0
1983	9,477,005	19.6	872,511	14.1	40,352	−5.6	8,564,142	20.3
1984	12,852,185	35.6	1,134,267	30.0	47,498	17.7	11,670,420	36.2
1985	17,833,097	38.8	1,370,462	20.8	84,827	78.6	16,377,808	40.0
1986	22,819,450	28.0	1,482,276	8.2	68,133	−19.7	21,267,041	29.9
1987	26,902,267	17.9	1,727,821	16.6	87.031	27.7	25,087,415	18.0
1988	31,700,000	17.8	1,840,000	6.3	n/a	–	n/a	–

* Percentage change over the previous year.
Source: Yearbook of China Tourism Statistics (1986–1989).

capacity, road conditions, power supplies and sewage provisions—would be solved in time. It is the purpose of this chapter to review current trends and to highlight deficiencies in the hotel and tourism industry in the People's Republic of China (PRC).

Development and history

The development and history of tourism to the PRC has been well documented (Zhang, 1985, 1989; Choy and Gee, 1983; Gao and Zhang, 1983; Uysal, Wei and Reid, 1986; Richter, 1983) and attempts at analysis and assessment have been completed (Zhang, 1989; Choy, Guan and Zhang, 1986). However, in a country both as large (it is the third largest and most populous country in the world) and as volatile as China, only very general analysis has been attempted. More specific research is now being undertaken at two centres—The Department of Tourism Studies, Beijing, and the Hospitality Research Unit at Hong Kong Polytechnic.

Growth

As a means of economic growth and a basis for international friendship and mutual understanding, tourism to China (now termed a *smokeless industry* by Chinese leaders) has found an important position in the grand plan for the realization of the *Four Modernizations*. Chinese leaders have stated

that to develop tourism actively in China there is a need to enhance the friendship and unity between the people of China and the rest of the world, a need to accumulate funds for modernization programmes, and a need to satisfy the growing demand for economic security so as to achieve a satisfactory standard of life.
. . . under unified State planning, we shall mobilize all quarters to develop the places of interest to tourists. We shall speed up the training of people engaged in the tourist industry and expand [the] production and sale of tourist commodities ('China's seventh Five-Year Plan for economic and social development (1986–90)').

Many travel industry experts speak of a *coming* boom in tourism (Zhang, 1985, 1989; Uysal *et al.*, 1986). Yet the total visitor count in 1988 was 31.7 million. Italy, the top tourist destination in the world, has only 52 million. This makes China about the fifth most popular destination in the world for foreign tourists.

International visitors to the PRC can be roughly classified into three categories.

1. **Foreigners**. This term is used to mean all those with non-Chinese passports, except holders of Hong Kong, Macao and RoC (Taiwan) passports. The National Tourist Authority (NTA) states that ethnic Chinese who travel

on passports other than those of Hong Kong, Macao and RoC are considered 'foreigners'.

2. **Overseas Chinese.** This term has been variously defined. It was first taken to mean ethnic Chinese living outside China. In 1988 the NTA provided a new definition, describing Overseas Chinese as nationals with Chinese passports.

3. **Compatriots.** These are ethnic Chinese living in Hong Kong, Macao or RoC. This does not include non-Chinese living in these areas.

In 1988 foreign tourist arrivals rose a mere 6% after averaging 18% a year for the past five years (Table 7.1). To put that in perspective with other countries in Asia, Hong Kong grew at 26%, Singapore 13%, RoC 12% and Thailand 24%. Even Japan, which lost business following price increases relating to the value of the yen, was growing at around 8% in 1988. If this disappointing figure for China is indicative of a trend, it means trouble for hotel ventures and tourism projects.

Foreign tourists tend to stay in the best hotels and bring in much-needed foreign exchange. Their distribution pattern, however, sees them concentrated in a dozen large cities and notably tourist areas, in spite of the implementation of a policy opening up new areas of historical or scenic interest.

Government infrastructure

A fundamental trend which has emerged during the past five years is decentralization and liberalization, breaking the hold that China Travel Service (CTS), China International Travel Service (CITS) and China Youth Travel Service (CYTS) had over group travel in the country. Since 1980 various unauthorized organizations, as well as certain provincial branches of CITS, have been offering visas and tours to overseas producers (Hunt, 1987).

In 1982 a State Council order attempted to stop this practice, but the order was largely ignored. Two years later the government decided to deregulate the industry, encouraging competition to CITS by allowing other state-sponsored agencies to be established with the same status as CITS (i.e. permission to negotiate directly with foreign producers, issue visas and receive payment in foreign currency). Amongst these are the China Civil International Tourist Corporation and China Swan International Tours, both run by ex-NTA and CITS personnel. At the beginning of 1988, the NTA announced that eighteen such agencies (categorized as class one) together with the provincial and municipal tourist bureaux, were approved, but because of the increasing accessibility to foreign visas, other agents are known to be operating in the same way.

Equally significant among CITS branches is a trend towards independence from head office. In 1983, some major CITS branches were permitted to issue their own visas, deal directly with foreign producers and run their own tours.

(They were not authorized to conduct nationwide tours in peak months, although this ruling was not rigidly followed.) Decentralization continued, and by 1985, CITS head office estimated that about 50% of the tour groups in China had been initiated by branch offices. Competition between some large CITS branches and head office—and even between the branches themselves—has intensified, making it difficult for some foreign producers to decide who they should be dealing with.

Domestic travel

Leisure travel became a possibility for the Chinese for the first time during the 1980s (Wang and Ge, 1985), resulting in sudden and overwhelming pressure on transport and destinations. Congestion and pollution have become major problems at all the main sights. The average spend of people in this category is very low (Mok, 1985; Fong, 1985), and due to heavily subsidized train fares there has been little economic benefit for the transport network.

According to the NTA, there were 290 million domestic tourists in 1987. A new department has been created to formulate strategies to cope with this new phenomenon.

Tourism economy

Travel and tourism have been given increasing priority since 1978, when the Third Plenary Session of the Eleventh Party Central Committee decided that they were a viable means to raising much-needed foreign currency. Between 1979 and 1984, earnings increased by 39%, and in 1984 foreign currency receipts amounted to the equivalent of 6% of China's export earnings, an acceptable figure (Table 7.2). In 1986, for the first time, travel and tourism were incorporated into China's Five-Year Plan. The then State Councillor, Gu Mu, reported that the Party Central Committee and the State Council viewed travel and tourism as stimulants to the expansion of light industry, transport, communications and other enterprises. They are also seen as a source of employment opportunities, and over the next five years are expected to be developed vigorously.

Between 1986 and 1990 central and local governments have invested Y13.2 billion in the tourism industry, according to the seventh Five-Year Plan. The investment has focused on consolidation of accommodation, transport facilities and personnel training in selected key cities. This compares with Y400 million invested between 1978 and 1983 (which concentrated on hotels, restaurants, archaeological and historic sights and the opening up of new tourist areas).

Table 7.2 *China's international tourism receipts (1978–1987)*

Year	Receipts US$ 100,000s	Growth rate %
1978	262.90	–
1979	449.27	70.9
1980	616.65	37.3
1981	784.91	27.3
1982	843.17	7.4
1983	941.20	11.6
1984	1131.34	20.2
1985	1250.00	10.5
1986	1530.85	22.5
1987	1845.27	20.5

Source: *Yearbook of China Tourism Statistics* (1986–1989).

Administration of travel

The deregulation of the travel industry shifted more responsibility onto the NTA, which until then had been concerned primarily with CTS, CITS and other smaller-scale travel organizations. In 1984, the NTA was charged with defining overall travel and tourism policy for the country, and then overseeing its implementation.

Despite these changes, it is doubtful that the NTA is equipped to cope with this massive directive. Its influence on the rapidly expanding and decentralizing industry is, at best, partial. Casual observation suggests that many hotels, transport facilities, travel agencies and other tourist amenities are being developed and operated without NTA's approval or knowledge. The NTA is still in the process of collecting basic data, such as a complete list of hotels considered suitable for foreign visitors (this is apparently decided at provincial level). Nor does it publish a comprehensive list of travel agencies who are authorized to deal with foreign visitors, even though this authorization is supposed to come from the NTA itself. (All travel agencies in China are required to register with the NTA, as of mid-1985.)

While much information on the NTA's activities remains internal, in 1986 a NTA spokesman made it clear that the NTA intends to tackle a wide range of tourism-related sectors. Its planning department handles overall policy and planning, including monitoring inbound volume and making arrival projections. The planning department also decides on areas to be developed for tourism, allocates the budget and deals with joint-venture projects with state-run organizations.

An NTA education department is in charge of travel training policy nation-wide. So far, however, its schemes—such as the plan to give everyone working in the industry on-the-job training—have shown little practical follow-through. An enterprise management department supervises hotel management nationwide, but again, there seems to be little obvious implementation of recommendations. A new department has been set up to deal with the massive problems created by the emergence of domestic tourism.

Promotion, a new concept to China's travel industry, is gradually developing. The NTA's promotional budget is US$7 million for 1986 to 1990. That averages out to US$1.4 million a year, and compares with US$1 million in 1985.

One indication that the government was aware of the NTA's shortcomings was the announcement in 1986, by the then State Councillor Gu Mu, that a tourism coordination committee was to be established. This committee, to function at State level (ie over the head of the NTA), was to coordinate leadership of the industry. Tourism infrastructure, acknowledged Gu, had not developed at a pace which could cater to rapid increases in both overseas arrivals and domestic tourism. However, no more has been heard of this committee.

In May 1988, Han Kehua, who had served as director general of China's National Tourism Administration for five years, was replaced. The new head is Liu Yi, a former minister for commerce. At the same time, China's new Premier Li Peng announced that the State Council would establish a Tourism Commission headed by Vice-Premier Wu Xueqian. Wu, who is 66, has been China's foreign minister for the last six years, and is now vice-premier, assisting Li Peng in the running of the country's foreign affairs.

The main responsibility of the commission, Li stated, would be to assist the NTA to coordinate with the communications ministry and civil aviation departments. Later, in June 1988, the State Council inaugurated this commission, now called a 'special committee', adding that its responsibilities were to 'formulate . . . principles, policies and legislation concerning [travel]; and examine 'large [travel] construction projects . . .'

The State Council criticized China's visitor industry for failing to implement regulations which have been in effect for the past three years. The regulations cover conditions for setting up travel services, price controls and the standardization of rights and responsibilities of China's tour guides. The NTA has announced that a basic tourism law is now being prepared. It will include regulations on hotels and travel agents with foreign involvement.

NTA 1986—1990

In January 1986, the NTA drew up broad plans for the period of the seventh Five-Year Plan, 1986–1990, which appear more realistic than previous projections. This was the first time that the travel industry had been included in the Five-Year Plan.

One positive sign is that the NTA has identified priorities, beyond the oft-repeated need to 'improve service, accommodation and transportation'. It intends to focus on consolidating tourism plans for the areas which have so far attracted most tourists: Beijing, Guangzhou, Hangzhou, Shanghai, Xian and the province of Jiangsu (which includes Suzhou, Wuxi and Nanjing). As a second priority, the NTA will continue to develop seventeen other areas, some of interest predominantly to foreigners (such as Lhasa and the Yangtze Gorges), and others currently visited mostly by Hong Kong and overseas Chinese (the sacred mountains, Qufu and Shandong).

The NTA projects an 11% increase in arrivals until 1990, when there will be five million visitors, of which three million will be foreigners (this does not include those visiting friends and relatives (VFR)). Between 1990 and 2000, the NTA projects a 7 to 8% annual growth rate to ten to twelve million tourists, of which seven to eight million will be foreign (not including VFRs).

The NTA announced in 1986 that China would double the number of rooms considered suitable for overseas visitors from 60,000 to 120,000 by 1990. But in March 1988, Han Kehua, outgoing head of the NTA, contradicted this, saying that China already had 200,000 rooms for overseas visitors. This incredible restatement is yet another indication of the gross inadequacy and unreliability of China's statistical data, as well as its planning. No revised estimate of rooms likely to be available in 1990 has yet been publicized.

The NTA says it will increase its efforts to improve quality and scale of training, which to date have been desperately lacking. It will put more funds (it does not say how much) into the country's two existing tertiary travel and tourism training institutes (subsidized by the NTA) and twelve travel and tourism departments in other colleges or universities. It will also subsidize a new National Tourism Centre in Tianjin, to be used for in-service training, and invest in more overseas training for managers. But these measures will not have short-term results, nor is the scale large enough to reach the 10,000 staff (NTA's figures) working in the state-sponsored sector of the industry. The International Labour Organization is also helping with training; a US$1.2 million grant from Spain for an advanced vocational training centre for hotels and tourism in Suzhou, Jiangsu, was due to open in late 1988.

Foreign investment

As yet, there is no breakdown of visitor-related foreign investment projects in China. Initially, however, they were considered by most investment analysts to be amongst the most attractive.

Hotels were regarded as the best investments in China in the first half of the 1980s. Capital returns were generally realized in seven to eight years. High demand, plus low construction costs and cheap labour, have made hotels an attractive prospect. The China hotel in Guangzhou, a joint venture with a Hong Kong consortium and managed by Hong Kong group New World

Hotels International, repaid 30% of its investment after two years' operation. As hotel earnings are mostly in foreign currency or foreign exchange certificates, hotels have not faced difficulties repatriating profits, unlike joint ventures in other spheres. However, a slowdown in hotel building followed curbs on Bank of China loans in 1986. By 1987, impending overcapacity in major cities combined with rising construction costs had further deterred new investors in this sector.

Transport

Transport is a bottleneck in China, and a high priority for development. State investment in transport (as well as posts and communications) was Y10.5 billion in 1984, up 34% on 1983, but this will allow only modest expansion in transport capacity, well below demand. For effective improvement, larger amounts—beyond China's existing means—are needed. However, private and collective ownership of boats, buses and aircraft (through air services) is now permitted, thus allowing competition with state-owned companies. Decentralization of air, rail and waterways is also likely to bring improvement.

Railways

China's railway network, the fifth largest in the world, has 52,500 kilometres of rail, half of it built since 1949. Most of its 11,000 locomotives are still steam-run, and the Government has announced that nearly 13,000 kilometres of track need replacing.

Over-crowded carriages and delays in getting tickets indicate that capacity on many lines is inadequate. In 1985 prices were increased 37% for journeys of less than 200 kilometres. Fares for foreigners are about 75% higher than fares for local Chinese or overseas Chinese.

Passenger capacity on China's trains is three million per day, but loads in 1987 were around 3.21 million. In the first five months of 1988, there were said to be 570 million passengers, up an incredible 21.1%. In 1986 there were 8.35 million foreign travellers on the railways, up 15.7%.

Waterways

Traditionally, waterways have provided China's main communication and trading links. The system carries some 19% of domestic freight volume, compared with 50% on the railways. About 30% of the navigable waterway system is in Jiangsu and Zhejiang provinces in intricate canal systems. Foreigner use of the system is on small stretches of the Grand Canal in Jiangsu and Zhejiang and through the Three Gorges of the Yangtze, between Chongquing and

Wuhan. Arrivals to Chinese ports—mostly by Hong Kong Chinese—are increasing significantly, however.

Roads

Highway transport is poor. Roads total only 930,000 kilometres (less than 12.6% of the density of the US road system) but are due to be increased to one million kilometres by 1990. Foreigners are permitted to use inter-city buses (previously discouraged), but road transport between cities is not normally used for tour groups unless there is no other alternative. Bus services between Hong Kong and Guangdong province were introduced in 1981. A motorway is being built linking Hong Kong, Guangzhou and Macao and is due to be open in 1992.

Airports

In May 1988, *China Daily* reported that China had only 80 civil airports. A month later, *China Features* said that there were only eight airports that could handle Boeing 747s and only 21 that could accommodate medium-sized aircraft. There are constant reports in publications such as *China Travel Trade* that China is ordering new jets of all configurations. But the facts are that the country's major internal fleet consists of ageing Russian propeller aircraft and some Tridents. The infrastructure to deal with new aircraft is not in place (Warwick, 1986).

The busiest airport in China is Guangzhou's Baiyun, which handled five million passengers in 1987. It has only just become computerized. Overbookings are commonplace in all regions, time-keeping is abysmal and wholesale cancellations of flights are regular occurrences. Safety standards—or rather, the lack of them—are legendary. Ernst Zimmerman, vice-president of Holiday Inn Asia Pacific, highlighted the problem while delivering a lecture to Chinese hotel managers at Hong Kong Polytechnic in November 1988. 'There can be no calculation in dollars of the damage that the Civil Aviation Administration of China (CAAC) has done to the hotel industry in China in the year 1987 to 1988,' he said. His remarks echoed the thoughts of the many tour operators and hotel managers who deal with China on a regular basis.

By June 1989, the final stage in the decentralization of CAAC came into place with the creation of Air China for international flights and the division of internal operations into separate companies. It is hoped that this reorganization will both change customer perception and make accountability easier to apportion.

Announcements regarding new or improved airports continue to be vague and/or contradictory. In 1987, Li Peng, now Prime Minister, proposed that the country should concentrate on transforming existing airports rather than building new ones. Signs are that less will be achieved than was indicated for the seventh Five-Year Plan (1986–1990). So far, all of the airport plans that have been approved are running behind schedule.

Between 1980 and 1985, 30 airports were built or expanded. In 1986 there were plans to build or expand seventeen more. Of particular importance to the foreign travel industry are the new airports in Xian—now three years delayed and currently due to open in 1990—Kunming—also delayed and due to open in 1990—and Chongquing, scheduled to open in 1989. Funding for a new runway in Guilin was approved by the State Council in June 1988. This, together with a much-needed terminal building, will be ready by 1990. A new domestic terminal opened in Guangzhou in 1987 and a new international terminal and extended apron are planned.

There has been much discussion about a new airport in Shenzen, on the border with Hong Kong. A go-ahead has been announced, but for a project much smaller than that originally proposed. If completed, the new airport, at Huangtian, will be for regional flights and will not compete with Hong Kong.

Arrival routes/methods

The most numerous access rootes to China are land routes. The most important are crossings from Hong Kong, and to a lesser extent, Macao. Other land crossings are from Nepal (officially opened to foreigners in March 1985, now closed due to political action in Tibet); North Korea (for special cases only; there is a flight and a train from Beijing to Pyongyang); Pakistan (officially opened to foreigners in May 1986, although temporarily closed again at the end of that year in order to upgrade facilities on the Chinese side of the border); and the USSR (for foreigners on the Trans-Siberian railway). But together these land crossings handle only a few thousand travellers a year.

The air service regime is closely controlled by China, and few services are offered on anything other than a reciprocal basis. Even when there is no reciprocal flight, as with Philippine Airlines' Manila to Xiamen route, there are reciprocal benefits, such as royalty payments. Only on routes to Hong Kong is air service formally structured to favour China. Here, China has gained agreement for a capacity ratio of six to one in favour of China against the UK (in legal terms, Hong Kong-based Cathay Pacific, and thus services from Hong Kong, are counted in the UK total). This is dramatically illustrated in terms of flight frequencies between Hong Kong and China. There are about 50 flights weekly for CAAC against seven for Cathay Pacific.

The other major air route into China is from Japan. This is about half the size of the Hong Kong–China air services. The figure was just over 5,000,000 seats in 1985.

The number of charter flights is small, apart from to and from Hong Kong, where the pattern is erratic but the flights are often regular enough to constitute scheduled services. Flights are sometimes operated as charters to overcome licensing problems or to avoid setting precedents. Cathay Pacific's Shanghai and Beijing air routes, for instance, both started as charter routes, and all of Dragonair flights into China are designated charter flights, even when they operate to a regular schedule.

Hotel overprovision

In China there is a flood of new hotel projects being planned and built in a market that is already saturated (Reynolds, 1989; HRI, October 1985; and others). The bulk of these are joint venture (JV) hotels with foreign investors in the major tourist cities and have been built without reference to any central planning.

Between 1979 and 1987, the national tourism authorities did not have any overall plan for hotel construction. By 1982 a new trend started, with foreign hotel management companies being brought in to set and maintain standards. By 1991, there will be more than 90 JV hotels run by 31 different hotel management companies (HMCs) (*China Travel Press*, March 1989). Low occupancy rates are already being recorded in all the major destinations, with Xian and Guilin the worst affected. The question may be raised as to why HMCs still persist in the Chinese market in the face of such adversity. There are two partial answers.

First, nearly all the HMCs have signed management contracts rather than equity stakes in the projects. The notable exception to this is the Hong Kong-based New World Hotels. The HMCs are, therefore, virtually guaranteed at least a modest profit. All expenses for senior expatriate staff and other costs are charged to the owner's account, while the management company takes its fee off the top. As a result, even when occupancies go below 50%, the operator still makes money. Second, foreign hotel operators, like other foreign companies doing business in China, claim that they are approaching their projects as long-term investments.

Conclusion

Although several writers have expressed great optimism regarding the future of China's tourism industry (notably Zhang, 1989 and Gao and Zhang, 1983) there has been a growing feeling of discontent amongst travellers, tour operators (*China Travel Press*, April 1989), and analysts (Hunt, 1987; Choy, 1986). The Chinese have always believed that their homeland offers unlimited interest. But it has been pointed out that it can be boring and monotonous for the average tourist (Hunt, 1987). Thus, the PRC may find itself facing a dilemma—that of having to provide expensive modern facilities in order to attract lower-spending visitors. Persistent problems with adequately servicing the foreign guest may aggravate the situation, as prices may have to be lowered to compensate for the lower standard of the holiday package relative to that of other international destinations. The realities of modern mass travel may force the Government to reassess the country's position as a tourist destination in the world market-place.

Postscript

Since the completion of this chapter, the student protests and subsequent Government reaction of May and June 1989 have taken place. There is no way, at this stage, to assess the damage that this will cause to China's links with the West, its trade and tourism. China has always been a volatile and difficult place in which to trade, but now we have new levels of risk and uncertainty. The slow downturn in tourist arrivals hinted at in this chapter has been transformed into a swift crash. It remains to be seen how quickly and how willingly companies involved with the tourist industry will pick up the pieces. By the autumn of 1989, a slow trickle of tourists had returned.

References

China Travel Press, Ismay Publications, 2204 C.C. Wu Bldg, Henessy Road, Hong Kong.

Choy, D. J. L., Gee, C. Y., 1983, 'Tourism in the PRC—five years after China opens its gates', *Tourism Management*, 4(2): pp. 85–93.

Choy, D. J. L., Guan, L. D., Zhang, W., 1986, 'Tourism in PR China', *Tourism Management*, 7(3): pp. 197–201.

Fong, M. K. L., 1985, 'Tourism: a critical review' in Wong, K. J., Chu, K. Y., *Modernisation in China: The Case of the Shenzen Economic Zone*, Oxford University Press, Oxford, pp. 79–88.

Gao, D., Zhang, G., 1983, 'China's tourism: policy and practice', *Tourism Management* 4(2): pp. 75–84.

HRI, 1985, *China's Hotel Boom*, Special issue, Vol. 19, Number 9, October 1985, Hotel & Restaurants International, USA.

Hunt, J., 1987, 'Competition comes to the industry', *Far Eastern Economic Review*, 19 March 1987, pp. 97–9.

Mok, M. K., 1985, 'Tourist expenditures in Guangzhou, PR China', in *Tourism Management*, 6(4): pp. 272–9.

Reynolds, P. C., 1989, 'Risk analysis in China's hotel industry', paper presented to Academy of International Business conference, June 1989, Nanjing, PRC.

Richter, L. K., 1983, 'Political implications of Chinese tourism policy', *Annals of Tourism Research*, 10(3): pp. 394–413.

Uysal, M., Wei, L., Reid, L. M., 1986, 'Development of international tourism in PR China', *Tourism Management*, 7(2): pp. 113–19.

Wang, T. S., Ge, L. C., 1985, 'Domestic tourism development in China', *Journal of Travel Research*, 14(2): pp. 13–30.

Warwick, G., 1986, 'The changing face of CAAC', *Flight International*, 23 August, pp. 37–9.

Zhang, G., 1985, 'China is ready for new prospect for tourism development,' *Tourism Management*, 6(2): pp. 141–3.

Zhang, G., 1989, 'Ten years of Chinese tourism', *Tourism Management*, 10(1): pp. 51–62.

8 Statistical trends in tourism and hotel accommodation, up to 1988

J. Latham

The collection of tourism statistics

The collection of tourism statistics is a complex and time-consuming process. Most countries now, as a minimum, estimate the volume and value of international arrivals across their borders. There are, however, difficulties in collating and comparing global figures due to the different definitions and methods of collection in use. (For a description of the current position and a review of the progress made in recent years in the collection and organization of tourism statistics, see Latham, 1989 and Allard, 1989.) Nevertheless, the World Tourism Organization (WTO) does provide an annual summary of the most important statistics for about 150 countries and territories in its *Yearbook of Tourism Statistics*, organizing its material so that comparisons can be made. Provisional figures for 1988 form the basis of much of this chapter.

The Organization for Economic Co-operation and Development (OECD) also produces an annual publication, *Tourism Policy and International Tourism in OECD Member Countries*. As a statistical source, this is more restrictive, as it covers only 25 countries. However, these do include the main generating and receiving countries of the world.

Due to the lack of reliable comparable data on domestic tourism, only trends in international tourism will be discussed. Many countries are in fact reluctant to measure domestic movements. Further, those figures that are available tend to be underestimates, as visits to friends and relatives (VFR), the use of commercial accommodation other than hotels and travel for recreational purposes are often not included. As a rough guide, domestic tourism world-wide accounts for about 90% of all tourism expenditure. Best estimates for the late 1980s are that annual expenditure on domestic and international tourism combined is more than US$2,000 billion, or 12% of gross domestic product at world level—more than twice what is spent on defence.

Historical trends

International tourism has grown steadily since World War II (Table 8.1). It has proved itself over several decades to be most resilient on a global scale to factors such as economic recession, variable exchange rates, terrorist

Table 8.1 *International tourism trends—arrivals and receipts world-wide*

	Arrivals (millions)	Receipts[1] (billions of current US$)
1950	25.3	2.1
1960	69.3	6.9
1970	159.7	17.9
1980	284.8	102.4
1981	288.8	104.3
1982	286.8	98.6
1983	292.8	98.8
1984	319.3	103.6
1985	333.8	108.6
1986	341.4	129.2
1987	358.7	158.7
1988	390.0[2]	195.0[2]

Notes: [1] Excludes international fare receipts.
  [2] Provisional estimates.
Source: World Tourism Organization.

activity and political unrest in many parts of the world. At worst, there has been a levelling-off of movements, for example, during the early 1980s. The 'total market' of international tourists is therefore an expanding one, and one which countries in most parts of the world view as extremely important. After all, incoming tourism is an invisible export, accounting for over 7% of world trade in goods and services and outperformed only by oil and motor vehicles (WTO, 1988).

The period up to 1980 saw the development of international tourism on a massive scale, with arrivals doubling every ten years or so. Large segments of the populations of the industrialized countries found that they had the time (paid leave from employment) and money (increased disposable income) to travel for pleasure. According to Poon (1989), mass, standardized and rigidly packaged tourism was created and nurtured by developments such as the arrival of the jet aircraft in 1958, promotional fares, cheap oil, demand for sun-lust tourism and the entry of multinational corporations into the tourism industry. Further, international travel was boosted by a growth in business travel stemming from increased economic activity. As a result, both industrial-ized and developing countries became fully aware of the potential of tourism to support an ailing balance of payments.

The early 1980s saw a temporary levelling of demand due to the difficult economic situation at the time. Although residents of the main generating countries continued to undertake foreign travel, they became more cautious in their spending patterns. This led to a switching of destinations (for example, to countries either nearby or ones with favourable exchange rates), greater use of accommodation other than hotels and shorter stays.

There is a time-lag between changes in economic activity and their effects on travel, and by late 1983 there was evidence that a recovery in international tourism was under way. This was confirmed in 1984 and 1985, which were record years, particularly for Europe. International movements were disrupted considerably in 1986 by terrorism and its lingering threat, the disaster at Chernobyl and a dramatic fall in the value of the US dollar against most other currencies. As a result, there was a shift in the choice of destination by many Americans away from Europe and North Africa in favour of countries in the Pacific and within North America itself. Other tourists simply postponed or cancelled trips.

Most parts of the world reported a rapid growth in international arrivals in 1987 and again in 1988. This represents some return to normality, not merely in terms of increasing numbers, but also in terms of the tourism flows prior to 1986.

International tourist arrivals have grown at an average rate of 4% per annum during the 1980s. This can be regarded as an average growth rate world-wide over the last decade and gives no indication of the considerable variation by region or continent, by country or by individual destinations within countries. Some destinations have successfully encouraged rapid growth (for example, Australia, China, Portugal and Turkey); whereas others have experienced no growth (Ireland) or even decreases in the number of international visitors (Sri Lanka). The market in overall terms is buoyant, though it is also dynamic in the sense that there is considerable interest in new forms of tourism. There are also new destinations and generating countries. In the long term, developing countries may benefit from a natural redistribution of tourist flows. For now, the established tourism destination countries are maintaining their market share.

Current trends and analysis

According to provisional estimates prepared by the WTO (1988), international tourist arrivals in 1988 numbered 390 million, an increase of just under 9% over the previous year. This establishes another all-time high and puts international tourism well in line to reach the half billion mark by the end of the century.

Receipts from international tourism world-wide rose in 1988 to US$ 195 billion, an increase of 23% over the previous year. This does not include expenditure on international transport. It is difficult to assess the value of tourism world-wide associated with payments to commercial passenger carriers for travel between countries; the International Civil Aviation Organization (ICAO), however, estimates that the total number of passengers on scheduled flights in 1988 was just over one billion, a year-on-year increase of 4.2%.

The OECD is an international organization of industrialized countries whose objective is to promote high rates of economic growth. It views tourism expenditure as an important catalyst of growth. International tourism to OECD countries was estimated at 245 million arrivals in 1988, an increase of just over 7%, contributing US$ 139 billion in receipts. OECD countries can therefore be seen to account for 63% of international arrivals and 71% of receipts.

Regional statistics

The growth trend revealed by the 1988 figures is shared by all regions of the world, though not equally (see Table 8.2). In terms of arrivals, Africa, East Asia and the Pacific performed especially well. When considering receipts, all regions achieved an annual increase of more than 24%, with the exception of the Americas and, for some reason, South Asia. Table 8.3 illustrates the trends since 1950, revealing significant growth in market share for international tourism to East Asia and the Pacific, largely at the expense of the Americas.

Europe and the Americas—and in particular, Western Europe and North America—are well-established receivers and generators of international tourism. The flows of 1988 confirmed their dominant position, as together they recorded a total of 324 million inbound tourists, or more than 80% of the world-wide total.

European countries as destinations now account for just under two-thirds of all international arrivals, a share that appears to have decreased over the last 30 years. However, Europe's share of international tourism receipts has been remarkably stable over the same period (Table 8.3). The European Economic

Table 8.2 *International tourism in 1988—regional summary statistics[1]*

	Arrivals (millions)	% Change over 1987	Receipts[2] (billions current US$)	% Change over 1987
Africa	12.0	+18.7	4.5	+24.3
Americas	72.6	+7.1	39.0	+17.0
East Asia & Pacific	42.0	+17.8	24.5	+27.7
Europe	251.5	+7.5	118.0	+24.0
Middle East	9.0	+8.2	7.0	+25.6
South Asia	3.0	+2.0	2.0	+7.7
World	390.0	+8.7	195.0	+22.9

Notes: [1] Based on provisional estimates for 1988.
[2] Excludes international fare receipts.
Source: World Tourism Organization.

Table 8.3 *Regional share of international tourism*

	1950 %	1960 %	1970 %	1980 %	1988[1] %
By arrivals:					
Africa	2.1	1.1	1.5	2.5	3.1
Americas	29.6	24.1	22.9	18.9	18.6
East Asia & Pacific	0.8	1.0	3.0	7.0	10.8
Europe	66.6	72.7	70.8	68.8	64.5
Middle East	0.8	0.9	1.2	2.0	2.3
South Asia	0.2	0.3	0.6	0.8	0.8
By receipts:					
Africa	4.2	2.6	2.2	2.6	2.3
Americas	50.5	35.7	26.8	24.9	20.0
East Asia & Pacific	1.4	2.8	6.1	7.3	12.6
Europe	42.3	57.1	62.6	60.2	60.5
Middle East	1.2	1.3	1.7	3.4	3.6
South Asia	0.3	0.5	0.6	1.5	1.0

Note: [1] Based on provisional estimates.
Source: World Tourism Organization.

Community alone hosts 40% of arrivals, accounting for 44% of receipts world-wide.

Such continued dominance can be explained in terms of the high incomes and paid leave of large segments of the population, the high priority given to travel, the wealth of attractions, the large tourist industry and the necessary infrastructure (Shackleford, 1987). Further, Europe consists of many relatively small countries, and so international travel need not involve great distances. The easing of border controls and the opening of the Channel Tunnel in the early 1990s may well add to its dominance in statistical terms.

Because of the sheer size of Canada and the USA, most of their populations prefer to take holiday trips within their own countries. Recent growth in arrivals to the Americas has been greatest to Central and South America and to the Caribbean. According to the WTO (1988):

Tourism [in the Americas] in 1988 was characterized by the enhanced standing of Europe and Japan as generating markets and a gradual shift of tourist flows originating in the United States, with more departures for South America and the Caribbean, a slight drop of travel to Europe and a positive trend in trips to East Asia and the Pacific.

Africa performed well as a receiver of international tourism in 1988, with arrivals up by 18.7% (the highest increase of any region) and receipts up by 24.3%. It now appears to have recovered completely from poor results in the previous two years brought about by strife and uncertainty in key areas. North

African countries, as destinations, account for just under half of all international arrivals to the continent, contributing significantly to the improved figures.

The market share of **East Asia and the Pacific** has grown dramatically over the last decade (Table 8.3) and 1988 saw further increases. The percentage increase in arrivals over the previous year was bettered only by Africa; receipts were up by nearly 28%. Recent growth is attributable to regional stability, favourable exchange rates and general improvements in market awareness. Hong Kong, Singapore and the People's Republic of China have all become increasingly popular as tourist destinations (Horwath and Horwath, 1988). International arrivals in 1988 to China were estimated at 1.7 million, an annual increase of 5.6%. The long-term impact on tourism to China of the events of 1989 are not yet known. In the short term, occupancies in major hotels in Beijing were reported to have plummeted to around 20% (see Jenkins in this volume).

In recent years, the Persian Gulf war and the American bombing of Libya have acted to inhibit travel to the **Middle East**. International tourist arrivals to the region have only now recovered the losses suffered in 1986, the most notable change being the increase in arrivals from the USA. The safety and protection—both real and perceived—of tourists has a strong influence on tourism, not only in the Middle East, but in many other parts of the world. It is interesting to note that current WTO data for the Middle East do not include Lebanon which, in 1975, was reported to account for 44% of arrivals to the region.

South Asia exhibited the smallest growth world-wide in international arrivals in 1988 (Table 8.2). However, this was an improvement on the reduction experienced in the previous year. In fact, the development of incoming tourism in the region has been somewhat depressed over the last five years. The overall performance of South Asia is closely linked to that of India, which receives half of the region's total arrivals.

Generating countries

A list of the major generators of international tourism, as measured by expenditure in current US dollars, appears as Table 8.4. The use of expenditure as a comparative measure is convenient, since not all governments publish information on international tourist departures.

With the exception of Japan and Australia, the only countries for which international tourism expenditure exceeds US$ two billion annually are to be found in Europe and North America. A list of the main generators for any particular destination country in any part of the world would typically include its neighbouring states, together with at least one of the group West Germany, USA and the UK. These countries, and the others listed in Table 8.4, are regarded world-wide as the most important international markets to attract.

Table 8.4 *International tourist expenditure by the main generating countries (1987)*

	Expenditure in current US$ Billion
West Germany	23.6
USA	20.5
UK	11.9
Japan	10.7
France	8.6
Netherlands	6.4
Austria	5.5
Canada	5.3
Italy	4.5
Switzerland	4.4
Belgium	3.9
Sweden	3.8

Source: Organization for Economic Co-operation and Development.

Purpose of visit

The split of international tourism by purpose of visit is difficult to assess on a world-wide scale due to the inconsistency of classifications and measures used by different countries, and, in many cases, the complete lack of information. The WTO, in its *Yearbook of Tourism Statistics*, provides details for some countries, but does not attempt to derive estimates on a broader scale. Categories used for purpose of visit are typically: holidays/recreation, business, visiting friends and relatives (VFR), and 'other' (such as health, study or 'in transit'). In cases where details are available, there is much variation from country to country'. In 1986, as much as 27% of international visits to Japan were for business purposes; at the other extreme, nearly 90% of tourist arrivals to Portugal were recorded as for holidays or recreation.

International transport

As with purpose of visit, it is not possible to derive with confidence global figures for the split of international tourism by transport used. A fair estimate might be that 70% of international arrivals world-wide are by road, 20% by air and the remaining 10% mainly by sea and rail. Again there is tremendous variation by country. For example, more than 99% of arrivals to Australia and

New Zealand are by air, whereas 85% of international visitors to West Germany come by road and only 6% by air.

Long-haul travel

Most international travel is within continents. However, long-haul journeys such as from European countries to destinations in Asia or from North America to Africa are now within the reach of large segments of the populations of the major generating countries. It is no longer the exclusive domain of the wealthy or adventurous independent traveller, and the future will see an increasing number of packages on offer. Recent figures for the UK suggest that growth in outward long-haul travel is running at about 8% per annum, with the USA and Hong Kong as the most popular destinations in 1987.

Air transport clearly holds the key. Initially long-haul travel was facilitated by the development of modern jet aircraft. Jets made it possible for long distances to be covered economically and without refuelling. Following deregulation in many countries, there is now more open competition on certain routes, leading to improved fare structures. New routes have also been developed. Of particular note is the recent rapid growth in Pacific-Asia airlines. In 1987 their share of scheduled world-wide international traffic was estimated at 28%. Given the likely future demand for long-haul travel and its increasing availability at a price that certain segments of the populations of countries such as West Germany, USA and the UK can afford, the trend towards increasing numbers of flights and air routes looks set to continue into the foreseeable future.

The hotel industry world-wide

The number of rooms in 'hotels and similar establishments' world-wide, as reported by the WTO (1988), is approximately ten million. About half are to be found in Europe (mainly in Western and Southern Europe), with a large proportion of the remainder in North America. This is not surprising given the pattern of international arrivals already described. The contribution in percentage terms of the supply of rooms made by the other parts of the world is small, but significant, nevertheless, when absolute numbers are considered (Table 8.5).

The 1980s have seen a significant increase in world-wide power and market share of hotel chains. Best estimates, for example, are that 60% of all US hotels belong to chains. US chains now dominate the global market, though European chains have strengthened their position in recent years through acquisitions and internal expansion. It is now difficult for independent hotels to compete in the major international markets without some association with a major chain or marketing consortium.

Table 8.5 *The supply of rooms in hotels and similar establishments, by region (1986)*

	Number of rooms millions	Share %
Europe	5.01	50.4
Americas	3.65	36.8
East Asia and Pacific	0.84	8.5
Africa	0.25	2.5
South Asia	0.10	1.0
Middle East	0.08	0.8

Source: World Tourism Organization.

According to Horwath and Horwath (1988), world-wide occupancy rates for hotels averaged 66.4% in 1987, an increase of just under 3% on the previous year. The average room rate, per available room, was US$62.13. Clearly such average figures are subject to great variation according to location and market. Table 8.6 exhibits the differences regionally.

Tables 8.7 and 8.8 demonstrate trends in hotel market data, world-wide and regionally. The split between domestic and international visitors is stable, with just under half of all visitors being international. Demand for hotel rooms in North America is predominantly domestic due to the high number of trips involving overnight stays taken by the large national population. In all other regions, international demand exceeds domestic, though not necessarily for individual countries (Australia, for example, is an exception).

Table 8.6 *Occupancy rates and room rates for hotels, 1987*

	Average occupancy Median %	Average room rate US$
Africa & Middle East	53.0	65.89
Asia & Australia	76.4	55.39
North America	66.5	61.45
Europe	64.9	64.72
Latin America/Caribbean	68.8	42.68
World-wide	66.4	62.13

Source: Adapted from Horwath and Horwath International, 1988, *Worldwide Hotel Industry*, New York.

Note: The statistics in the Horwath and Horwath report are based on 1,051 questionnaires returned by hotels (representing 272,500 hotel rooms) following a mailshot of 3,500. The sample represents, as far as is reasonably possible, a broad picture of the hotel industry in terms of location and market segment.

126   J. Latham

Table 8.7 *Hotels world-wide—trends in market data (1983–1987)*

	1983	1984	1985	1986	1987
Source of business:					
Domestic	51.3	51.2	50.2	52.1	50.7
International	48.7	48.8	49.8	47.9	49.3
Percentage of repeat business	40.3	38.4	40.0	37.2	36.2
C mposition of market:					
Business travellers	42.1	42.7	38.3	38.7	36.0
Tourists (pleasure)	27.3	26.4	34.4	34.4	38.0
Conference participants	13.2	13.4	10.5	12.1	12.7
Government officials	6.2	5.3	7.1	4.4	4.1
Other	11.2	12.2	9.7	10.4	9.2

Notes: For each year, figures are percentages. See note to Table 8.6.
Source: Adapted from Horwath and Horwath International, 1988, *Worldwide Hotel Industry*, New York.

Table 8.8 *Market data for hotels by region, 1987*

	Africa & Middle East	Asia & Australia	North America	Europe	Latin America and Caribbean
Source of business:					
Domestic	24.6	35.0	84.6	47.3	38.8
International	75.4	65.0	15.4	52.7	61.2
Percentage of repeat business	35.5	30.7	42.8	36.0	26.6
Composition of market:					
Business travellers	35.5	30.6	39.4	39.8˙	28.1
Tourists (pleasure)	32.1	51.1	25.8	36.4	55.5
Conference participants	6.5	5.8	22.7	12.3	7.6
Government officials	9.4	3.9	4.2	2.5	2.9
Other	16.5	8.6	7.9	9.0	5.9

Notes: For each year, figures are percentages. See note to Table 8.6.
Source: Adapted from Horwath and Horwath International, 1988, *Worldwide Hotel Industry*, New York.

The level of repeat business to individual hotels in recent years has declined. The most loyal visiting pattern is to be found in North America, with Latin American and Caribbean hotels reporting the lowest proportion of repeat visits.

The composition of the market for hotels world-wide is seen to have changed considerably over the years 1983 to 1987, with an increase in the proportion of tourists on pleasure trips, mainly at the expense of business traffic. Hotels in Australia, the Pacific and the Caribbean are particularly strong in terms of attracting a high proportion of guests on pleasure trips.

Conclusion

There has been steady growth in international travel since the end of World War II, and there is little evidence to suggest that such growth is likely to be arrested in the near future. The average annual growth in international arrivals during the 1980s has been 4%; growth for 1987 and 1988 was in fact at 5 and 9% respectively. Such global figures do however hide the fact that the performance of individual regions and countries has exhibited much variation from these 'averages'. The East Asia and Pacific Region, for example, has increased its share of the market in dramatic fashion, largely at the expense of the Americas.

Provisional estimates for 1988 are that there were 390 million international tourist arrivals, worth US$195 billion in receipts. The contribution towards these receipts made by travellers from West Germany, the USA, the UK and Japan was over 40%. This high level of concentration helps to explain why many countries all over the world seek to attract tourists from the main generating countries.

Whatever their limitations (in terms of, for example, lack of comparability of data), statistics for international tourism are abundant, enabling detailed analyses to be carried out. On the other hand, the measurement of domestic tourism and its characteristics, on a global scale, is subject to guesswork and takes the form of estimates, often resulting in very large errors. Nevertheless, countries other than the industrialized states are beginning to take seriously some monitoring of domestic movements. For this to be undertaken world-wide, and in a consistent manner, the resulting benefits must be clearly seen to outweigh the costs involved.

References

Allard, L., 1989, 'Statistical measurement in tourism', in Witt, S. and Moutinho, L. (eds), *Tourism Marketing and Management Handbook*, Prentice Hall, London, pp. 419–24.

Horwath and Horwath International, 1988, *Worldwide Hotel Industry*, Horwath and Horwath International, New York.

Latham, J., 1989, 'The statistical measurement of tourism', in Cooper, C. P., (ed.), *Progress in Tourism, Recreation and Hospitality Management*, Vol. 1, Belhaven, London, pp. 55–76.

Organization for Economic Co-operation and Development, annual, *Tourism Policy and International Tourism in OECD Member Countries*, OECD, Paris.

Poon, A., 1989, 'Competitive strategies for a new tourism', in Cooper, C. P. (ed.), *Progress in Tourism, Recreation and Hospitality Management*, Vol. 1, Belhaven, London, pp. 91–102.

Shackleford, P., 1987, 'Global tourism trends', *Tourism Management*, 18(2): pp. 98–101.

World Tourism Organization, annual, *Yearbook of Tourism Statistics* (2 volumes), WTO, Madrid.

World Tourism Organization, 1988, *Current Travel and Tourism Indicators*, 1988, (4), WTO, Madrid.

9 Marketing of the service process: state of the art in tourism, recreation and hospitality industries

F. Go and K. M. Haywood

Introduction

Marketing as applied to hospitality and tourism has generated a large literature, though the literature is only beginning to develop in recreation. This vigorous activity is a direct result of the tremendous interest, growth and competition in these three leisure-driven service industries that are becoming increasingly integrated (Jansen-Verbeke and Dietvorst, 1987). It is more than a little ironic, however, that this growing interest in marketing coincides with an equally widespread concern about the deleterious social, cultural, environmental and economic effects attributed to marketing's attempt to generate growth in tourist traffic (Mathieson and Wall, 1982). As a consequence, there are those who repudiate marketing. In this context, then, it is important to determine the extent to which marketing thought—particularly in the area of tourism—is responding to these concerns and providing evidence of progress. For example, is there an emerging vanguard of socially conscious marketers who are anxious to project more humanism, enlightened practice and thought into marketing? (Kotler, 1987; Fennell, 1987; Krippendorf, 1987.)

In assessing the state of the art of marketing, therefore, we feel obliged to assume that it is both an applied managerial technology and a social process (Fisk, 1986). Although the systematic bias towards the applied technology direction is acknowledged, it is important to recognize that marketing has micro/macro, profit/non-profit, as well as positive/normative perspectives (Hunt, 1975). With the emergence of a service marketing paradigm we are also interested in determining the extent to which marketers within the hospitality, tourism and recreation fields are recognizing the wider perspective in which some social constructs of marketing cannot help but be included.

There are obvious links between tourism, hospitality and recreation (Go, 1984), but marketing for them has developed almost entirely separately. They have also developed outside the emerging study of services marketing. Therefore, each will be discussed individually.

Hospitality marketing

In commercial terms, hospitality includes accommodation and foodservice businesses (profit and non-profit) that cater to people who are away from home. Most of the early marketing literature was written to assist independent and invariably smaller *mom and pop* businesses to attract and hold customers or guests. Based on industry need, and borrowing somewhat from the retail industry, early emphasis was placed on merchandizing and sales promotion.

In fact, it is virtually impossible to pick up an industry trade journal published during the 1960s and 1970s that is not replete with articles on *how to attract customers* or make more effective use of the media. The popular texts of the period have a similar focus. For the foodservice industry, the discussion focuses on food or the menu (Kotschevar, 1975; Seaburg, 1973), while in the hotel sector the emphasis is on how to effectively sell rooms. Books by Stein (1971) and the consummate marketing professional, Dewitt Coffman (1970, 1980), became the standard marketing texts for the 1970s. So strong was their practical approach that attempts by marketing academics to break into the field were thwarted. Breaking free from this mould was the conceptually original and landmark, *Marketing of the Meal Experience* (Campbell-Smith, 1967). Though largely unheralded, particularly in North America, it is fair to say that this consumer-oriented book was far ahead of its time. Only recently has there been a renewed interest in the *experiences* of customers (Bitner *et al.*, 1985).

With the exception of two conceptually sound and well-written texts (Buttle, 1986; Lewis and Chambers, 1989), the books on marketing have been unspectacular and burdened with heavy doses of advertising and promotional ideas (Taylor, 1964; Laine and Laine, 1972; Taylor, 1981; Gottlieb, 1982; Feltenstein, 1983; Abbey, 1989). Attempts at writing more inclusive marketing texts have been made (Kotas, 1975; Astroff and Abbey, 1978; Eisen, 1980; Summer, 1982; Greene, 1982; Fisher, 1982; Nykiel, 1983; Reid, 1983; Lewis, *et al.*, 1986; Hart and Troy, 1987) but by and large they provide superficial and unsatisfactory coverage of many complex marketing issues. At a time when hospitality businesses were expanding and the complexity of managing chain organizations (Wyckoff and Sasser, 1978), fast-food corporations (Emerson, 1979) and hotel conglomerates, such as Holiday Inn (Pearce and Robinson, 1982), was intensifiying, marketers, academics and students at the university level were inevitably drawn towards the more rigorous and thorough general-marketing texts written by authors such as Kotler (1980).

Upset by the formidable ignorance of marketing within the industry and the lack of empirically defensible marketing research, several marketing professionals and academics moved into the vacuum. The prodigious output of authors such as Peter Yesawich and Robert Lewis is especially noticeable. Their contributions have been major; almost single-handedly they have pulled the field of hospitality marketing into the mainstream of marketing thought. As a consequence, hospitality marketing has taken on more strategic focus (Sasser and Morgan, 1977; Blomstrom, 1983) with increasing attention being given to such topics as:

— market segmentation (Lewis, 1980; Moller *et al.*, 1985; Swinyard and Struman, 1986; Garvey, 1986);
— positioning (McNaughton, 1981; Lewis, 1982; Lewis, 1985);
— a new marketing mix (Renaghan, 1981; Booms and Bitner, 1982; Goffe, 1986);
— marketing planning (Yesawich, 1979; Doswell and Gamble, 1979; Yesawich, 1988);
— research techniques (Welch, 1985; Lewis, 1985; Ritchie and Goeldner, 1987; Yesawich, 1987);
— environment (Booms and Bitner, 1982; Noble and Olsen, 1986);
— demand and capacity management (Hart and Lawless, 1983; Yesawich, 1984; Jeffrey and Hubbard, 1986);
— consumer buying behaviour (Swinyard, 1977; Lewis, 1984; Lewis and Klein, 1985; Dhir, 1987; Wilensky and Buttle, 1988);
— life cycles (Hart, Casserly and Lawless, 1984; Leven, 1985; Haywood, 1985);
— new product development (Withiam, 1985; Haywood, 1985; Feltenstein, 1986);
— pricing and discounting (Kreul, 1982; Abbey, 1983; Miller, 1987; Greenburg, 1985; Carroll, 1986; Lewis, 1986; Lefever and Morrison, 1988; Lewis and Roan, 1986);
— competition (Akehurst, 1986; Haywood, 1986);
— promotional strategies (Lewis, 1987; Renaghan and Kaye, 1987; Morrison, 1989; Haywood, 1988; Haywood, 1989);
— consumer feedback and complaint handling (Doltas, 1977; Cadotte, 1979; Lewis and Pizam, 1981; Lewis, 1983; Trice and Layman, 1984; Lewis and Morris, 1987; Davis and Horney, 1988);
— customer satisfaction (Lewis, 1987; Renaghan and Kaye, 1987; Cadotte and Turgeon, 1988);
— service delivery systems (Levitt, 1972; Pickworth, 1988; Haywood and Pickworth, 1989).

In addition, attention should be drawn to the consumer omnibus studies on eating-out behaviour. Most of these studies, commissioned by the major foodservice, catering and lodging associations (such as the National Restaurant Association and the American Hotel and Motel Association), have advanced our market knowledge tremendously. However, we are still largely ignorant about the marketing behaviour of hotel and restaurant companies. A few attempts have been made to determine how the hospitality marketing function is pursued or managed (Haywood, 1975), and there is a growing body of well-researched case studies developed at both Harvard and the University of Guelph that identify important marketing issues.

With the burgeoning of services, in general, it is interesting to note that more marketing researchers are including hospitality services in their surveys. The following list is a way of highlighting topics of interest and sources in the more general business/marketing literature:

— consumer decision-making processes (Lewis, 1981; Meryer, 1981; Wolf and Latane, 1983; Louviere and Woodsworth, 1983; Filiatrault and Ritchie, 1983; Bon and Pras, 1984; McDougall, 1986; June and Smith, 1987);
— customer satisfaction (Swan, Trawick and Carroll, 1981; Cadotte, Woodruff and Jenkins, 1987);
— business location analysis (Arbel and Pizam, 1977; Smith, 1985, 1986; Wall *et al.*, 1985; Pillsbury, 1987);
— market segmentation (Boote, 1981);
— risk-taking and development (Bartram, Cox and Southgate, 1980).

In this review it is evident that a lack of attention has been given to the marketing of institutional foodservice. Clearly this is a growth area in many companies (Comacho, 1988) and interest in marketing is evident. For example, there are bibliographies on school foodservice marketing (Shanklin *et al.*, 1987) and dietetics (Pickworth and Pickworth; 1984); the marketing of nutrition has become a topic of great contemporary interest (Carlson, 1986; Regan, 1987); and, the state of the art in marketing hospital foodservice departments has been studied (Pickens and Shanklin, 1985). Particular note should be made of the current interest in health care marketing (Berkowitz and Flexner, 1978; Rice, Slack and Garside, 1981; Rubright and MacDonald, 1981).

With the rapid expansion of other service industries, the similarity between hospitality management and the management of other service businesses has not gone unnoticed (Haywood, 1987; Barrington and Olsen, 1987). While there is still a tendency to borrow heavily from the marketing literature flowing from the consumer goods industries, service marketing literature is booming. For obvious reasons that stem from the unique characteristics of services, a new set of ideas concerning the hospitality marketing process has been suggested. For example, the involvement of the customer in the simultaneous production and consumption of services has raised concern over the issue of service quality, particularly as it relates to its management and measurement (Haywood, 1983; Wykoff, 1984; King, 1984; Hart and Casserly, 1985; Moores, 1986), the development of food products (Drew and Lyons, 1986) and the links with capacity, productivity and service delivery systems (Pickworth, 1988; Haywood and Pickworth, 1989; Jones, 1988).

The importance of finding out what service customers really want and how they evaluate services has already been noted, but the area of customer-employee relations or relationship marketing, for example, still needs to be developed (Stringer, 1981; Haywood, 1989; Lockwood and Jones, 1989). In essence, the service management/marketing models show that hospitality marketing is inextricably tied to aspects of human resource management, training and operations management. During the next decade, therefore, we can anticipate that more effort will be made to link marketing research with these areas. Indeed, a more multicutural and international focus will be required (Shames and Glover, 1989).

Tourism marketing

As in the hospitality field, societal and economic changes during the past two decades have resulted in rapid expansion and growth of domestic and international tourism in many countries. Competition among destinations, economic instabilities, oil crises and political events have demonstrated the vital significance of marketing in the development and operation of a whole range of tourism services. For example, transportation and lodging businesses, tour operators, travel agencies, as well as towns, cities, regions and nation states are all actively involved in encouraging tourists. The scope of tourism marketing, therefore, is enormous and extends into both the public and private sectors of the economy. Large amounts of money are being allocated to tourism marketing research (though the amounts are still viewed as inadequate at the corporate level (Rovelstad and Blazer, 1983)), so a rich empirical base is being established.

Among the earliest publications relating to tourism marketing were market studies (Bjorkman, 1963); analyses of tourist markets (Schmidhauser, 1962; Crampton, 1966); and demand-forecasting studies and econometric modelling (Lickorish, 1972; Archer, 1976; Baron, 1979). Mention should be made of the studies and reports published by the IUOTO (International Union of Travel Organizations) later. to become the WTO (World Tourism Organization). Since the 1970s, information on marketing has also been disseminated through many national and international tourism seminars sponsored by such organizations as the Pacific Area Tourist Association (PATA), and the Travel and Tourism Research Association (TTRA) and its various chapter organizations. Furthermore, researchers or research institutes at numerous universities (Colorado, Texas A&M, Utah, George Washington, Hawaii and Surrey, to name a few) have provided a wealth of marketing knowledge. The *Journal of Travel Research* has become the world's leading research journal, publishing many articles relating to the subject area. A brief retrospective of the existing literature in marketing reveals that research interest seems to be focused on the following topics:

— developing marketing programs (McCleary, 1987; Frechtling, 1987);
— identifying the tourist or segmenting the market (Crask, 1981; Calatone and Johar, 1984; Woodside and Jacobs, 1985; McQueen and Miller, 1985; Pearce, 1985; Koynak, 1985; Davis and Sternquist, 1987; Weaver and McCleary, 1984; Dybka, 1987; Woodside *et al.*, 1987; Snepenger, 1987; McCleary, 1987; Mcguire *et al.*, 1988);

- understanding consumer behaviour and tourists' decision-making processes (Woodside and Sherrell, 1977; Gittelson and Crompton, 1983; Bronner and deHoog, 1984; Shih, 1986; Pitts and Woodside, 1986; Moutinho, 1987; Nickels and Snepenger, 1988; Woodside and Carr, 1988; Cook, 1989);
- measuring tourist demand and improving forecasting procedures (Merlo, 1985; Hess and Voink, 1986; Witt and Martin, 1987; Uysal and Crompton, 1985; Ritchie and Sheridan, 1988; Calatone *et al.*, 1987);
- advertising/communications and conversion studies (Woodside and Motes, 1981; Pritchard, 1982; Bellman *et al.*, 1984; Yochum, 1985; Silberman and Klock, 1986; Mazanec, 1986);
- understanding images of destinations (Hunt, 1975; Haati and Yayas, 1982; Wee *et al.*, 1986; Phelps, 1986; Gartner and Hunt, 1987):
- attractiveness of tourist areas (Gearing *et al.*, 1974; Var *et al.*, 1977; Husbands, 1983; Squire, 1988);
- evaluating tourist satisfaction (Pizam *et al.*, 1978; Hannigan, 1980; Pearce, 1980; Pearce and Moscardo, 1985);
- issues in product development, attractions and life cycles (Ritchie and Beliveau, 1974; Ritchie and Zins, 1978; Butler, 1980; Go, 1981; Stough and Feldeman, 1982; Riley, 1983; Mercer, 1985; Haywood, 1986; Patton, 1986; Makens, 1987; Hall, 1987; Lew, 1987);
- marketing of package tours and tour operators (Allen, 1985; Sheldon and Mak, 1987; Kent *et al.*, 1987; Kale *et al.*, 1985).

Tourism marketing activities have not gone unnoticed by academics in other disciplines. Studies published deserve separate mention here because of the criticism or fresh perspective they provide. Of particular note are articles by Thurot and Thurot (1983), Uzzell (1984), Dilley (1986) and Nord (1986); their attention to tourism advertising is especially enlightening. Urban geographers and planners are paying attention to the marketing of cities as it pertains to tourism (Jansen-Verbeke, 1988; Ashworth and Voorgd, 1988) focusing on a much neglected topic—the dynamics of location (the place component in the marketing mix). The literature on recreational geography (Smith, 1983) provides useful insights here.

With regard to product development, tourism marketers should not neglect the importance of their sister discipline, tourism planning. Of particular note is Gunn's (1988) work. Also linked to the area of product development is recognition of recent studies made in information and communication technologies. Not only are new links among the various component businesses of tourism being created, there are also tremendous opportunities for marketing—the identification and delivery of better services and the creation of customer loyalty.

There are other oversights in the tourism marketing literature. The spate of tourism studies dealing with tourism impacts, whether upon citizens living in a tourist destination community, on tourists themselves as victims of crime or disease, or upon the quality of tourism's physical and natural resources, suggest problems inherent in marketing activities. Other than in studies written by critics of marketing (see Nord, 1986), the literature has inadequately addressed such concerns as the creation of false perceptions, the problems of overcrowding and difficulties involved in host/guest encounters. With the recent interest in business ethics, the ethical questions inherent in tourism marketing demand attention, especially as they relate to destinations in developing countries (Go *et al.*, 1989). A revision of the marketing concept as it applies to tourism may be in order (Haywood, 1990).

Part of the problem is that the whole issue of what is meant by tourism marketing is unclear. The texts and manuals on the subject are not much help. Many have been prepared primarily for tour operators or travel agencies (Reilly, 1980; Bishop, 1981; Davidoff and Davidoff, 1983; Mahoney and Warnell, 1986; Harris and Katz, 1987; NTA, 1987). Wahab's *Tourism Marketing* (1976) is based on a consumer-goods marketing model and is woefully out-of-date, while Schmoll's *Tourism Promotion* (1977) is too narrowly focused. Only a few books stand out. One is Ritchie and Goeldner's *Travel, Tourism and Hospitality Research* (1987), which offers an excellent compendium of articles on research techniques written by experts in their field. Another useful book, although it is classified as a handbook, is *Tourism Marketing and Management* (Witt and Moutinho, 1989). It contains a wealth of interesting articles by practitioners and academics from many parts of the world. Recently, several authors have responded to the need to define the field of tourism marketing. Jefferson and Lickorish (1988) provide a practical guide with a destination emphasis, and Mill (1989), Mill and Morrison (1985) and Middleton (1988) have produced marketing tourism texts which will serve as models for further development.

Recreation marketing

Most experts in the recreation, parks and arts fields will readily admit that marketing has yet to be embraced as a vitally important management function—particularly in the not-for-profit sector. Marketing has, however, found its way into some of the major texts in the field (Howard and Crompton, 1980; Orenstein and Nunn, 1980; Bullaro and Edginton, 1986) and is being actively discussed at many conferences.

A spattering of articles that have appeared over the years argue for the adoption of a marketing approach (Uysal, 1986; Dearden and Andressen, 1987), a greater role for market research (Cowell, 1981) and a marketing role in developing new programmes (Crompton, 1983; Davis, 1983). The relatively new *Journal of Park and Recreation Administration* is significant because it has published a variety of marketing-related articles on such topics as: user fees (Becker *et al.*, 1985); market potential (Howard, 1985); target markets (Crompton, 1983); marketing audits (Crompton and Lamb, 1986) and leisure activities

(Cato and Kunstler, 1988). In the recreation/leisure literature at large there are, of course, a variety of articles on motivation and satisfaction levels (Tinsley and Kass, 1977; Howes, 1978; Ragheb and Beard, 1979; Beard and Ragheb, 1983; Cato, 1986); and even in the tourism literature, recreation articles are now making an appearance. For example, specific visitor management techniques are being discussed (Graham *et al*., 1988). It is interesting to note that an interest in 'quality' is also emerging (Crompton, 1988; Ferguson and Malone, 1988).

The involvement of marketing with the arts should be mentioned. Its history can be traced to Baumol and Bowen (1966), who identified economic problems in the performing arts. Since then marketers have embraced this area in the marketing of non-profit organizations. The most extensive review and coverage of this topic to date appears in *Advances in Non-Profit Marketing* (Vols. 1 and 2). Of special importance is the article by Semenik, 'State of the art of arts marketing' (1987). Also worth mentioning is Tighe (1985), who has been an active promoter of a partnership between arts and tourism. All in all, the expanding body of information on the marketing of cultural industries is fascinating, as it embraces quality-of-life issues, which are of growing importance to marketers in tourism and recreation (McNulty and Penne, 1984; Ritchie, 1987).

Finally, recreation marketers are being attracted to the concepts of service marketing; Mahoney's article (1987) is of particular relevance here. He suggests a fresh approach to marketing based upon understanding interactions between employees and customers, customers and customers and customers and environment. He argues that these interactions are essential to building a new model of recreation marketing—a model that will allow marketers to more fully understand the experiences that result in customer satisfaction and repeat-purchase decisions.

Emerging marketing paradigms

In a now classic article, Kotler and Levy (1969) argue for a broadened concept of marketing. The article has had far-reaching consequences and prompted a re-thinking of the marketing discipline. Unfortunately, the impact of this re-thinking has not yet been felt with full force in the hospitality, tourism and recreation industries. In this final section, four emerging and mutually supportive paradigms of importance to hospitality/tourism/recreation marketing are identified. Application of service marketing in a strategic marketing context, implemented with a social marketing conscience and viewed in a global context, can have profound implications for the field. It could help restructure the concept of marketing and help set new research agendas.

Throughout this paper, the extent to which the service marketing concept has made inroads into the literature has been noted. The pioneering efforts of such people as Levitt (1972), Rathmell (1974), George and Barksdale (1974),

Donnelly (1976), Sasser (1976), Shostak (1977), Thomas (1978) and many others have been overwhelming. To summarize:

— services are performances which tend to be produced in real time, often in the presence of the customer;
— the creation and delivery of a performance is unlike that of a manufactured good; more attention needs to be given to developing, testing and introducing new services;
— customers may be actively involved in creating the service product;
— the intangibility of services makes their pricing difficult, particularly with respect to the perception of risk, search costs and prices for similar services;
— capacity and demand management require special attention;
— quality assurance is a persistent problem and needs to be better understood, measured and managed;
— distribution channels will be controlled increasingly through information and communications technologies;
— tourism services need to be more effectively bundled.

All of these concerns need to be addressed more thoroughly, but the concern which is of utmost importance is the service encounter. Not only does this affect how a service can be best marketed (Czepiel *et al.*, 1985; Lovelock, 1988), but how a service business should be organized and operated (Mills, 1986). For anyone who has tried to keep up on just this area of service marketing, the information available is overwhelming; and a whole new approach to marketing is being dictated (Lehtinen, 1986). Given this interest in encounters, marketing researchers would be wise to study the problems associated with cross-cultural marketing or the role of marketing intermediaries (Maister and Lovelock, 1982; Rao and Ovmlil, 1988; Shames and Glover, 1989).

Service marketing, however, does not happen in a vacuum; serious issues regarding the effective management of service organizations need to be addressed (Haywood, 1987). The recent slew of service management texts provides a useful start (Normann, 1984; Albrecht and Zemke, 1985; Heskett, 1986; Albrecht, 1988). The unique characteristics of services and the intensely competitive environment of hospitality, tourism and recreation organizations demand a more strategic approach (Hodgson, 1987). As Allen (1988) points out, five critical aspects to managing a service business have a strategic orientation: renewing the service offering; localizing the point of service system; leveraging the service contract; using information power strategically; and determining the strategic value of a service business. Evidence also suggests that positioning strategies (Shostak, 1987) and competitive strategies (Wilson, 1988) may be quite different for service businesses.

While there is no denying that hospitality, tourism and recreation organizations operate in an increasingly competitive world, the results orientation can be problematic. Fixation with results can focus the marketer and other managers on achieving the results to the near exclusion of recognizing other benefits and problems derived from the process itself. To the extent that we believe tourism and recreation are community-based and community-driven activities (Murphy, 1985), there is a need to be concerned with longer-term results. As Kotler (1980) says, 'The sensitive marketer has to take responsibility for the totality of outputs (and outcomes) created'. The propensity for marketing to displace or even consume human values along with exchange values needs rectifying. Witt and Moutinho's *Tourism Marketing and Management Handbook* (1989) identifies a range of 'the most crucial issues in tourism marketing and management' likely to be of concern to us well into the 1990s.

In conclusion, the adoption of a more service-oriented approach to marketing—in particular, the implementation of customer-centred systems designed to deliver quality in service more consistently—seems most likely. This should be coupled with a strategic approach that begins by looking at customer needs and aims to build profits through integrating marketing efforts to satisfy consumers. This can be best accomplished if tourism and hospitality marketers can learn to be sensitive to societal needs—by fitting into the fabric of the host community (Go, 1982) and a diversity of cultures (Hirschman, 1985), for example. Marketing professionals must give careful consideration to these issues if we are to avoid the undesirable consequences of marketing techniques gone awry.

We expect that in the 1990s the *globalization* phenomenon will drive new tourism, recreation and hospitality developments even more than in the 1980s. The removal of most of the remaining barriers in the European Economic Community in 1992 and the anticipated takeover of Hong Kong by China in 1997 are but two examples that will spell both upheaval and opportunity in world travel markets. Furthermore, the frenzy of mergers and acquisitions coupled with the emergence of computerized reservation systems (CRS) and the growth of international franchising (Go and Christensen, 1989) will require marketing professionals to have a much better *global grasp* in addition to understanding marketing as a specific business function.

In summary, the main challenge for the future will be to develop managers who will be able to deal with constant, rapid change and a multitude of issues. If creativity and innovation can be successfully applied to the challenge ahead in tourism, recreation and hospitality management, there is no reason why service marketing should not ascend to new heights.

References

Abbey, J., 1983, 'Is discounting the answer to declining occupancies?', *International Journal of Hospitality Management*, 2(2): pp. 77–82.

Abbey, J., 1989, *Hospitality Sales and Advertising*, The Educational Institute, East Lansing, Michigan.

Akehurst, H., 1986, 'Identification of the reactions of hotel managers to new competition', *International Journal of Hospitality Management*, 5(4): p. 189.

Albrecht, K., 1988, *At America's Service: How Corporations Can Revolutionize the Way They Treat Their Customers*, Dow Jones-Irwin, Homewood, Illinois.

Albrecht, K., Zemke, R., 1985, *Service America: Doing Business in the New Economy*, Dow Jones-Irwin, Homewood, Illinois.

Allen, M., 1988, 'Strategic management of consumer services', *Long Range Planning*, 21(6): pp. 20–5.

Allen, T., 1985, 'Marketing by a small tour operator in a market dominated by big operators', *European Journal of Marketing*, 19(5): pp. 83–90.

Arbel, A., Pizam, A., 1977, 'Some determinants of urban hotel location: the tourists' inclinations', *Journal of Travel Research*, 15(3): pp. 18–22.

Archer, B. H., 1976, *Demand Forecasting in Tourism*, Bangor Occasional Papers in Economics, No. 9, University of Wales Press, Cardiff.

Ashworth, G. J., Voorgd, H., 1988, 'Marketing the city: concepts, processes and Dutch applications', *Town Planning Review*, 59(1): pp. 65–79.

Askari, H., 1971, 'Demand for package tours', *Journal of Transport Economics and Policy*, 5(1): pp. 40–51.

Astroff, M. T., Abbey, J. R., 1978, *Convention Sales and Service*, Wm. C. Brown, Dubuque, Iowa.

Bellman, G. *et al.*, 1984, 'Toward higher quality conversion studies: refining the numbers game', *Journal of Travel Research*, 22(4): pp. 28–33.

Baron, R., 1979, 'Forecasting tourism: theory and practice', in *TTRA—A Decade of Achievement*, Tenth Annual Conference proceedings, Bureau of Economic and Business Research, University of Utah, Salt Lake City.

Barrington, M. N., Olsen, M. O., 1987, 'Concept of service in the hospitality industry', *International Journal of Hospitality Management*, 6(3): pp. 131–8.

Bartram, M. *et al.*, 1980, 'Researching future developments in hotels', *The Market Research Society Conference*, March, pp. 101–11.

Beard, J., Ragheb, M., 1983, 'Measuring leisure motivation', *Journal of Leisure Research*, 15(3): pp. 219–28.

Becker, R. H., Berrier, D., Barker G. D., 1985, 'Entrance fees and visitation levels', *Journal of Park and Recreation Management*, 3(1): pp. 28–32.

Bishop, J., 1981, *Travel Marketing*, Bailey Bros. and Seinfen Ltd., Folkestone.

Bitner, M., Nyquist, B., Booms, B., 1985, 'The critical incident as a technique for analyzing the service encounter', in T. Block *et al.*, *Services Marketing in a Changing Environment*, AMA Marketing Association, Chicago, pp. 48–51.

Bjorkman, B., 1963, 'Market studies in the field of international tourist traffic', *The Tourist Review*, 18(4): pp 142–9.

Blackwell, J., 1970, 'Tourist traffic and the demand for accommodation: some projections', *Economic and Social Review*, 1(3): pp. 323–43.

Bon, J., Pras, B., 1984, 'Dissociation of the roles of buyer, payer, and consumer', *International Journal of Research in Marketing*, 1(1): pp. 7–16.

Booms, B. H., Bitner, M. J., 1982, 'Marketing services by managing the environment', *Cornwell HRA Quarterly*, May, pp. 35–9.

Boote, A. S., 1981, 'Market segmentation by personal values and salient product attributes', *Journal of Advertising Research*, 21(1): pp. 29–35.

Bronner, A. A., de Hoog, R., 1984, 'Computer assisted decision-making: a new tool for market research', *Esomar Congress*, Rome, pp. 171–91.

Bullaro, J. J., Edginton, C. R., 1986, *Commercial Leisure Services: Managing for Profit, Service and Personal Satisfaction*, Macmillan Publishing, New York.

Buttle, F., 1986, *Hotel and Food Service Marketing: A Managerial Approach*, Holt, Rinehart and Winston, London.

Cadotte, E. R. *et al.*, 1987, 'Expectations and norms in models of consumer satisfaction', *Journal of Marketing Research*, August, pp. 305–14.

Calatone, R., Johar, J. S., 1984, 'Seasonal segmentation of the tourism market using a benefit segmentation framework', *Journal of Travel Research*, 23(2): pp. 14–24.

Calatone, R., *et al.*, 1987, 'A comprehensive review of the tourism forecasting literature', *Journal of Travel Research*, 26(2): pp. 28–39.

Camacho, F. E., 1988, 'Meeting the needs of senior citizens through lifecare communities: Marriott's approach to the development of a new business', *The Journal of Services Marketing*, 2(1): pp. 49–53.

Campbell-Smith, G., 1967, *Marketing of the Meal Experience*, University of Surrey, London.

Carlson, B., 1986, 'Meeting consumer needs—the basis for successful marketing of nutrition in foodservice', *International Journal of Hospitality Management*, 5(4): p. 163.

Carroll, J. O., 1986, 'Focusing on discounting hotel rack rates', *Cornell H.R.A. Quarterly*, August, p. 13.

Cato, B., 1986, 'Happiness: the missing link of marketing in a technological society', *Visions in Leisure and Business*, 5(1 and 2), pp. 64–73.

Cato, B., Kunstler, R., 1988, 'Preferred leisure activities and reasons for participation: a comparison study with implications for marketing leisure services', *Journal of Park and Recreation Management*, 6(1): pp. 54–65.

Coffman, D., 1970, *Marketing for a Full House*, Cornell University, Ithaca, New York.

Coffman, D., 1980, *Hospitality For Sale*, Cornell University, Ithaca, New York.

Cowell, D., 1981, 'The role of market research in the development of public policy in the field of recreation and leisure', *Journal of the Market Research Society*, 23(3): pp. 72–83.

Cowell, D., 1984, *The Marketing of Services*, Heinemann, London.

Crampton, L. J., 1966, 'A new technique to analyze tourist markets', *Journal of Marketing*, 30(2): pp. 27–31.

Crask, M. R., 1981, 'Segmenting the vacationer market: identifying the vacation preferences, demographics and magazine readership of each group, *Journal of Travel Research*, 20(1): pp. 29–34.

Crompton, J. L., 1983, 'Developing new recreation and parks programs', *Recreation Canada*, July, pp. 27–33.

Crompton, J. L., 1983, 'Selecting target markets—a key to effective marketing', *Journal of Park and Recreation Management*, 1(1): pp. 7–26.

Crompton, J. L., Lamb, C. W., 1986, 'The marketing audit—a starting point for strategic management', *Journal of Park and Recreation Management*, 4(1): pp. 19–34.

Czepiel, J. A., Solomon, M. R., Surprenant, C. F. (eds), 1985, *The Service Encounter: Managing Employee/Customer Interaction in Service Businesses*, Lexington Books, Lexington, Massachusetts.

Dann, G., 1981, 'Tourist motivation: an appraisal', *Annals of Tourism Research*, 8(2): pp. 187–219.

Davidoff, P. G., Davidoff, D. S., 1983, *Sales and Marketing for Travel and Tourism*, National Publishers of the Black Hills, Rapid City, South Dakota.

Davis, B. D., Sternquist, B., 1987, 'Appealing to the elusive tourist: an attribute cluster strategy', *Journal of Travel Research*, 25(4): pp. 25–31.

Davis, L., 1983, 'Recreation marketing: a common sense approach to program planning', *Recreation Canada*, September, pp. 6–11.

Davis, R. V., Horney, N., 1988, 'Guest feedback and complaint handling in the hospitality industry', *International Conference on Services Marketing, Vol. 5*, Cleveland State University, Cleveland, Ohio.

Dhir, K. S., 1987, 'Analysis of consumer behaviour in the hospitality industry: an application of social judgement theory', *International Journal of Hospitality Management*, 6(3): pp. 149–61.

Dilley, R. S., 1986, 'Tourist brochures and tourist images', *Canadian Geographer*, 30(1): pp. 59–65.

Donnelly, J. H., Jr, 1976, 'Marketing intermediaries in channels of distribution for services', *Journal of Marketing*, 40: pp. 55–70.

Doswell, R., Gamble, P. R., 1979, *Marketing and Planning Hotels and Tourism Projects*, Barrie and Jenkins, London.

Drew, K., Lyons, H., 1986, 'The dimensions of quality in food product development', in Beharr, R. *et al*. (eds), *Marketing in the Food Chain, Conference Proceedings, Part 1, Food Marketing*, 2(3).

Drinkwater, R., Davies, I., 1987, 'Leisure marketing in action: selling; sponsorship', *Leisure Management*, 7(11): pp. 42–3, 49–50.

Dybka, J. M., 1987, 'A look at the American traveller: the US pleasure travel market study', *Journal of Travel Research*, 25(3): pp. 2–4.

Eisen, I. I., 1980, *Strategic Marketing in Food Service—Planning for Change*, Lebhar Friedman Books, New York.

Emerson, R. L., 1979, *Fast Food—The Endless Shakeout*, Lebher Friedman Books, New York.

Feltenstein, T., 1983, *Restaurant Profits Through Advertising and Promotion—The Indispensable Plan*, CBI Publishing, Boston.

Fennell, G., 1987, 'A radical agenda for marketing science: represent the marketing concept', in Firat, A. F. *et al*. (eds), *Philosophical and Radical Thought in Marketing*, Lexington Books, Lexington, Massachusetts, pp. 289–306.

Ferguson, J. M., Malone, K. M., 1988, 'Quality service in health clubs: do employees know what customers want?', *International Conference on Services Marketing, Vol. 5*, Cleveland State University, Cleveland, Ohio.

Ferraro, F. F., 1979, 'The evaluation of tourist resources: an applied methodology', *Journal of Travel Research*, 17(4): pp. 24–32.

Filiatrault, P., Ritchie, J. R. B., 1980, 'Joint purchasing decisions: a comparison of influence structure in family and couple decision-making units', *Journal of Consumer Research*, 7(2): pp 131–40.

Fisk, G. (ed.), 1986, *Marketing Management Technology as a Social Process*, Praegar, New York.

Frechtling, D. C., 1987, 'Five issues in tourism marketing in the 1990s', *Tourism Management*, 8(2): pp. 177–8.

Gartner, W. C., Hunt, J. D., 1987, 'An analysis of state image change over a twelve-year period, 1971–1983', *Journal of Travel Research*, 26(2): pp. 15–19.

Garvey, J., 1986, 'Outlook and opportunities in market segmentation', in Lewis, R., *et al*. (eds), *The Practice of Hospitality Management II*, AVI, Westport, Connecticut.

Gearing, C. E. *et al*., 1974, 'Establishing a measure of touristic attractiveness', *Journal of Travel Research*, 12(4): pp. 1–8.

George, W. R., Barksdale, H. C., 1974, 'Marketing activities in the service industry', *Journal of Marketing*, 38: pp. 65–70.

Gittelson, R. J., Crompton, J. L., 1983, 'The planning horizons and sources of information used by pleasure vacationers', *Journal of Travel Research*, 21(3): pp. 2–7.

Go, Frank M., 1981, 'Development of new service products for the leisure travel market—a system's view', *Revue de Tourisme*, 36(2): pp. 9–18.

Go, Frank M., 1982, 'Hospitality and heritage—a profitable partnership', in Pizam, A. *et al*. (eds), *The Practice of Hospitality Management*, AVI, Westport, Connecticut.

Go, Frank M., 1984, 'The hospitality/tourism connection: a cooperative plan of action', in Brymer, Robert A. (ed.), *Introduction to Hotel and Restaurant Management*, Kendall/Hunt, Dubuque, Iowa.

Go, Frank M., 1988, 'Appropriate marketing for travel destinations in developing nations', in Vir Singh, Tej, Theuns, H. Leo, Go, Frank M. (eds), *Towards Appropriate Tourism: The Case of Developing Countries*, Verlag Peter Lang GmbH, Frankfurt.

Go, Frank M., Christensen, Julia, 1989, 'Going global', *Cornell H.R.A. Quarterly*, 30(3), forthcoming.

Goffe, P., 1986, 'Replacing place in the marketing mix strategy for hospitality services', *F.I.U. Hospitality Review*, spring, p. 24.

Gottlieb, L., 1982, *Foodservice/Hospitality Advertising and Promotion*, Bobbs Merrill Educational Publishing, Indianapolis, Indiana.

Graham, R. *et al*., 1988, 'Visitor management in Canadian national parks', *Tourism Management*, 9(1): pp. 44–62.

Greenberg, C., 1985, 'Room rates and lodging demand', *Cornell HRA Quarterly*, November pp. 10–11.

Greenley, G. E., Matcham, A. S., 1986, 'Marketing orientation in the service of incoming tourism', *European Journal of Marketing*, 20(7): pp. 64–73.

Gronroos, C., 1980, 'Designing a long range marketing strategy for services', *Long Range Planning*, 13(4): pp. 36–42.

Gunn, C. A., 1988, *Tourism Planning*, second edition, Taylor and Francis, New York.

Haati, A., Yayas, U., 1982, 'Tourists' perception of Finland and selected European countries as travel destinations', *European Journal of Marketing*, 17(2): pp. 34–42.

Hall, C. H., 1987, 'The effects of hallmark events on cities', *Journal of Travel Research*, 26(2): pp. 44–5.

Hannigan, J. A., 1980, 'Reservations cancelled: consumer complaints in the tourist industry', *Annals of Tourism Research*, 7(3): pp. 366–84.

Harris, G., Katz, K. M., 1987, *Promoting International Tourism*, Americas Group, Los Angeles.

Hart, C. W. L., Lawless, M. J., 1983, 'Forces that shape restaurant demand', *Cornell HRA Quarterly*, November, pp. 7–17.

Hart, C. W. L., Casserly, G. D., Lawless, M. J., 1984, 'The product life cycle: how useful?', *Cornell HRA Quarterly*, November, 58: pp. 61–3.

Hart, C. W. L., Casserly, G. D., 1985, 'Quality: a brand-new, time-tested strategy', *Cornell HRA Quarterly*, November, pp. 52–63.

Hawes, D., 1978, 'Satisfaction derived from leisure-time pursuits: an exploratory nationwide survey', *Journal of Leisure Research*, 10(4): pp. 247–64.

Haywood, K. M., 1975, *Marketing and Merchandizing Practices in the Canadian Hospitality Industry, Volume 1, The Accommodation Sector*, University of Guelph, Guelph, Ontario.

Haywood, K. M., 1975, *Management and Merchandizing Practices in the Canadian*

Hospitality Industry, Volume 2, The Foodservice Sector, University of Guelph, Guelph, Ontario.

Haywood, K. M., 1983, 'Assessing the quality of hospitality services', *International Journal of Hospitality Management*, 3(4): pp. 164–77.

Haywood, K. M., 1985, 'Overcoming the impotency of marketing', *F.I.U. Hospitality Review*, Fall, p. 30.

Haywood, K. M., 1985, 'The Go system: generating opportunities for hospitality businesses', *International Journal of Hospitality Management*, 4(1): pp. 15–26.

Haywood, K. M., 1986, 'Scouting for competition for survival and success', *Cornell H.R.A. Quarterly*, November, pp. 80–7.

Haywood, K. M., 1986, 'Can the tourist-area life cycle be made operational?', *Tourism Management*, 7(3): pp. 154–67.

Haywood, K. M., 1987, 'Service management concepts: implications for hospitality management', *FIU Hospitality Review*, 5(2): pp. 43–60.

Haywood, K. M., 1988, 'Repeat patronage: cultivating alliances with customers', *International Journal of Hospitality Management*.

Haywood, K. M., 1989, 'Managing word of mouth communications', *Journal of Service Marketing*, forthcoming.

Haywood, K. M., 1990, 'Revising and implementing the marketing concept as it applies to tourism', *Tourism Management*, forthcoming.

Heskett, J. L., 1986, *Managing in the Service Economy*, Harvard Business School Press, Boston.

Hess, T., Voink, T., 1986, 'The uncommitted tourist', *Proceedings of the Esomar Congress*, Monte Carlo, pp. 69–84.

Hirschman, E., 1985, 'Marketing as an agent of change in subsistence cultures: some dysfunctional consumption consequences', in Lutz, R. J. (ed.), *Advances in Consumer Research*, Vol. 13, Association for Consumer Research, Provo, Utah, pp. 99–104.

Hodgson, A. (ed.), 1987, *The Travel and Tourism Industry: Strategies for the Future*, Pergamon Press, Oxford.

Howard, D. R., Crompton, J. L., 1986, *Financing, Managing and Marketing Recreation and Park Resources*, William C. Brown Publishers, Dubuque, Iowa.

Howard, D. R., 1985, 'An analysis of market potential for public leisure services', *Journal of Park and Recreation Management*, 3(1): pp. 33–40.

Hunt, J. D., 1975, 'Image as a factor in tourism development', *Journal of Travel Research*, 13(3): pp. 1–7.

Hunt, S.D., 1975, 'The nature and scope of marketing', *Journal of Marketing*, 40, July, pp. 17–28.

Husbands, W. C., 1983, 'Tourist space and tourist attraction: an analysis of the destination choices of European travellers', *Leisure Sciences*, 5(4): pp. 289–307.

Jansen-Verbeke, M., 1988, *Leisure, Recreation and Tourism in Inner Cities: Explorative Case Studies*, Nijmegen, Amsterdam.

Jansen-Verbeke, M., Dietvorst, A., 1987, 'Leisure, recreation and tourism—a geographic view on integration', *Annals of Tourism Research*, 14, pp. 361–75.

Jefferson, A., Lickorish, L., 1988, *Marketing Tourism—A Practical Guide*, Longman, Harlow.

Jeffrey, D., Hubbard, N., 1986, 'Weekly occupancy fluctuations in Yorkshire and Humberside hotels, 1980–1984: patterns and prescriptions', *International Journal of Hospitality Management*, 5(4): p. 177.

Jones, P., 1988, 'Quality, capacity and productivity in service industries', *International Journal of Hospitality Management*, (7) and (2): pp. 104–12.
Joseph, W. B. *et al.* (eds), 1986, *Tourism Services Marketing: Advances in Theory and Practice*, Special Conference Series, Volume 2, Cleveland State University, Cleveland, Ohio.
June, L., Smith, S. L. J., 1987, 'Service attributes and situational effects on customer preferences for restaurant dining', *Journal of Travel Research*, 26(2): pp. 20–7.
Kale, S. H. *et al.*, 1987, 'Marketing overseas tour packages to the youth segment', *Journal of Travel Research*, 25(4): pp. 20–4.
Kaynak, E., 1985, 'Developing marketing strategy for a resource-based industry', *Tourism Management*, 6(3): pp. 184–93.
Kent, W. E. *et al.*, 1987, 'Reassessing wholesaler marketing strategies: the role of travel research', *Journal of Travel Research*, 25(3): pp. 31–3.
King, C. A., 1984, 'Service-oriented quality control', *Cornell HRA Quarterly*, November, pp. 92–8.
Kotas, R. (ed.), 1975, *Market Orientation in the Hotel and Catering Industry*, Surrey University Press, London.
Kotler, P., 1980, *Marketing Management: Analysis, Planning and Control*, Prentice Hall, Englewood Cliffs, New Jersey.
Kotler, P., 1987, 'Humanistic marketing: beyond the marketing concept', in Firat, A. F. *et al.* (eds), *Philosophical and Radical Thought in Marketing*, Lexington Books, Lexington, Massachusetts, pp. 271–88.
Kotler, P., Levy, S. J., 1969, 'Broadening the concept of marketing', *Journal of Marketing*, 33(1): pp. 10–15.
Kotschevar, L. H., 1975, *Management by Menu*, National Institute for the Foodservice Industry, Chicago.
Kreul, L. M., 1982, 'Magic numbers: psychological aspects of menu pricing', *Cornell HRA Quarterly*, August, pp. 70–5.
Krippendorf, Jost, 1987, *The Holiday Makers—Understanding the Impact of Leisure and Travel*, Heinemann, Oxford.
Laine, S., Laine, I., 1972, *Promotion in Foodservice*, McGraw-Hill, New York.
Lefever, M., Morrison, A., 1988, 'Couponing for profit', *Cornell HRA Quarterly*, February, pp. 57–63.
Lehtinen, J. R., 1986, *Quality Oriented Services Marketing*, University of Tampere, Finland.
Leven, M. A., 1985, 'Hotel life cycle', *Cornell HRA Quarterly*, February, 1985, p. 10.
Levitt, T., 1972, 'The production line approach to service', *Harvard Business Review*, Sept–Oct., pp. 41–52.
Lew, A. A., 1987, 'A framework of tourist attraction research', *Annals of Tourism Research*, 14: pp. 553–75.
Lewis, R. C., 1980, 'Benefit segmentation for restaurant advertising', *Cornell HRA Quarterly*, November, pp. 6–12.
Lewis, R. C., 1981, 'Restaurant advertising: appeals and consumers' intentions', *Journal of Advertising Research*, 21(5): pp. 69–74.
Lewis, R. C., 1982, 'Positioning analysis for hospitality firms', *International Journal of Hospitality Management*, Fall, pp. 115–18
Lewis, R. C., 1983, 'When guests complain', *Cornell HRA Quarterly*, August, pp. 23–32.
Lewis, R. C., 1984, 'Theoretical and practical considerations in research design', *Cornell HRA Quarterly*, February, pp. 25–35.

Lewis, R. C., 1984, 'Isolating differences in hotel attributes', *Cornell HRA Quarterly*, November, pp. 64–77.

Lewis, R. C., 1984, 'The basis of hotel selection', *Cornell HRA Quarterly*, May, pp. 54–69.

Lewis, R. C., 1985, 'The market position: mapping guests' perceptions of hotel operations', *Cornell HRA Quarterly*, August, p. 86.

Lewis, R. C., 1986, 'Customer-based hotel pricing: many of the hotel industry's pricing policies run counter to economic wisdom and market realities', *Cornell HRA Quarterly*, August, p. 18.

Lewis, R. C., 1987, 'The measurement of gaps in the quality of hotel services', *International Journal of Hospitality Management*, 6(2): pp. 83–8.

Lewis, R. C. *et al.* (eds), 1984, *The Practice of Hospitality Management II*, World Hospitality Conference, AVI Publishing, Westport, Connecticut.

Lewis, R. C., Chambers, R. E., 1989, *Marketing Leadership in Hospitality—Foundation and Practices*, Van Nostrand Reinhold, New York.

Lewis, R. C., Klein, D. M., 1985, 'Personal constructs: their use in marketing of intangible services', *Psychology and Marketing*, 2(3): pp. 201–16.

Lewis, R. C., Morris, S. V., 1987, 'The positive side of guest complaints', *Cornell HRA Quarterly*, February, pp. 13–15.

Lewis, R. C., Roan, C., 1986, 'Selling what you promote', *Cornell HRA Quarterly*, May, pp. 13–15.

Lickorish, L. J., 1972, 'Forecasting in tourism', *The Tourist Review*, 27(1): pp. 28–30.

Lockwood, A., Jones, P., 1989, 'Creating positive service encounters', *Cornell HRA Quarterly*, February, pp. 44–50.

Lovelock, C. H., 1988, *Managing Services—Marketing, Operations and Human Resources*, Prentice Hall, Englewood Cliffs, New Jersey.

Louviere, J. J., Woodsworth, G., 1983, 'Design and analysis of simulated consumer choice or allocation experiments', *Journal of Marketing Research*, 20(4): pp. 350–67.

Mackay, K. J., Crompton, J. L., 1988, 'A conception model of consumer evaluation of recreation service quality', *Leisure Studies*, 7(1): pp. 41–9.

Mahoney, E. M., Warnell, G. R., 1986, *Tourism Marketing*, Extension Bulletin, Co-operative Extension Service, Michigan State University.

Maister, D. H., Lovelock, C. H., 1982, 'Managing facilitator services', *Sloan Management Review*, summer, pp. 19–31.

Makens, J. C., 1987, 'The importance of US historic sites as visitor attractions', *Journal of Travel Research*, 25(3): pp. 8–12.

Mathieson, A., Wall, G., 1982, *Tourism—Economic, Physical and Social Impacts*, Longman, London.

Mazanec, J. A., 1986, 'Allocating an advertising budget to international travel markets', *Annals of Tourism Research*, 14(4): pp. 609–34.

McCleary, K. W., 1987, 'A framework for national tourism marketing', *International Journal of Hospitality Management*, 6(3): pp. 169–75.

McCleary, K. W., 1987, 'Marketing the United States to foreign tourists: America's greatest challenge', *Hospitality Education and Research Journal*, 11(2): pp. 223–31.

McDougall, G. H. G., 1986, 'Products and services: some insights into consumer decision making', *ASAC Conference*, Whistler, British Columbia, pp. 212–21.

Mcguire, F. *et al.*, 1988, 'Attracting the older traveller', *Tourism Management*, 9(2): pp. 161–4.

McNaughton, R. W., 1981, 'How to develop a positioning strategy on a small restaurant's budget', *Cornell HRA Quarterly*, February, pp. 10–14.

McNulty, R., Penne, L., 1984, *Economics of Amenity*, Partners for Livable Places, Washington, D.C.

McQueen, I., Miller, K. E., 1985, 'Target market selection of tourists: a comparison of approaches', *Journal of Travel Research*, 24(1): pp. 2–6.

Mercer, J. A. T., 1985, 'Product life cycles of the windsurfer market', *European Journal of Marketing*, 19(4): pp. 13–22.

Merlo, L., 1985, 'Marketing adaptation to the changing trends in tourist behaviour', in *Trends of Tourism Demand*, 35, the AIEST Conference, pp. 103–7.

Meryer, R. J., 1981, 'A model of multiattribute judgements under attribute uncertainty and informational constraint', *Journal of Marketing Research*, 28(4): pp. 428–41.

Miller, J., 1987, *Menu Pricing and Strategy*, second edition, Van Nostrand, New York.

Mill, R. C., Morrison, A. M., 1985, *The Tourism System: An Introductory Text*, Prentice Hall, New York.

Mills, P. K., 1986, *Managing Service Industries: Organizational Practices in a Post-industrial Economy*, Balinger Publishing Company, Cambridge, Massachusetts.

Moller, K. E. K. *et al*., 1985, 'Segmenting hotel business customers: a benefit clustering approach', in Blah, T. *et al*. (eds), *Services Marketing in a Changing Environment*, American Marketing Association, Chicago, pp. 72–6.

Moores, B. (ed.), 1986, *Are They Being Served? Quality Consciousness in Service Industries*, Philip Allan, Oxford.

Morrison, A. M., 1989, *Hospitality and Travel Marketing*, Delmar Publishers Inc., Albany, New York.

Moutinho, L., 1987, 'Consumer behaviour in tourism', *European Journal of Marketing*, 21(10), whole issue.

Murphy, P. E., 1985, *Tourism—A Community Approach*, Methuen, New York.

Nickels, C. M., Snepenger, D. J., 1988, 'Family decision making and tourism behaviour and attitudes', *Journal of Travel Research*, 26(4): pp. 29–37.

Noble, K., Olsen, M., 1986, 'Foodservice industry environment: market volatility analysis', *FIU Hospitality Review*, Fall 1989.

Nord, D. C., 1986, 'Canada perceived: the impact of Canadian tourism advertising in the United States', *Journal of American Culture*, 9(1): pp. 23–30.

Normann, R., 1984, *Service Management: Strategy and Leadership in Service Businesses*, John Wiley and Sons, Chichester.

NTA (National Tour Association), 1987, *Partners in Profit: An Introduction to Group Travel Marketing*, Lexington, Kentucky.

Nykiel, R. A., 1983, *Marketing in the Hospitality Industry*, CBI Publishing, Boston.

Orenstein, E., Nunn, A., 1980, *The Marketing of Leisure*, Associated Business Press, London.

Patten, S. G., 1986, 'Factory outlets and travel industry development: the case of Reading, Pennsylvania', *Journal of Travel Research*, 25(1): pp. 10–17.

Pearce, J. A., Robinson, R. B., 1982, *Strategic Management: Strategy Formulation and Implementation*, Richard D. Irwin, Homewood, Ill.

Pearce, P., 1980, 'A favorability–satisfaction model of tourists' evaluations', *Journal of Travel Research*, 19(1): pp. 13–17.

Phelps, A., 1986, 'Holiday destination image—the problem of assessment. An example developed in Menorca', *Tourism Management*, 7(3): pp. 163–80.

Pickens, C. W., Shanklin, C. W., 1985, 'State of the art in marketing hospital food-service departments', *Journal of the American Dietetic Association*, 85(11): pp. 1474–8.

Pickworth, J., Pickworth, B. 1984, *An Annotated Bibliography of Food Service Articles in the Journal of American Dietetic Association from 1965–1983*, American Dietetic Association, Chicago.

Pickworth, J., 1988, 'Service delivery systems in the food service industry', *International Journal of Hospitality Management*, 7(1): pp. 43–62.

Pillsbury, R., 1987, 'From hamburger alley to hedgerose heights: toward a model of restaurant location dynamics', *The Canadian Geographer*, 39(3): pp. 326–44.

Pizam, A. *et al.*, 1978, 'Dimensions of tourist satisfaction with a destination area', *Journal of Tourism Research*, 5(3): pp. 314–22.

Pritchard, G., 1982, 'Tourism promotion: big business for the States', *Cornell HRA Quarterly*, 23(2): pp. 48–52.

Ragheb, M., Beard, J., 1979, 'Leisure satisfaction: concept, theory and measurement', in Iso-Ahola, S., *Social Psychology Perspectives in Leisure and Recreation*, Charles C. Thomas Co., Springfield, Ill.

Rao, C. P., Ovmlil, A. B., 1988, 'Some critical distribution problems in services marketing', *International Conference on Services Marketing*, Vol. 5, Cleveland State University, Cleveland, Ohio.

Rathmell, J. M., 1974, *Marketing in the Service Sector*, Winthrop Publishers, Cambridge, Massachusetts.

Regan, C., 1987, 'Promoting nutrition in commercial foodservice establishments: a realistic approach', *Journal of the American Dietetic Association*, 87(4): pp. 486–8.

Reid, R. D., 1983, *Foodservice and Restaurant Marketing*, CBI Publishing, Boston.

Reilley, R. T., 1980, *Travel and Tourism, Marketing Techniques*, Merton House Publishing, Wheaton, Ill.

Renaghan, L. M., 1981, 'New marketing mix for the hospitality industry', *Cornell HRA Quarterly*, August, pp. 30–5.

Renaghan, L. M., Kaye, M., 1987, 'What meeting planners want: the conjoint analysis approach', *Cornell HRA Quarterly*, May, pp. 67–76.

Riley, C., 1983, 'The contribution of research to new product development in package tour operating', in *Seminar on the Importance of Research in the Tourism Industry*, Esomar, pp. 135–47.

Ritchie, J. R. B., Goeldner, C. R., 1987, *Travel Tourism and Hospitality Research: A Handbook for Managers and Researchers*, Wiley, New York.

Ritchie, J. R. B., 1987, 'Tourism marketing and the quality-of-life', in Samli, A. C. (ed.), *Marketing and the Quality-of-Life Interface*, Quorum Books, New York.

Ritchie, J. R. B., 1988, 'Consensus policy in tourism: measuring residence views via survey research', *Tourism Management*, 9(3): pp. 119–22.

Ritchie, J. R. B., Sheridan, M., 1988, 'Developing an integrated framework for tourism demand data in Canada', *Journal of Travel Research*, 27(1): pp. 3–9.

Ritchie, J. R. B., Zins, M., 1978, 'Culture as determinant of the attractiveness of a region', *Annals of Tourism Research*, 5(2): pp. 252–67.

Rovelstad, J. M., Blazer, S. R., 1983, 'Research and strategic marketing in tourism: a status report', *Journal of Travel Research*, 22(2): pp. 2–7.

Sasser, W. E., Morgan, I. P., 1977, 'The Bermuda Triangle of food service chains', *Cornell HRA Quarterly*, February, pp. 56–61.

Sasser, W. E., Olsen, R. P., Wyckoff, P. D., 1978, *Management of Service Operations: Text, Cases and Readings*, Allyn and Bacon, Boston.

Schmidhauser, H. P., 1962, *Marketforschung im Fremdenverkehrsverband*, Lang, Bern.

Schmoll, G. A., 1977, *Tourism Promotion*, Tourism International Press, London.

Seaburg, A. G., 1973, *Menu Design, Merchandising and Marketing*, second edition, CBI Publishing, Boston.

Semenik, R. J., 1985, 'State of the Art of Arts Marketing', in *Advances in Non-Profit Marketing*, Vol. 1.

Shames, G. W., Glover, G., 1989, *World Class Service*, Intercultural Press, Yarmouth, Maine.

Shanklin, C. W. *et al.*, 1987, 'Marketing in school food service—bibliography', *School Food Service Research Review*, 11(2): pp. 120–6.

Sheldon, P. J., Mak, J., 1987, 'The demand for package tours: a mode choice model', *Journal of Travel Research*, 24(4): pp. 2–11.

Shoemaker, S., 1984, 'Marketing to older travellers', *Cornell HRA Quarterly*, September, pp. 84–91.

Shostack, L., 1977, 'Breaking free from product marketing', *Journal of Travel Marketing*, 41(4): pp. 75–80.

Shostack, L., 1987, 'Service positioning through structural change', *Journal of Marketing*, January, pp. 34–43.

Silberman, J., Klock, M., 1986, 'An alternative to conversion studies for measuring the impact of travel ads', *Journal of Travel Research*, 24(2): pp. 12–16.

Smith, S. L. G., 1983, *Recreation Geography*, Longman, London.

Smith, S. L. G., 1985, 'Location patterns of urban restaurants', *Annals of Tourism Research*, 12(4): pp. 581–602.

Smith, S. L. G., 1986, 'Population threshold and capacity in the tourism and hospitality industry: analysis of specialty urban restaurants', *Journal of Travel Research*, 24, spring, p. 29.

Smith, S. L. G., 1989, *Tourism Analysis—A Handbook*, Longman, Harlow.

Snepenger, D. J., 1987, 'Segmenting the vacation market by novelty-seeking role', *Journal of Travel Research*, 26(2): pp. 8–14.

Squire, S. J., 1988, 'Wordsworth and Lake District tourism: romantic reshaping of landscape', *The Canadian Geographer*, 32(3): pp. 237–47.

Stein, B., 1971, *Marketing in Action for Hotels, Motels and Restaurants*, Ahrens Publishing, New York.

Stough, R. R., Feldman, M., 1982, 'Tourism attraction development modelling: public sector policy and management case', *Review of Regional Studies*, 12(3).

Stringer, P. F., 1981, 'Hosts and guests: the bed-and-breakfast phenomenon', *Annals of Tourism Research*, 8(3): pp. 357–76.

Summer, J. R., 1982, *Improve Your Marketing Techniques: A Guide for Hotel Managers and Caterers*, Northwood Publications, Sussex, U.K.

Swan, J. E. *et al.*, 1981, 'Effect of participation in marketing research on consumer attitudes toward research and satisfaction with a service', *Journal of Marketing Research*, 28(3): pp. 356–63.

Swinyard, W., 1977, 'A research approach to restaurant marketing', *Cornell HRA Quarterly*, February, pp. 62–5.

Swinyard, W. R., Struman, K. D., 1986, 'Market segmentation: finding the heart of your restaurants market', *Cornell HRA Quarterly*, May, pp. 89–96.

Taylor, D., 1981, *How to Sell Banquets—the Key to Conference and Function Promotion*, second edition, CBI Publishing, Boston.

Thomas, D., 1978, 'Strategy is different in service businesses', *Harvard Business Review*, July–August, pp. 58–65.

Thurot, J. M., Thurot, G., 1983, 'The ideology of class and tourism: confronting the discourse of advertising', *Annals of Tourism Research*, 10(1): pp. 173–89.

Tighe, A. S., 1985, 'Cultural tourism in the USA', *Tourism Management*, Winter, pp. 235–51.

Tinsley, H., Kass, R. A., 1977, 'Leisure activities and need satisfaction', *Journal of Leisure Research*, 9, pp. 110–20.

Uysal, M., Crompton, J. L., 1985, 'An overview of approaches used to forecast tourist demand', *Journal of Travel Research*, 23(4): pp. 7–15.

Uysal, N., 1986, 'Marketing for tourism—a growing field', *Parks and Recreation, USA*, 21(10): pp. 57–61.

Uzzell, D., 1984, 'An alternative structuralist approach to the psychology of tourism marketing', *Annals of Tourism Research*, 11(1), pp. 79–99.

Var, T. *et al.*, 1977, 'Determination of touristic attractiveness of the touristic areas in British Columbia', *Journal of Travel Research*, 15(3): pp. 23–9.

Wahab, S., 1976, *Tourism Marketing—A Destination Oriented Programme for the Marketing of International Tourism*, Tourism International Press, London.

Wall, G. *et al.*, 1985, 'Point pattern analyses of accommodation in Toronto', *Annals of Tourism Research*, 12(4): pp. 603–18.

Weaver, P. A., McCleary, K. W., 1984, 'A market segmentation study to determine the appropriate and/model format for travel advertising', *Journal of Travel Research*, 23(1): pp. 12–16.

Wee, C. H. *et al.*, 1986, 'Temporal and regional differences in image of a tourist destination: implications for promoters of tourism', *Service Industries Journal*, 6(1): pp. 104–44.

Welch, J. L., 1985, 'Focus groups for restaurant research', *Cornell HRA Quarterly*, August, pp. 75–85.

Wilson, I., 1988, 'Competitive strategies for service business', *Long Range Planning*, 21(6): pp. 10–12.

Wilensky, L., Buttle, F., 1988, 'A multivariate analysis of hotel benefit bundles and choice trade-offs', *International Journal of Hospitality Management*, 7(1): pp. 29–41.

Withiam, G., 1985, 'Hotel companies aim for multiple markets: the current proliferation of brand names to an effort by hotels to become', *Cornell HRA Quarterly*, November, p. 39.

Witt, S. F., Martin, C. A., 1987, 'Econometric models for forecasting international tourism demand', *Journal of Travel Research*, 25(3): pp. 23–30.

Witt, S. F., Moutinho, L., 1989, *Tourism Marketing and Management Handbook*, Prentice Hall, New York.

Wolf, S., Latane, B., 1983, 'Majority and minority influence on restaurant preferences', *Journal of Personality and Social Psychology*, 45(2): pp. 282–92.

Woodside, A. G., 1984, 'How serious is non-response bias in advertising conversion research?', *Journal of Travel Research*, 22(4): pp. 34–7.

Woodside, A. G., Jacobs, L. W., 1985, 'Step two in benefit segmentation: learning the benefits realized by major travel markets', *Journal of Travel Research*, 24(1): pp. 7–13.

Woodside, A. G., Jeffrey, A., 1988, 'Consumer decision making and competitive marketing strategies: applications for tourism planning', *Journal of Travel Research*, 26(3): pp. 2–7.

Woodside, A. G., Motes, W. H., 1981, 'Sensitivity of market segments to separate advertising strategies', *Journal of Marketing*, 16(1): pp. 63–73.

Woodside, A. G., Sherrell, D., 1977, 'Traveller evoked, inept and inert sets of vacation destinations', *Journal of Travel Research*, 16(1): pp. 14–18.

Woodside, A. G. *et al.*, 1987, 'Profiling the heavy traveller segment', *Journal of Travel Research*, 25(4): pp. 9–14.

Wyckoff, D. D., Sasser, W. E., 1978, *The Chain-Restaurant Industry*, 2, Lexington Books, Lexington, Massachusetts.

Yesawich, P. C., 1977, 'Know your prime prospects: marketing research for the lodging industry', *Cornell HRA Quarterly*, February, pp. 11–16.

Yesawich, P. C., 1978, 'Post-opening marketing analysis for hotels', *Cornell HRA Quarterly*, November, pp. 70–81.

Yesawich, P. C., 1979, 'The execution and measurement of a marketing program', *Cornell HRA Quarterly*, May, pp. 41–52.

Yesawich, P. C., 1980, 'Marketing in the 1980s', *Cornell HRA Quarterly*, February, pp. 35–8.

Yesawich, P. C., 1981, 'Marketing in an inflationary economy', *Cornell HRA Quarterly*, February, pp. 35–8.

Yesawich, P. C., 1984, 'A market-based approach to forecasting', *Cornell HRA Quarterly*, November, pp. 47–53.

Yesawich, P. C., 1987, 'Hospitality marketing for the 90s: effective marketing research', *Cornell HRA Quarterly*, May, pp. 48–57.

Yesawich, P. C., 1988, 'Planning: the second step in market development', *Cornell HRA Quarterly*, February, pp. 71–81.

10 Managers in hospitality: a review of current research

Y. Guerrier and A. Lockwood

Introduction

'Management makes a difference . . . and it can be developed', writes Charles Handy (NEDO, 1987). He claims, based on research in West Germany, the USA, France, Japan and the UK, that corporations in all these countries share the view that what managers do is important, that some managers are more effective than others and that it is possible to learn to become a better manager. There is now a body of research data stretching back over 30 years which addresses the questions of what managers do, who managers are, how management styles vary, how managers learn management skills and how effective managers may be distinguished from ineffective managers. However, with the exception of some key studies (Whyte, 1948; Bowey, 1976; Shamir, 1978; Mars and Nicod, 1984; Gabriel, 1988), there are few references in the general management literature to problems of management and organization in the hospitality industry. Most of the research which relates to this industry has been conducted by people who are specifically involved in teaching vocational courses in hospitality management and is published in specialized journals such as the *International Journal of Hospitality Management* and the *Cornell Hotel and Restaurant Administration Quarterly*.

Recently, however, writers in the specialized journals have placed less emphasis on the uniqueness of the hospitality industry and more on the way in which ideas drawn from general management theory may be applied to this industry (see, for example, Mullins, 1988). At the same time, management researchers and developers based in business schools and general management departments are showing increasing interest in management within the service sector and there are a growing number of publications focused in this area (for example, Jones, 1989; Moores, 1986; Fitzsimmons and Sullivan, 1982; Voss *et al.*, 1985). As hospitality companies such as Trusthouse Forte (THF), Grand Metropolitan and Accor and Marriott continue to expand both in the diversity of their product range and in the scope of their international interests, so their needs will be less focused on the specific technical content of hospitality operations and more on professional general management skills and techniques. If research on hospitality management is to be useful to such companies it needs to be conducted with the same rigour as research in the general management field and needs to take account of the latest developments and ideas.

In the next section, current themes in general management research will be reviewed. Then an attempt will be made to relate recent research studies on management in the hospitality sector to these themes, identifying possible avenues for future research.

Themes in management research

In the 1960s and 1970s, academic notions about the nature of managerial work evolved as a result of a series of studies into what managers actually do as against what was the ideal image of managerial work. The best-known study in this area was that of Henry Mintzberg (1973) who, based on intensive research on a small number of chief executives, emphasized the fragmented and reactive nature of managerial work. Mintzberg's managers, coping with frequent interruptions, making quick decisions in response to events and seeking out contacts with a wide range of people, seemed a world away from the typical image of the manager, associated with classical theorists such as Fayol (1949). Fayol's manager was a man who sat in his office planning, organizing and directing. However, Mintzberg and Fayol had in common a belief that managerial work could be reduced to a general set of definitive characteristics.

Hales (1986), in an article reviewing some 20 years of research into the nature of managerial work, concludes that there are few useful generalizations that can be made about what managers do. 'Managerial jobs seem, in general,' he claims, 'to be sufficiently loosely defined to be susceptible to choice in both style and content.' Part of a manager's job, therefore, is to define his or her role and to decide how to allocate tasks and responsibilities to others. Managers inevitably have to respond to conflicting pressures and expectations, so an important part of management work is about compromise and negotiation and *keeping things going*. Much of what managers do is also, necessarily, about reacting to events, thinking on one's feet and *doing* rather than *thinking*. However, beyond this, Hales chooses to emphasize the variety and diversity in managerial jobs and argues that 'managerial work is contingent upon *inter alia*: function, level, organization (type, structure and size) and environment' (including cultural context).

Hales also points out that the analysis of what managers actually do is only one part of the study of managerial work. What managers actually do may or may not be the same as what managers think they do. Studies based on managers' own reports of their work may tell more about managers' beliefs and myths about their work than about the nature of the work itself (although these beliefs and myths may form part of the process of defining the work). And what managers actually do may or may not be the same as what they ought to do, however that may be defined.

What managers do is likely to be influenced by who they are. An alternative approach to the study of management work is to focus on the managers themselves and to ask the following questions: 'Who becomes a manager and why?'

'What is known about the educational and class background of managers?'
'What types of families do managers come from?' 'What types of qualification
improve the chances of managerial success?' 'How much of an advantage is it to
be male rather than female and are the backgrounds and qualifications of
female managers markedly different from those of their male counterparts?'
'What type of marriage and family arrangements do managers have?'

A number of studies have attempted to answer these questions (for example,
Melrose-Woodman, 1978; Alban-Metcalfe and Nicholson, 1984; Lee, 1981;
Whitley, *et al.*, 1981; Cox and Cooper, 1988), and they demonstrate how
management success can be influenced by factors which may have little connection with the skills and style of managers themselves. However, management success is presumably also influenced by the personal qualities of the
manager, and other studies have attempted to answer the question of who
managers are by examining the personalities and personal values of managers
(England, 1975; Cox and Cooper, 1988). Personal values are, of course, influenced by the manager's background and up-bringing. Recent cross-cultural
studies of managers have emphasized just how different the values and beliefs
of Hong Kong Chinese managers may be from those of British managers, of
French managers from American managers, of Japanese managers from
German managers (Hofstede, 1984; England, 1975; Laurent, 1986; Fukada,
1988).

Research into the nature of management work has been dominated by the
Americans, supplemented by contributions from the British and other
Europeans. However, there are tremendous variations not only in management
values from country to country but also in the route to becoming a manager.
Only 24% of British top managers have degrees compared with 85% of top
managers in Japan and the USA (NEDO, 1987). A qualification in accountancy
is seen to benefit the British top manager, while his West German counterpart
is more likely to possess a doctorate in engineering, science or law. A *social-effect*
viewpoint would argue that the process through which a country selects or
trains its managers would be one factor affecting the success of specific
industries in that country; for example, that British managers are particularly
well suited to run large-batch and mass or process production operations while
the German style of management is better set to pursue differentiated quality
and craft production (Maurice *et al.*, 1980).

How managers manage, then, is influenced by their background, their
education and their personal values. However, much of what a manager knows
and does is organization-specific and learnt *on-the-job* (Whitley, 1989). It
seems likely, therefore, that the types of jobs managers have experienced—their
career development—will affect their approach to their work. Patterns of job
change may be influenced by societal trends and cultural values. For example,
studies of British managers over the last 30 years have shown increasing rates
of employer changes (Guerrier and Philpot, 1978; Nicholson and West, 1988).

However, organizational needs also affect career paths. Gunz (1989)
proposes that organizations have different career logics, depending on the

firm's structure and growth patterns. A service sector company, such as a retail or restaurant chain, made up of a large number of similar units, would, according to Gunz, have a *command-centred career logic*, in which managers develop by moving from 'command' to ever bigger 'command'. The type of management skills developed through this type of progression would be different to the skills and approach developed in a company with a *constructional career logic*, where managers make a series of complex movements across a firm aiming to get as broad a background as possible without getting *trapped* in any one function or product area.

Common sense tells us that some managers are better at managerial work than others, but what do *effective* managers do which is different from what *ineffective* managers do? Hales (1986) defines effectiveness as the match between what a manager is expected to do and what he or she actually does; a manager is effective to the extent to which he or she manages to satisfy possibly conflicting expectations. However, this begs the qustion of how *good* are the expectations. A manager may be very successful in organizational terms because he is behaving exactly as expected, but if the organization fails and a contributor to that failure is the way in which managerial work has been defined, can he really be said to have been effective?

The issue of what an effective manager is and does is clearly a complex one. It is also a crucial issue for practitioners concerned about improving the performance of organizations as opposed to researchers interested in the academic study of managerial work. Therefore, it is not surprising if approaches which aim to *scientifically* assess the work performance of individual managers generate considerable interest. The notion of management *competencies* is currently popular and has provided a basis for the development of methods of assessment and development of managers in many large companies (Jackson, 1989; Greatrex and Phillips, 1989). In the UK , with the Management Charter Initiative, there have been attempts to develop a set of transferable and general management competencies which can form the basis of an initial chartered management qualification (Day, 1988; Hornby and Thomas, 1989). However, this approach has its critics (Jacobs, 1989). Can one really produce a list of things that the effective manager does, any more than one can produce a list of things which managers actually do? By breaking down a manager's skills into their component parts, do we lose sight of the whole person?

In this section, a number of themes have been developed through a review of recent research into managers and management. Broadly, researchers have attempted to answer the following four questions: 'What do managers do?' 'Who are managers?' 'How are managers' careers developed?' 'What is meant by managerial effectiveness?' The following sections will review the research which has been conducted into hospitality management and managers in each of these areas.

What do hospitality managers do?

A number of studies have attempted to examine the activities of hospitality managers using the approaches to activity analysis pioneered by Carlson (1951), Horne and Lupton (1965), Stewart (1967) and Mintzberg (1973). The earliest study, conducted by Nailon (1968), was intended to test out a self-completion questionnaire which could be used as a tool in the analysis of hospitality managers' work. As the focus was on the methodology, the sample size was restricted to three general managers within a single chain of hotels. The results indicated an even greater fragmentation of the working day than previous studies of managers in other sectors. Hotel managers were also more heavily involved with the external environment, in particular with customers, than with their own staff. They monitored the hotel's performance through fleeting contact and frequent movement about the establishment.

An alternative approach was adopted by Ley (1978, 1980). His work, based on detailed observation of seven general managers (GMs) in medium-sized hotels in the US, each belonging to the same chain, attempted to relate Mintzberg's managerial roles to the hotel industry. Ley was also interested in management effectiveness and whether the GMs who were rated as the most effective by their Head Office emphasized different roles and structured their time in different ways to those GMs who were rated as less effective. His major finding was that those managers judged more effective allocated relatively more time to the *entrepreneurial* role. All managers saw the *leadership* role as important, but there was no clear-cut relationship between the time devoted to the leadership role and manager effectiveness. However, the managers who worked the longest hours were those who were rated most effective by Head Office. This raised questions about the validity of Head Office effectiveness ratings. Ley (1978) comments that 'innkeepers would remain close to their office until 6 pm, which is 5pm Head office time'. This was in spite of the fact that little, if any, work of consequence was conducted during this additional hour. Innkeepers joked about it, but apparently felt that they 'should be there in case a call came in from head office'.

Ferguson and Berger's (1984) study of restaurant managers also raised questions about how what managers actually do is related to what they should do. Once again, this study drew heavily on Mintzberg and, as with Ley's work, was based on detailed observation of the work activities of a small number (nine) of restaurant owner/managers and managers in the US. In retrospect, Ferguson and Berger felt that Mintzberg's classification system had confined their thinking and had not been particularly appropriate to this type of management work.

For restaurant managers, they wrote, 'planning seems to have been eclipsed by reacting; organizing might be better described as carrying on; co-ordinating appears more like juggling; and controlling seems reduced to full-time watching' (Ferguson and Berger, 1984). There was little evidence that managers spent time on systematic forward planning, monitoring or controlling although, as the researchers point out, the observation method is not able to identify thinking time spent in solitary away from the business. Once at work, the managers constantly worked in an *interrupt mode*, with fewer and shorter desk sessions than managers in Mintzberg's study but making many more contacts with others (an average of ten or eleven contacts each hour). As with Nailon's managers, they monitored the performance of the restaurant by watching and being around and, in many cases, slipped into the role of operations supervisor by default. Although the sample was made up of managers who were judged successful by their peers, the researchers raise questions about whether the managers were really using their time in the most effective way.

Two further studies have made use of the Mintzberg classification based on self-report questionnaires. Arnaldo (1981) surveyed 194 US hotel chain GMs who were asked to classify their duties according to Mintzberg's roles and according to how they allocated their time between them. The most important roles were identified as *leader, monitor, disseminator* and *entrepreneur*. The least important roles were *negotiator, figurehead, spokesman* and *liaison*. Clearly, collecting data by the self-report method may reveal more about managers' beliefs about how they should be spending their time than about how they actually spend their time. Shortt (1989) conducted a similar exercise on 62 general managers of inns in Northern Ireland. They saw their most important roles as *disturbance handler, leader*, and *entrepreneur* and their least important as *figurehead, disseminator* and *negotiator*. His attempts to predict managers' ratings through regression analysis, examining such factors as age, educational background, level and number of employees, proved inconclusive.

Hales (1987), starting from the view that managerial effectiveness may be regarded as the relationship between actual and expected behaviour, emphasizes that managers have to meet a number of possibly conflicting demands from a variety of *role senders*. He argues that 'most studies of managerial work are limited by their exclusive focus upon actual managerial behaviour rather than upon the role prescriptions of the managerial job'. He therefore advocates the use of the *managerial wheel*—a method of examining the role demands made on managers by defining the expectations of each role sender as well as the manager's own perception of his or her role. The main conclusion he draws from his research into six unit management jobs in the hospitality industry is that 'the character of unit management is determined at least as much by the specific nature of what is being managed (i.e. what kind of "unit") as by characteristics of the management process in general'. The role of a hospital catering unit manager, for example, is much more ambiguous, subject to many more conflicting demands and therefore much more political, than that of the unit manager in a family restaurant chain.

With the exception of Hales' work, all the studies discussed above have focused on the analysis of managerial activities, it is perhaps surprising how much use has been made of the Mintzberg classification of management roles. Although Shortt (1989) argues for a replication of this methodology in alternative hospitality settings, the results of the studies that have been conducted are limited because of their almost exclusive emphasis on what managers actually do. The most interesting questions about the nature of management work focus on the relationship between what managers do, what they think they ought to do and why and what they need to do to be effective.

Who hospitality managers are

Any research study concerned with managers in the hospitality industry should start with an attempt to define the population from which a sample can be selected. In an industry composed of a large number of units ranging in size from the very small to the very large, across a wide range of different sectors and a geographical spread covering the whole of a country, this is bound to be difficult. In those countries where there is limited industrial classification and little attempt at registration of units, this is even more complicated.

Ideally, a demographic description of who hospitality managers are would include details of age and sex distribution, educational background and qualifications, national background and place of birth, family background and current family status and some details of previous work experience. This demographic breakdown could then be applied to different levels of management with different levels of responsibility covering the different sectors of the industry and different geographical locations.

These figures would be likely to differ significantly from country to country, if indeed they were available at all. This section will review the statistics available on hospitality managers in the UK in order to identify the approaches adopted and any problems or omissions that arise, allowing readers to make comparisons with their own countries.

In 1978, a survey was conducted to establish certain basic facts about the types of people managing in Britain (Melrose-Woodman, 1978). This survey, which attempted to represent all of the approximately 1,500,000 managers in the UK, was based on a sample of the 10,000 members of the British Institute of Management and had a response rate of around 45% (with 4,525 members returning questionnaires). The comprehensive survey covered most of the areas identified above in order to build a profile of the *average* manager and identify trends for future development. It is unfortunate that no such comprehensive survey has been conducted to cover the estimated 250,000 managers in the hospitality industry in Britain.

In 1976, in order to support its training policies, the UK's Hotel and Catering Industry Training Board (HCITB) undertook a major study of manpower in the industry based on a weighted sample of some 4,206 employers. This study (HCITB, 1978), called Tier 1, provided much-needed estimates of the total number of employees in the industry engaged in full and part-time work, by region and sector. The study also outlines the distribution of establishments by size and by sector and includes a detailed occupational breakdown seg-regated into seven broad classifications, including managers. Although it does not provide substantial detail about managers in the industry, the study offers a firm foundation for further work.

The foundation was developed through work on Tier 2, which was based on a longitudinal study over an eighteen-month period of some 400 to 600 employers (who had been included in the original study, and weighted by the number of establishments in each sector identified in Tier 1. Two major reports on this work were published. The first report (HCITB, 1983) was con-cerned with manpower changes in the industry and provided some additional detail. The workforce profile included length of service, hours of work and qualifications, but was only broken down by industry sector and not by occupa-tional group; an age, sex and nationality distribution was provided by occupa-tional group, but in this case a sector comparison was not included. The main part of the study examined the impact of seasonality, previous employment, length of service, sex, age and qualifications on the pattern of turnover, but again only analysed the results by industry sector. The second report (HCITB, 1984) combined the data on staff turnover with detailed forecasts of industry growth (ETAC/HCITB, 1984) to produce a manpower model which could calculate recruitment needs for the industry up to 1987. In order to achieve this objective, the report examined manager flows into, out of and within each industry sector, combining this with an estimated age structure to predict turn-over patterns and hence recruitment and training needs.

It is disappointing to note that the valuable field research provided by Tier 1 and Tier 2 has not been fully exploited. The latest available information (HCITB, 1985) is based on published data from the population census, the employment census and updates from the employment gazette, all of which lack the detail of the previous work. These provide only estimated numbers of managers in various sectors and a limited breakdown by sex and regional distribution.

Another source of information about managers comes from the professional body of the industry—the Hotel, Catering and Institutional Management Asso-ciation (HCIMA). The HCIMA have conducted an annual salary survey since the late 1970s. As well as looking at salary levels and conditions of employment for managers, originally the questionnaire collected data about length of service in the industry, length of service with present employer and levels of decision-making at different levels of management, analysed by industry sector (see HCIMA, 1980). The present survey, however, now conducted in conjunc-tion with consultants Greene Belfield-Smith, is restricted to a review of salary and benefit levels but includes detailed results analysed by industry sector, location, age, sex and qualifications (Greene Belfield-Smith, 1988).

Some biographical data is available as an adjunct to other studies mentioned in this paper, for example, Arnaldo (1981) and Shortt (1989), but there is remarkably little information about the nationality of hospitality managers. The studies that have provided basic data have concentrated primarily on domestic hotel chains and there is a distinct lack of information about the international hotel chains and about senior-level management. Yet informal observation of the international industry suggests that certain nationalities of manager, especially the Swiss and German, seem to have been unusually successful. Establishing basic international data about the biographies and style of senior management and the factors contributing to their success would seem to be a fruitful area for further research. It is a pity that some studies that have attempted to look at the management style of senior hotel managers (Ruddy's (1988) work on Hong Kong managers, for example) have omitted to include this basic biographical data.

An alternative approach to examining who managers are considers their personality traits. One approach is to ask managers to rate themselves against a series of personality characteristics (Swanljung, 1981; Ruddy, 1988); however, the validity of this method is questionable. A more serious study has been conducted by Worsfold (1989a). Based on a sample of 28 hotel general managers (GMs) working for the same UK hotel chain, he compared the managers' self ratings against their personality profile as measured through Cattell's 16PF test. Compared with the general management norms provided by Cattell (Cattell *et al.*, 1970), the hotel managers were more assertive, more venturesome and imaginative and placed a greater emphasis on 'people' skills and working in groups. Replicating Worsfold's approach, Stone (1988) surveyed 140 UK GMs, 71 from chain hotels and 69 from independents. His results were similar to Worsfold's. He found they were more assertive, more tough-minded and more competitive than Cattell's management sample and also scored significantly lower on the intelligence dimension. However, this dimension is commonly regarded as the most problematic in the test.

As part of the same study, Worsfold (1989b) looked at the leadership style of the general managers using the Fleishman LOQ Leadership Opinion Questionnaire. This measures leadership style on two dimensions—the extent to which a manager develops trusting relationships with subordinates and initiating structure or the extent to which a manager organizes and defines group activities. Worsfold's sample scored relatively high on both factors leading him to define their style as that of benevolent autocrats. It is interesting to compare these results with those of White (1973), who asked staff in hotels to identify their preferred management style by choosing between the autocrat, the persuasive manager, the consultative manager and the participative manager. He also asked them to indicate their perceptions of their current manager's style. His sample was split between those preferring the autocratic style and those preferring the consultative style. However, the majority perceived their bosses' actual style as autocratic. White comments that while older, long-standing staff may like this autocratic style, it may lead to high levels of turnover in younger staff. It is a pity that the article offers no details of the size and composition of the sample.

These studies all seem to point in the same general direction and to confirm some of the established beliefs about how hotel managers manage (Guerrier and Lockwood, 1989b). They also correspond closely with the results from studies about what managers do. However, while Worsfold and Stone would argue that their studies are potentially useful in improving the selection process for hotel managers and potential managers, Guerrier and Lockwood (1989b) argue that the existing style is not necessarily the most appropriate and may have consequences in terms of staff morale, development and retention similar to those highlighted by White more than sixteen years ago. It must be emphasized again that all these studies have focused on the general managers of hotels in the UK domestic market and that research in other sectors of the hospitality industry and on an international basis might show very different results.

One study conducted in a very different setting looks at hoteliers in Ireland (Baum, 1988). Predominantly based in small establishments, these managers emphasize the *mine host* element of their role and have little interest in developing general business management skills. It is interesting that nearly 60% of this sample had no formal hospitality education and had either worked their way up from service positions or moved into hotel management from some other career late in life. This study illustrates the interconnections between who managers are, what they do and how their careers develop. In the next section, the research into careers in hospitality will be reviewed.

Managers' careers in hospitality

Managers' careers can be studied from a number of different perspectives. The subject can be approached through large-scale surveys of the extent and types of mobility both within and between industries (Guerrier and Philpot, 1978; Nicholson and West, 1988). In these types of surveys, general trends in the distribution of inter-industry, inter-firm, intra-firm and geographical moves can be examined. The limitation of the survey method is the difficulty of collecting sufficient detail about managers' moves and the reasons for these moves to allow the patterns and logic of career progression to be clearly identified. Although it is possible to generate data about the frequency and direction of career moves, certain types of job change—for example, where a job expands but the job title remains the same—will not be highlighted.

Small-scale studies based on in-depth interviews of managers can provide insights into the motivation behind career moves and allow a picture of the individual's career logic to emerge. Such studies can either focus on the individual and his career in relation to life-cycle stages (Levinson, 1978; Marshall and Cooper, 1976) or on the organization, attempting to build a picture of the way in which careers work within a particular organization or group of organizations (Sofer, 1970; Gunz, 1989) and the factors that affect the career progression of certain types of managers. An alternative route into the study of careers is through the practice of manpower planning and the design of organizational career structures. The study of internal and external labour markets can also provide insights into career patterns.

An example of a questionnaire-based study in the hospitality industry is provided by Pickworth (1982). His survey of 40 foodservice chains and fourteen hotel companies in North America was concerned with managers occupying thirteen key positions. One of his more interesting conclusions was to distinguish between two categories of managerial positions. Transient jobs were occupied by younger managers and seemed to be seen as stepping stones to more senior posts. Of the managers in the survey under 30 years of age, 84% occupied the posts of assistant general manager, food and beverage manager, front office manager or personnel manager in hotels, or foodservice manager in fast-food operations or restaurants. Permanent career jobs were occupied by older managers and were not seen as providing a route for further advancement. These jobs included general manager, executive housekeeper and executive chef in hotels and foodservice managers in institutional feeding.

Riley and Turam (1989) approached the study of career paths in the hotel industry from a manpower planning perspective. Their survey of 115 UK hotel managers attempted to identify the length of time taken and the stages of development involved in progressing to the job of hotel general manager. Their results indicate that it takes eight to ten years from age 21 to reach hotel GM status. Typically, the GM will have moved every three years and spent eight years as an assistant or deputy manager, having started in a hotel with more than 200 rooms. The authors found little mobility between sectors or across industries. They also argued that, for the most part, hotel managers took control of their own careers; 60% of their job moves were self-initiated. Another interesting finding was that the job of supervisor or departmental head does not seem to provide a route to more senior positions. These results support the model developed by Guerrier and Lockwood (1989(a)). They distinguish between *company core* staff in hotels, who see their careers developing within the chain, move frequently between different units as they progress and are expected to be skilled in a variety of hotel functions, and *unit core* staff who are anchored to the unit rather than the company.

Guerrier (1987) conducted in-depth interviews with sixteen GMs and regional managers in three UK hotel companies in order to gain an insight into the career paths to general manager. Her results complement the Riley and Turam (1989) survey in confirming that GMs make an early commitment to the hotel industry and then remain within it. She identifies three stages of development: the training stage, which might involve formal study but certainly involves gaining operative experience, particularly in top-class European hotels; followed by the assistant-manager stage, during which there are frequent moves as the manager acquires different types of experience in different locations. Her respondents had usually reached the general manager stage by age 30, starting with a small hotel and progressing to larger, more complex properties and moving approximately every three years. She comments that this traditional route to developing the hotel manager has the effect of anchoring the manager to the occupation and not to an individual company and produces managers who define themselves as hoteliers and not as managers, priding themselves on their craft and guest-relations skills rather than their marketing, management and financial skills. An alternative route emphasizing professional management skills and organizational commitment may be emerging.

Baker (1988), based on a small-scale study of ten female managers in functional or operational positions in eight hotel companies, hypothesizes that hotels may be divided between those with a traditional orientation, where the emphasis is on craft training, especially in food and beverage, and those with a rooms orientation, where it is possible to become a general manager without having food and beverage experience. She argues that hotels with the latter may offer a more favourable career experience for women managers. Guerrier (1986) also explores the way in which the traditional approach to the development of careers in hotels places women at a disadvantage. The HCTB study (HCTB, 1987) provides further evidence that women are pushed into careers in front office, housekeeping, sales and marketing, whereas men are encouraged to concentrate on food and beverage, a function which is currently viewed as central to career success. The same study also shows how women start to fall behind men in the important first two years of employment in the industry. Women are less likely to make rapid progress into the junior management posts that form the first rung of the ladder to GM and more likely to fall into the hole of supervisory and departmental head positions, from which it is difficult to escape.

A substantial amount of data has now been collected concerning career paths in domestic hotel chains, particularly in the UK, but there is still room for further research, especially about the links between career paths and company culture and comparisons between career paths in different organizations. No substantial work has been done regarding companies or careers that cross international boundaries or concerning staff at the senior management and director level. There is also a need for research into other sectors of the hospitality industry.

Identifying hospitality management competencies

Companies and educational establishments needing to make strategic decisions about provisions for the training and development of hospitality managers will find many points of interest in the academic studies described above. However, there is also a need for more specific research into the knowledge and skills that hospitality managers require in order to be effective in their work. As noted above, what managers actually do may not lead to the most effective performance. Once these management competencies have been determined, there is a need to develop appropriate measures to evaluate managerial performance.

The HCIMA, the professional body for hospitality managers in the UK, has devoted considerable time and effort to surveying practising managers on the skills and knowledge they use in their work in order to define the curriculum for their professional examinations (HCIMA, 1974; Johnson, 1977; Jones, 1989; Gamble and Messenger, 1989). While the earlier studies emphasized hospitality-specific technical skills at the expense of general management, the more recent work has highlighted the need for a business and analytical management approach that also takes account of the *soft* functions of management, particularly in relation to dealing with people, both customers and staff. Despite the traditional emphasis on operations, managers in the industry have been more concerned with operating the unit than with applying the operations management techniques that have been successfully used in manufacturing (Martin and Clark, 1989).

This more recent work has also moved away from a view of hospitality management as discrete *bits* of largely technical knowledge towards a more integrated approach which combines competencies in managing activities, managing people, managing the environment and personal skills with an awareness of factors bringing change and an ability to relate these to the specific context in which the manager works (Jones, 1989). In the hospitality industry, educational establishments have shown most interest in developing this approach and there are published studies from a number of countries (Rutherford and Schill, 1984; Tas, 1988; Baum, 1989). However, in other industries, most of the development work has been initiated by the companies themselves. One might expect to see hospitality companies exhibiting a similar interest in the development and assessment of company-specific competencies.

It is clear, then, that the effectiveness of managers cannot be assessed purely by relying upon *hard* financial measures (Kaplan, 1983) and that, especially in service industries, a combination of *hard* and *soft* measures is more appropriate (Fitzgerald, 1988). These would also include some assessment of the service process and customers' expectations and satisfactions. Umbreit's attempts (1986 and 1987) to relate *soft*, behaviourally anchored scales for evaluating managerial performance to *harder* indicators of operational outcomes show how difficult this is to achieve in practice.

Conclusions

In some respects, the research reviewed in this chapter paints a remarkably consistent picture of the hospitality industry. A recurrent theme has been the *traditional* style of operations of the hotel industry. This style is characterized by a high level of activity, a bias towards the practicality of the operation linked to an emphasis on technical and craft skills and a benevolent and autocratic style of staff management. The authors have reviewed the limitations of this style and questioned its appropriateness in the current environment elsewhere (Guerrier and Lockwood, 1989(b)). There does, however, appear to be a slow move towards a business orientation.

Much of the research so far has been focused on a particular sector of the industry. While we may know a lot about domestic hotel operations, especially in the UK and the US, there is still a distinct lack of information about other sectors of the industry and we have not found any studies which make comparisons across international boundaries. There are obvious methodological and practical problems in conducting such research but there are major benefits to be derived in terms of a better understanding of this increasingly globalized industry. This review has also highlighted the lack of very simple and basic data about how many managers there actually are in the industry, where they are based and who they are. Such a database would be of considerable assistance to future researchers.

It is encouraging that researchers into hospitality management are increasingly drawing on the general management literature at the same time that researchers in general management are showing more interest in hospitality—clearly a consequence of the greater interest in service industries in general. Perhaps undue attention has been paid to certain theories and theorists. With the richness of management research available to draw upon, it is hoped that hospitality researchers will continue to broaden the scope of their studies.

References

Alban-Metcalfe, B., Nicholson, N., 1984, *The Career Development of British Managers*, British Institute of Management, London.

Arnaldo, M., 1981, 'Hotel general managers: a profile', *Cornell HRA Quarterly*, November, pp. 53–6.

Baker, S., 1988, 'Hotel management—a disadvantaged profession for women', *Proceedings of International Association of Hotel Management Schools Autumn Symposium*, Leeds Polytechnic.

Baum, T., 1988, 'Toward a new definition of hotel management', *Cornell HRA Quarterly*, October, pp. 36–9.

Baum, T., 1989, 'Managing hotels in Ireland: research and development for change', *International Journal of Hospitality Management*, 8(2): pp. 131–44.

Bowey, A. M., 1976, *The Sociology of Organizations*, Hodder and Stoughton, London.

Carlson, S., 1951, *Executive Behaviour: A Study of the Workload and Working Methods of Managing Directors*, Strombergs, Stockholm.

Cattell, R., Eber, H., Tatsuoka, M., 1970, *Handbook for the 16 Personality Factor Questionnaire (16 PF)*, Institute for Personality and Ability Testing, Ill.

Cox, C. J., Cooper, C. L., 1988, *High Flyers: An Anatomy of Managerial Success*, Basil Blackwell, Oxford.

Day, M., 1988, 'Managerial competence and the charter initiative', *Personnel Management*, August.

England, G. W., 1975, *The Manager and His Values: An International Perspective from the United States, Japan, Korea, India and Australia*, Ballinger, Cambridge, Massachusetts.

ETAC/HCITB, 1984, *Manpower Forecasts for the Hotel and Catering Industry*, Hotel and Catering Industry Training Board, London.

Fayol, H., 1949, *General and Industrial Management* (translated by C. Storrs), Pitman, London.

Ferguson, D., Berger, F., 1984, 'Restaurant managers: what do they really do?', *Cornell HRA Quarterly*, 25(1), May: pp. 27–34.

Fitzgerald, L., 1988, 'Management performance measurement in service industries', in Johnson, R. (ed.), *The Management of Service Operations*, IFS Publications/Springer-Verlag, London.

Fitzsimmons, J., Sullivan, R., 1982, *Service Operations Management*, McGraw-Hill, New York.

Fukada, K. J., 1988, *Japanese-style Management Transferred: The Experience in East Asia*, Routledge, London.

Gabriel, Y., 1988, *Working Lives in Catering*, Routledge & Kegan Paul, London.

Gamble, P., Messenger, S., 1989, *Revised Professional Courses—Consultation with Industry and Education*, HCIMA, London.

Greatrex, J., Phillips, P., 1989, 'Oiling the wheels of competence', *Personnel Management*, August, pp. 36–9.

Greene Belfield-Smith, 1988, *Salaries and Benefits in the Hotel and Catering Industry—1988 Survey*, Touche Ross, London.

Guerrier, Y., 1986, 'Hotel manager: an unsuitable job for a woman?', *Service Industries Journal*, 6(2): pp. 227–40.

Guerrier, Y., 1987, 'Hotel managers' careers and their impact on hotels in Britain', *International Journal of Hospitality Management*, 6(3): pp. 121–30.

Guerrier, Y., Lockwood, A., 1989(a), 'Core and peripheral employees in hotel operations', *Personnel Review*, 18(1): pp. 9–15.

Guerrier, Y., Lockwood, A., 1989(b), 'Developing hotel managers—a reappraisal', *International Journal of Hospitality Management*, 8(2): pp. 82–9.

Guerrier, Y., Philpot, N., 1978, *The British Manager: Careers and Mobility*, British Institute of Management, London.

Gunz, H., 1989, *Careers and Corporate Cultures: Managerial Mobility in Large Corporations*, Basil Blackwell, Oxford.

Hales, C., 1986, 'What do managers do? A critical review of the evidence', *Journal of Management Studies*, 23(1): pp. 88–115.

Hales, C., 1987, 'The manager's work in context: a pilot investigation of the relationship between managerial role demands and role performance', *Personnel Review*, 16(5): pp. 26–33.

Hales, C., Nightingale, M., 1986, 'What are unit managers supposed to do? A contingent methodology for investigating managerial role requirements', *International Journal of Hospitality Management*, 5(1): pp. 3–11.

HCIMA, 1974, *Tomorrow's Managers*, HCIMA, London.

HCIMA, 1980, *Survey of Management Jobs, Salaries and Conditions of Service in Hotels, Catering and Institutional Services*, Hotel, Catering and Institutional Management Association, London.

HCITB, 1978, *Manpower in the Hotel and Catering Industry*, Hotel and Catering Industry Training Board, London.

HCITB, 1983, *Manpower Changes in the Hotel and Catering Industry*, Hotel and Catering Industry Training Board, London.

HCITB, 1984, *Manpower Flows in the Hotel and Catering Industry*, Hotel and Catering Industry Training Board, London.

HCITB, 1985, *Hotel and Catering Manpower in Britain 1984*, Hotel and Catering Industry Training Board, London.

HCTB, 1987, *Women in the Hotel and Catering Industry*, Hotel and Catering Training Board, London.

Hofstede, G., 1984, *Culture's Consequences: International Differences in Work-related Values*, Sage Publications, Beverly Hills, California.

Hornby, D., Thomas, R., 1989, 'Towards a better standard of management', *Personnel Management*, January, pp. 52–5.

Horne, J., Lupton, T., 1965, 'The work activities of middle managers—an exploratory study', *Journal of Management Studies*, Vol. 2, pp. 14–33.

Jackson, L., 1989, 'Turning airport managers into high-fliers', *Personnel Management*, October, pp. 80–92.

Jacobs, R., 1989, 'Getting the measure of management competence', *Personnel Management*, June, pp. 32–7.

Johnson, P., 1977, *The Corpus of Professional Knowledge in Hotel, Catering and Institutional Services*, HCIMA, London.

Jones, P. A., 1989, 'A profile for management development in the hotel and catering industry', *Proceedings of the Launch Conference of the Journal of Contemporary Hospitality Management*, Dorset Institute, Poole.

Jones, P. L. M. (ed.), 1989, *Management in Service Industries*, Pitman, London.

Kaplan, R., 1983, 'Measuring manufacturing performance: a new challenge for accounting research', *Accounting Review*, Vol. 58(4).

Laurent, A., 1986, 'The cross-cultural puzzle of international human resource management', *Human Resource Management*, Spring, 25(1): pp. 91–102.

Lee, G., 1981, *Who Gets to the Top?* Gower, London.

Levinson, D., 1978, *The Seasons of a Man's Life*, Knopf, New York.

Ley, D., 1978, 'An empirical examination of selected work activity correlates of managerial effectiveness in the hotel industry using a structured observation approach', PhD. thesis, Department of Management, Michigan State University.

Ley, D., 1980, 'The effective GM: leader or entrepreneur?', *Cornell HRA Quarterly*, November, pp. 66–7.

Mars, G., Nicod, M., 1984, *The World of Waiters*, Allen & Unwin, London.

Marshall, J., Cooper, C., 1976, *The Mobile Manager and His Wife*, MCB Monographs Edition, MCB, Bradford.

Martin, C., Clark, B., 1989, 'The use of production management techniques in the tourism industry', *Proceedings of the 4th Annual International Conference of the Operations Management Association*, University of Glasgow, Glasgow.

Maurice, M., Sorge, A., Warner, M., 1980, 'Societal differences in organizing manufacturing units. A comparison of France, West Germany and Great Britain', *Organization Studies*, 1(1): pp. 59–85.

Melrose-Woodman, J., 1978, *Profile of the British Manager*, Management Survey Report No. 38, British Institute of Management.

Mintzberg, H., 1973, *The Nature of Managerial Work*, Harper and Row, New York.

Moores, B. (ed.), 1986, *Are They Being Served?*, Phillip Allan, Oxford.

Mullins, L., 1988, 'Managerial behaviour and development in the hospitality industry', *Proceedings of International Association of Hotel Management Schools Autumn Symposium*, Leeds Polytechnic.

Nailon, P., 1968, 'A study of management activity in units of an hotel group', MPhil. thesis, University of Surrey.

NEDO, 1987, *The Making of Managers*, MSC/NEDO, London.

Nicholson, N., West, M., 1988, *Managerial Job Changes: Men and Women in Transition*, Cambridge University Press, Cambridge.

Pickworth, J. R., 1982, 'Managerial jobs in chain organizations', *Cornell HRA Quarterly*, February, pp. 30–3.

Riley, M., Turam, K., 1989, 'The career paths of UK hotel managers: a developmental approach', *Signet Quarterly*, 1(1): pp. 1–13.

Ruddy, J., 1988, 'How hotel general managers succeed', *Proceedings of International Association of Hotel Management Schools Autumn Symposium*, Leeds Polytechnic.

Rutherford, D., Schill, W., 1984, 'Theoretical constructs in practice: managers rate their importance', *International Journal of Hospitality Management*, 3(3): pp. 101–6.

Shamir, B., 1978, 'Between bureaucracy and hospitality—some organizational characteristics of hotels', *Journal of Management Studies*, Vol. 15, October, pp. 285–307.

Shortt, G., 1989, 'Work activities of hotel managers in Northern Ireland: a Mintzbergian analysis', *International Journal of Hospitality Management*, 8(2): pp. 121–30.

Sofer, C., 1970, *Men in Mid-career*, Cambridge University Press, Cambridge.

Stewart, R., 1967, *Managers and Their Jobs*, Macmillan, London.

Stone, G., 1988, 'Personality and effective hospitality management', *Proceedings of International Association of Hotel Management Schools Autumn Symposium*, Leeds Polytechnic.

Swanljung, M., 1981, 'How hotel executives made the climb to the top', *Cornell HRA Quarterly*, May, pp. 30–4.

Tas, R., 1988, 'Teaching future managers', *Cornell HRA Quarterly*, October, pp. 41–3.

Umbreit, W., 1986, 'Developing behaviourally-anchored scales for evaluating job performance of hotel managers', *International Journal of Hospitality Management*, 5(2): pp. 55–61.

Umbreit, W., Eder, R., 1987, 'Linking hotel manager behaviour with outcome measures of effectiveness', *International Journal of Hospitality Management*, 6(3): pp. 139–47.

Voss, C., Armistead, C., Johnson, R., Morris, B., 1985, *Operations Management in Service Industries and the Public Sector*, Wiley, Chichester.

Whitley, R., 1989, 'On the nature of managerial tasks and skills: their distinguishing characteristics and organization', *Journal of Management Studies*, 23(3): pp. 209–24.

Whitley, R., Thomas, A., Marceau, J., 1981, *Masters of Business: The Making of a New Elite?*, Tavistock, London.

Whyte, W. F., 1948, *Human Relations in the Restaurant Industry*, McGraw-Hill, New York.

Worsfold, P., 1989(a), 'A personality profile of the hotel manager', *International Journal of Hospitality Management*, 8(1): pp. 51–62.

Worsfold, P., 1989(b), 'Leadership and managerial effectiveness in the hospitality industry', *International Journal of Hospitality Management*, 8(2): pp. 145–55.

11 Restaurant marketing
F. Buttle and M. Mehrotta

Introduction

This summary of research into restaurant marketing has been compiled from many sources. Several on-line and documentary searches were conducted. Two years' issues (1987–1988) of 50 American and British academic journals and trade magazines were surveyed. Industry associations, consulting organizations and government publications from both sides of the Atlantic were audited. A census of American marketing research agencies claiming expertise in this field was also undertaken. Empirical findings grounded in either a positivistic/quantitative or a humanistic/qualitative methodology were sought. That this chapter is so brief points to the scarcity of published and/or publicly accessible research meeting these criteria.

Much of what is published takes the form of '*how-to-run-a-profitable-restaurant*' protocols, helpful tips, rehashes of well-established normative marketing theory and PR-generated case histories. Industry reports detailing trends in product-markets as varied as breakfast dining, barbecues and Cajun food appear regularly in trade magazines such as *Restaurant Business* (United States of America) and *Caterer and Hotelkeeper* (United Kingdom). Other journals, such as the *Cornell Hotel and Restaurant Administration Quarterly* and the *International Journal of Hospitality Management*, are targeted at more of an academic readership and often carry articles discussing conceptual issues such as service, quality and customer satisfaction. Many are opinion pieces unsupported by data. Several articles of this genre are listed in the bibliography at the end of the chapter, although they are not cited in the text. Sadly, but inevitably, we were unable to gain access to proprietary information, which is possibly where the most significant research is undertaken.

The chapter begins with an introduction to sources of restaurant market research data and some observations about the changing environment in which restaurants operate. But for the most part, it is organized around a conceptual framework developed by Booms and Bitner (1981). They suggested that the marketers of services use seven variables to influence consumer purchasing. Nick-named 'the seven Ps', these variables are product, price, promotion, place, process, participants and physical evidence. While some of the research we report does not fit neatly into this scheme, it is a useful organizing device and heuristic.

Restaurant market research

The British Library's holdings of market research reports include a number which are of particular significance to restaurant marketers (Ashpitel, 1988). Amongst them are the following:

The Consumer Catering Report (Euromonitor, 1986)
The Hotel and Catering Industry (Euromonitor, 1983)
The Pub Report (Euromonitor, 1985)
UK Hotels in the 1980s (Euromonitor, 1987)
Catering Industry, third edition (ICC Business Ratio Reports, 1987)
Hotel Industry, fifth edition (ICC Business Ratio Reports, 1987)
Catering Prices—costs and subsidies and other information (Industrial Society, 1986)
Catering Industry: Basic Market Data (Insight Research, 1983)
Catering: The Demands of Diversity (Insight Research, 1984)
Catering: Serving A Service (Institute of Grocery Distribution, 1983)
The British Catering Industry (Jordan & Sons, 1984)
Catering, first edition (Key Note Publications, 1985)
Contract Catering, first edition (Key Note Publications, 1985)
Fast Food Outlets, fifth edition (Key Note Publications, 1987)
Public Houses, fifth edition (Key Note Publications, 1985)
Restaurants, second edition (Key Note Publications, 1985)
Catering: UK Database (Marketing Strategies for Industry, 1987)
Fast Food: UK Database (Marketing Strategies for Industry, 1987)
Catering for Profit (Ministry of Agriculture, Fisheries and Food, 1986).

Many of these reports are serially updated on a regular basis, as is the British Library's listing. They contain a wealth of data concerning market size, segments, consumption and expenditure patterns and trends. Trade publications such as *Caterer and Hotelkeeper* often abstract these reports. In 1986, for example, the magazine reported the results of a survey by the Gallup research organization (Stacey, 1986). Gallup had investigated customers' opinions about standards of restaurant service; spending patterns; where to go for a business lunch, with a family or when shopping; eating at work and value for money. Similar data are available about other markets. Dun and Bradstreet (1986) supply substantial amounts of data about the American restaurant industry. Financial data, consumer and marketing statistics and demographics are reported for over 6,000 restaurants. The data reveal a new era of growth and burgeoning competition. For example, the report shows how shifting demographics affect patronage patterns, describes the effect of two-income households and often projections of restaurant growth as related to population, age and ethnic distributions. *Restaurants and Institutions*, the American trade magazine, produces an annual data set comprising historical and forecast market data (Bartlett, 1989). Equivalent data are available about the New

Zealand market (Ameyde and Brodie, 1984). Some international comparisons are also available. Jeffries (1988), for example, compares the American, British, West German, French, Japanese and other European markets for fast-food.

Marketing environment

For many years, the restaurant industry has been product-oriented. However, the recent shift to stronger brand names, franchising and multinational operations has accompanied a reorientation towards marketing. It is clear that having an innovative product concept is no guarantee of profitability. According to Welch (1985), 'having a good idea is probably no longer enough for success. The restaurant must be in a favourable comparative position, its advertising must clearly differentiate it from other operations, and the mix of product, price, service, location and atmosphere must consistently meet consumer needs and desires.' This is the function of marketing, but it is an attitude to business which has not permeated the entire industry. One empirical study of the Canadian restaurant market concluded that restaurant owners had not fully adopted the marketing concept (a business orientation which claims that customer satisfaction is the most important element in business success). Specifically, the research concluded that product mixes, especially menu items, were designed on the basis of operational criteria rather than upon market needs (Stewart, 1986).

The concept of market segmentation is becoming accepted in the restaurant industry. Market segmentation recognizes that restaurants cannot be all things to all people. Swinyard and Struman (1986) wrote that, 'by applying a market segmentation approach, your marketing effort will be more precise. . . . A precisely aimed marketing effort is usually more profitable than a broadly defined campaign. By their nature, different customer segments have distinctive desires in restaurants. . . . a knowledge of the needs of each customer segment allows you to judge how well the competition is meeting those needs. . . . if you identify the high potential segments, determine the products and services attractive to them, and then promote those products and services in the most effective media, you will achieve a higher return for each promotional dollar spent.'

Bahn and Granzin (1985) have tested the merit of one form of segmentation to restaurant marketers. Benefit segmentation has been employed elsewhere for more than 20 years. The basic approach is to partition markets into segments based upon the benefits that customers think are important and then to relate those sub-populations to demographics, consumption patterns, media habits, life style and so on. The researchers found that benefits are an important element in restaurant choice.

A number of socio-demographic trends, many of which have been noted by the compilers of the reports listed above and reported in other places (see Lawless and Hart, 1983; American Demographics, 1987), are likely to be significant to tomorrow's restaurateurs, particularly as they affect market segmentation opportunities. There are changes in age and ethnic profiles, family and household size and numbers of women in the workforce. Not least, there is some evidence that consumers are becoming more inner-directed; social conformity is being sacrificed for greater self-expression. There is a greater willingness to experiment with new foods. Some (but not all) market segments are more health and appearance conscious. These changes have various and conflicting implications for restaurant marketers. Granzin and Bahn (1983), for example, show how nutritional concerns can affect restaurant patronage. Carlson (1986) agrees that nutritional information is used in restaurant selection, but also foresees a growing demand for nutritional quality. Menu item choice, both of food and beverage, is increasingly subject to health considerations.

The growing percentage of women in the workforce suggests that eating out and consumption of prepared foods will increase. One challenge, therefore, is to develop packaging material that keeps take-out or home-delivered food hot or cold for longer periods of time.

Notwithstanding greater consumer experimentation, in the USA American fare continues to be the leading ethnic cuisine and is reported as having the greatest growth potential for the 1990s (Research Performance Inc., 1988). Mexican, Chinese, Cajun and Italian are the ethnic cuisines that come next in terms of growth potential. The continued popularity of Cajun food along with the emergence of Caribbean cuisine seems to suggest that spicy food may not prove to be a fleeting fad. This prediction is based on American demographic projections showing shifts in ethnic population sizes and proportions. Nationally, it is expected that the percentage of whites will decrease, while that of blacks, Hispanics and other minorities will increase. Zelinsky (1987) has written about the relationship between ethnic populations and restaurant sales.

However, national trends may not reflect local patterns. Consequently, some chain operations are pursuing regional marketing strategies reflecting local conditions. According to Meyer (1988), 'Regional marketing involves tailoring the marketing mix to a specific location or region. This often means the selection of different products or different prices for a new location; altering the advertising or promotional message to heighten the appeal to local audiences; or even choosing a location where the customer base matches the product or advertising style. Suppliers frequently need to customize products or alter distribution for a new market. Regional marketing is simply a response to the reality that retailers and their suppliers are captive to the trade areas surrounding each outlet.' Meyer goes on to note that though the drive for economies of scale has forced restaurant firms into mass marketing strategies, many are beginning to question whether the costs associated with regional marketing will be more than compensated by extra revenues. Coppress (1988) endorsed these comments.

The survey by Research Performance Inc. (1988) mentioned earlier also pinpointed other factors which pose great challenges to tomorrow's restaurateurs. These include scarce and expensive labour, higher food costs, the threat of burdensome legislation on wages and health benefits and uncertainty about consumer spending. Of these, the labour shortage is causing the greatest concern. The inadequate supply of young, semi-skilled or unskilled people prepared to work in this service industry is encouraging restaurateurs to recruit older people, often retirees, and to investigate options such as job-sharing and corporate day care (see, for example, Huffman and Schrock, 1987). Also, multi-site low-average check operations are looking at ways of further mechanizing food production and service. Kujava (1988) has reported how satellite foodservice operations working out of a central kitchen go some way to solving the high costs of energy, food waste and labour. A further threat is the imbalance of supply and demand; too many restaurants are chasing too few customers. An industry shakeout is expected.

Researching the '7 Ps'

The 7 Ps—product, price, promotion, place, process, participants and physical evidence—are the variables that service marketers use to influence consumer demand (Booms and Bitner, 1981). What follows is a summary of published research findings classified according to this schema.

Product

In a conventional marketing sense, products are defined as the bundle of satisfactions or dissatisfactions that a customer consumes. In restaurants, this has become known as the *meal experience*. In this classification of the 7 Ps, some parts of the meal experience are dealt with elsewhere. Food was examined earlier. Service, locational convenience and price are also examined later.

The failure rate of new restaurants is dramatically high. Researchers have been able to cast some light on the causes. Toft (1986) reports that 'undercapitalization is the prime cause of restaurant failure.' It is naïve to enter a new market and not expect to suffer a loss during the first year or two. Too many restaurateurs fail to capitalize sufficiently in order to survive these traumatic months. Lee (1987) points to a number of other contributory causes of restaurant failure. Some, such as poor product quality, lack of inter-unit standardization and failure to adapt, are of concern to marketers.

Cost-Volume-Profit (CVP) analysis is a method which researchers have touted as a means of identifying menu items to promote or drop. CVP analyses the relationship between profit, unit sales, price and cost. In addition to aiding menu planning, it can be used to pinpoint abnormal levels of activity to specific areas such as purchasing, inventory or operations and then nip the problem in the bud. According to Greenberg (1986), CVP analysis 'takes restaurant performance evaluation one step beyond the operating statement. Its functions are both informational and practical. CVP can help you understand your establishment's cost structure and help improve your decision-making by quantifying the effect of specific policy decisions on the bottom line'.

The increase in the number of women in the workforce has caused restaurants to become more 'feminine'. Open kitchens are becoming increasingly popular in restaurants. This is because customers are more educated and curious about food preparation methods.

A restaurant's core product can be augmented in various ways to make the operation more competitive and attractive to customers. Many restaurants employ music. Research has been conducted into the impact on consumers of restaurant music. In the research done by Milliman (1986), groups of customers were treated to slow and fast tempo music and the different reactions were observed. With the slow-tempo music used in this study, patrons stayed longer, ate about the same amount of food, but consumed more alcoholic beverages. The study concludes that 'background music can significantly affect the behaviour of restaurant customers'.

Price

According to Rose (1988), who was writing largely about institutional feeding, all pricing systems correspond to one of the three broad categories of pricing: fixed factor, prime costing and recovery-plus-profit. He says, 'in **fixed factor** pricing, the raw food cost of each item is multiplied by a predetermined factor that allows an operator to determine all associated costs and achieve a desired net profit. This factor—at least theoretically—usually represents labour, supply and raw food costs, as well as projected profits'.

Prime costing accounts specifically for food cost and labour cost in its pricing formula. Both costs are calculated for each menu item, then they are divided by the desired percentage, called the prime cost target, to establish optimum levels. Under certain circumstances, calculating labour cost per menu item can be very time-consuming, especially since costs can also vary markedly in relation to the volume being produced and the level of labour completing the task.

According to Rose, 'the **recovery-plus-profit** pricing system almost always yields exactly the same results as the prime costing system. In reality, the systems are very similar, but this system also clearly maps out expectations for all expenses.'

Recently the literature has called into question such mechanical approaches to price setting; if price is of concern to marketers then, it is argued, some consideration needs to be given to customer expectations. Ferguson (1987) has called for restaurateurs to study consumer behaviour in setting price, while Pavesic (1989) has argued that pricing of menu items should take into account subjective and psychological factors.

Recent studies in restaurants have called into question the value of discounting menu prices. Unless the number of covers served rises to compensate, lower prices may well lead to reduced profit (Pavesic, 1985).

Promotion

The promotional mix includes advertising, sales promotion, selling, direct mail, merchandizing, sponsorship and public relations. Fast-food organizations spend heavily in the electronic media. *Advertising Age* (1986) ranked McDonalds as the ninth largest USA advertiser, spending some $700 million world-wide on advertising and promotion. The evidence suggests that mid-scale restaurant promotional budgets are no longer being deployed in TV and display advertising. Rather, proprietors are turning to promotional vehicles which offer cost-effective, measurable results. Couponing, using carefully targeted direct mail (with redemption rates between 4% and 30%) has become popular (Andereck, 1988). Chapman (1986) has reported experimental research which investigates the effect of couponing on take-out pizza sales. Results suggest that it is an effective promotional medium.

In general, dealing is becoming more commonplace in restaurant marketing. Despite this, there is some evidence that the value of the average check is increasing (Crest Marketing Services, 1988).

A key issue today is that of bringing customers back and rewarding repeaters (Haywood, 1988). Continuity promotions work to this end. What began with the airlines as frequent-flyer programmes in the early 1980s, has spread via hotel chains to restaurants. Multi-unit restaurant operators are now being attracted by the potential of frequent dining programs to encourage repeat customers. Some restaurants are distributing membership cards entitling customers to special privileges or discounts, while others offer points which are variable against spending levels. Still others give credit for every visit to the restaurant. After customers reach a certain level of accrued points or credits, they are offered bonuses. These may be gifts, cash discounts or free meals.

Place

There are two dimensions of place which influence consumer purchasing: location and the channels of distribution which restaurateurs use to make their products more convenient and accessible.

Location

The best restaurant sites change hands very quickly and at great cost. Consequently, restaurant firms are attempting to develop secondary locations away from downtown, high street, highway and mall areas. Military bases, colleges, workplaces and schools have been investigated. The unwillingness of some hoteliers to regard foodservice as a profit centre provides other opportunities. For example, most restaurants within casino-hotels are traditional coffee shops, gourmet dining rooms and buffets. Recently, however, Burger King has taken up a concession in a Las Vegas, Nevada property in an innovative locational move (Swerdlow, Strate and Brown, 1987), and Days Inns of America has tied in with Wendy's (Simon, 1987). Burger King has also introduced 20 mobile foodservice vehicles (Baker, 1986).

In a defensive response to losing some of their food business to restaurants, many supermarkets, delicatessens, bakeries and convenience stores have introduced a limited prepared-food menu (Agnew, 1986, 1987). The structural relationship between retail food stores, restaurants and other foodservice businesses has been empirically studied (Ingene, 1983), as has the spatial relationship between competitors in five different classes of restaurant operation (Smith, 1985). Whitehall (1985) and Chitty (1986) have both reported how restaurant operators presently evaluate trading areas and sites prior to making location decisions. Min's work (1987) has resulted in the development of an innovative locational model which can be calibrated for the achievement of various business objectives.

Franchising is a common mechanism for restaurateurs wishing to rapidly increase in size. *Restaurant Business*, the American trade magazine, annually reviews franchising trends in the ten major menu segments of the fast-food industry—hamburger, steak, chicken, pizza, Mexican, seafood, pancake, sandwich, ice-cream and doughnut.

Distribution channels

Despite conditions of supply exceeding demand, restaurants have not innovated much in distribution channel design. Tie-ins with video stores, theatres, airlines and hotels have been used to increase the number of points of distribution.

Participants and process

Booms and Bitner (1981) describe participants as 'all human actors who play a part in service delivery and thus influence the buyer's perceptions: namely, the firm's personnel and other customers in the service environment'. Process involves 'the actual procedures, mechanisms, and flow of activities by which the service is delivered'. In restaurant marketing research, investigators have customarily confounded participants and process. After all, service providers (participants) very often do not adhere to process policies. Indeed, policies frequently do not exist in smaller chain and independent operations. Of the 7 Ps, participants and process, and particularly the dimension of service, have probably been subjected to the most research.

Barrington and Olsen (1987) observe that 'the concept of service today can be better understood by dividing it into categories representing three distinct groups of people who experience service with different and sometimes conflicting points of view: (1) the customer, (2) the provider of service, and (3) the theorist/researcher'.

The customer's perspective

The authors note that there is no shortage of customers who claim that service is poor to non-existent. A number of factors appear to account for this belief about service, particularly as it applies to the hospitality industry:

1. Demographic changes—the current baby-boomer population is more aware of the world around them and possesses increased disposable income, because of which their expectations for service are more precise and demanding;
2. Greater emphasis on the price/value relationship;
3. Increased competition—the maturation of the industry has created a situation wherein many competitors are struggling to differentiate their product on the basis of service;
4. Increased knowledge on the part of the consumer;
5. The shift from an industry-based to a service-based economy;
6. Rapid growth in the hospitality industry, resulting in tremendous demand for entry-level positions as well as managers, causing premature promotions from service positions;
7. Society modernization—managers are more comfortable dealing with quantitative analyses than with people.

These observations are endorsed by Lydecker (1986): 'People no longer take good service for granted. When service meets or exceeds expectations, they perceive it as an added benefit.' He notes that some commentators have traced the origins of the problem back to the 1960s, when the franchise boom brought droves of young, inexperienced servers and managers into the industry.

The service provider's perspective

There are few good examples of management in the service area. This, when coupled with a high labour turnover, tends to reduce effectiveness. Also, restaurants are so highly capitalized that management tends to focus primarily on the bottom line. Everything else, including the customers, is often neglected because of senior management's overwhelming performance orientation. This is more of a manufacturing industry approach to business, perhaps inappropriately applied to the service industry.

Barrington and Olsen (1987) offer several reasons for service providers' failure to overcome the poor public image of service:

1. Limited time to manage both production and service.
2. The relative lack of time and ability to properly recruit, screen and hire prospective service employees.
3. The lack of knowledge and time for proper training of service personnel.
4. A high turnover rate of service employees, which makes training a constant problem.
5. The uncontrollable reward system of tipping.

6. The fact that the manager's performance is often measured by factors other than the quality of service.

The perspective of the theorist/researcher

Theoreticians have written about the subject from different perspectives, such as the link between services and the manufacturing industry; consideration of the customer as part of the service production and delivery process (see, for example, Jones' (1988) overview of trends in foodservice delivery systems design); the level of self-supervision on the part of the personnel; and finally, viewing service as an information exchange medium.

The issue of quality in service is a topical one. Quality service is a very complex concept. It is not inconceivable that restaurateurs hold a wide variety of viewpoints on what constitutes quality, largely because they seek to serve different clienteles. According to Martin (1986), service quality can be conceptualized as comprising a combination of the two factors—service procedures and conviviality. The procedural dimension consists of the flow of service, timeliness, accommodation (the ability to deal with the individual customer's whims and fancies), anticipation of customer needs, communication, customer feedback and supervision. The convivial dimension consists of attitude, body language, tone of voice, tact, mode of address, attentiveness, guidance, suggestive selling and assistance in solving the customer's problems. Restaurateurs can set their service standards using these service indicators.

However, each dimension must be ranked in terms of its importance for the particular establishment and performance graded. According to Martin, evaluation should be done by everybody involved with the service—both the service user and the service provider. Martin's opinions about service appear to be highly ethnocentric. Dore's (1988) research, which is grounded in a positive anthropological frame rather than merely a normative perspective, clearly indicates that there are many local interpretations and variations as to what constitutes good service.

The importance of service to patronage decisions has been investigated. The October 1984 *Gallup Monthly Report on Eating Out* found that service not only influences whether customers return, it also determines whether they will recommend the restaurant to others. 'It's incredible how much diners will put up with if they are treated properly. Mediocre food, too much noise, cramped tables all appear to be accepted as long as people are greeted with a welcoming smile and are made to feel that the management cares about them,' Gallup reports. But if the service is bad and the experience is bad, then 34% of the respondents said that they would tell other people about it. Additional research by June and Smith (1987) focuses on the impact of service and situational factors on customer preferences for restaurant dining. The product of their research is a consumer choice behavioural model.

178 F. Buttle and M. Mehrotta

Physical evidence

According to Booms and Bitner (1981), this comprises 'the environment in which the service is assembled and in which the firm and customer interact; and any tangible commodities which facilitate performance or communication of the service'.

Opinions about the impact of design elements upon customer feelings and behaviour are abundant. For example, without producing supporting data, Wolson (1986) claimed that uniforms are as important as interior design to restaurant marketing strategy.

Summary

There is a dearth of research on restaurant marketing. Very little good quality work has been produced. This is not to say that nothing can be learned from the literature. Case histories and industry surveys can help restaurateurs decide what sort of operation to run and how to market it. However, there is little which would satisfy those of a more mainstream scientific leaning. The established methods of analysing restaurant marketing fall far short of what constitutes good quantitative or qualitative research.

References

Advertising Age, 1986, '100 leading national advertisers, McDonald's Corp./Mobil Corp./Monsanto Co.', *Advertising Age*, 57(47): pp. 128–31.

Agnew, J., 1986, 'Convenience stores testing fast-food market', *Marketing News*, Vol. 20: p. 10.

Agnew, J., 1987, 'Eating at home and away', *Marketing News*, Vol. 21: p. 7.

American Demographics, 1987, 'Taking to taking out', *American Demographics*, 9, 13.

Andereck, K. O., 1988, 'Let's make a deal', *Restaurant Hospitality*, 72(4): pp. 166–70.

Ameyde, A., van, Brodie, R. J., 1984, *The Christchurch and New Zealand Eating-out Markets*, Research Report, Agricultural Economics Research Unit, Lincoln College, University of Canterbury, New Zealand.

Ashpitel, S., 1988, *Market Research: A Guide to British Library Holdings*, fifth edition, Science Reference and Information Service, British Library, London.

Bahn, K. D., Granzin, K. O., 1985, 'Benefit segmentation in the restaurant industry', *Journal of the Academy of Marketing Science*, 13(3): pp. 226–47.

Baker, R. K., 1986, 'Remote cuisine', *American Demographics*, 8(6): p. 72.

Barrington, M. N., Olsen, M. D., 1987, 'Concept of service in the hospitality industry', *International Journal of Hospitality Management*, 6(3): pp. 131–8.

Bartlett, M., 1989, 'Annual forecast 1989', *Restaurants and Institutions*, 99: pp. 32–5.

Booms, B. H., Bitner, M.-J., 1981, 'Marketing strategies and organization structures for service firms', in Donnelly, J. H., George, W. R. (eds), *Marketing of Services*, American Marketing Association, Chicago.

Carlson, B. L., 1986, 'The marketing of nutrition in foodservice', *International Journal of Hospitality Management*, 5(4): pp. 163–70.

Chapman, R. G., 1986, 'Assessing the profitability of retailer couponing', *Journal of Retailing*, 62(1): pp. 19–41.

Chitty, G., 1986, 'Finding a site: the scientific approach', *Caterer and Hotelkeeper*, 177(3442): pp. 99–101.

Coppress, M. H., 1988, 'Regional marketing: translating national trends for your local audience', *Restaurants USA*, 8(4): pp. 30–1.

Crest Marketing Services, 1988, *Executive Top-line Report*, June–August 1988.

Dore, C. D., 1988, 'The interpretation of service: an anthropological view', *Hospitality Education Research Journal*, 12(1): pp. 81–91

Dun & Bradstreet, 1986, *The Restaurant Industry Study—A Strategic and Financial Analysis of Full Service and Fast Food Restaurants*, second edition, Dun & Bradstreet, Murray Hill, New Jersey.

Ferguson, D. H., 1987, 'Hidden agendas in consumer purchase decisions', *Cornell HRA Quarterly*, 28(1): pp. 30–8.

Granzin, K. L., Bahn, K. D., 1983, 'The differential importance of nutrition in the offerings of two types of restaurants', *American Marketing Association Proceedings*, pp. 291–4.

Greenberg, C., 1986, 'Analyzing restaurant performance: relating cost and volume to profit', *Cornell HRA Quarterly*, 27(1): pp. 9–11.

Haywood, K. M., 1988, 'Repeat patronage: cultivating alliances with customers', *International Journal of Hospitality Management*, 7(3): pp. 225–38.

Huffman, L. M., Schrock, J. R., 1987, 'Corporate day care: an answer to the labor shortage', *Cornell HRA Quarterly*, 28(1): pp. 22–4.

Ingene, C. A., 1983, *Structural Determinants of Competition in Food Retailing*, American Marketing Association Proceedings, pp. 251–6.

Jeffries, D. A, 1988, *International Fast Food Market*, Leatherhead Food Research Association, April.

Jones, P., 1988, 'Trends in foodservice delivery systems', *International Journal of Operations and Production Management*, 8(7): pp. 23–31.

June, L. P., Smith, L. J., 1987, 'Service attributes & situational effects on customer preferences for restaurant dining', *Journal of Travel Research*, 26(2): pp. 20–7.

Kujava, G., 1988, 'Trends in satelliting foodservice', *Consultant*, 21(2): pp. 39–40.

Lawless, M. J., Hart, C. W., 1983, 'Forces that shape restaurant demand', *Cornell HRA Quarterly*, 24(3): pp. 6–17.

Lee, D. R., 1987, 'Why some fail where others succeed', *Cornell HRA Quarterly*, 28(11): pp. 32–7.

Lydecker, T., 1986, 'The crisis in service', *NRA News*, March: pp. 13–16.

Martin, W. B., 1986, 'Defining what quality service is for you', *Cornell HRA Quarterly*, pp. 32–87.

Meyer, T. G., 1988, 'The regional marketing strategy', *Restaurant Hospitality*, 72(4): pp. 170–1.

Milliman, R. E., 1986, 'The influence of background music on the behaviour of restaurant patrons', *Journal of Consumer Research*, 13(9): pp. 286–8.

Min, H., 1987, 'A location model for fast-food restaurants', *Omega*, 15(5): pp. 429–42.

Pavesic, D., 1985, 'The myth of discount promotions', *International Journal of Hospitality Management*, 4(2): pp. 67–73.

Pavesic, D., 1989, 'Psychological aspects of menu pricing', *International Journal of Hospitality Management*, 8(1): pp. 43–9.
Research Performance, Inc., 1988, *Research News*, Tarrytown, New York.
Rose, J. C., 1988, 'Pricing I: the three menu pricing systems', *Food Management*, Jan.: p. 40.
Simon, R., 1987, 'Fast food and fast lodging', *Forbes*, 139(2): p. 78.
Smith, S. L. J., 1985, 'Location patterns of urban restaurants', *Annals of Tourism Research*, 12(4): pp. 581–602.
Stacey, C., 1986, 'Customer survey 1986', *Caterer and Hotelkeeper*, 177(3419): pp. 26–47.
Stewart, D. B., 1986, 'Marketing strategy in the Canadian restaurant market: an empirical review of the marketing ethic in retailing', *International Journal of Retailing*, 1(3): pp. 43–53.
Swerdlow, S., Strate, L., Brown, F. X., 1987, 'Fast-food franchises: an alternative menu for hotel-casinos', *Hotel & Casino Law Letter*, 4(1): pp. 68–71.
Swinyard, W. R., Struman, K. D., 1986, 'Market segmentation: finding the heart of your restaurant's market', *Cornell Hotel and Restaurant Association Quarterly*, pp. 89–96.
Toft, M., 1986, 'Independent restaurants', *Canadian Hotel and Restaurant*, Oct.: pp. 17–18.
Welch, J. L., 1985, 'Focus groups for restaurant research', *Cornell HRA Quarterly*, pp. 78–85.
Whitehall, B., 1985, 'Marketing methods to target on customers', *Caterer and Hotelkeeper*, 176(3366): pp. 63, 65, 67.
Wolson, S., 1986, 'Working wardrobes', *Restaurant Institutions*, 96(9): pp. 181–3.
Zelinsky, W., 1987, 'You are where you eat', *American Demographics*, 9(7): p. 30.

Further sources, not listed in the text

Boyle, K., 1985, 'Anniversary celebrations', *NRA News*, May: pp. 26–8.
Boyle, K., 1986, 'The crisis in service training', *NRA News*, March: pp. 17–19.
Boss, D., Schechter, M., 1987, 'Serving the next generation', *Food Management*, Oct.: pp. 118–37.
Curlook, C., 1986, 'Restaurant trends of the 80s', *Canadian Hotel and Restaurant*, June: pp. 32–48.
Farrell, K., 1988, 'Put on promotions', *Restaurant Business*, March 1: pp. 111–32.
Garel, E. M., 1987, 'Creating mood for the food', *Canadian Hotel and Restaurant*, Nov.: pp. 34–7.
Gillespie, B., 1988, 'Do-it-yourself research', *Restaurant Business*, Sept.: pp. 68–80.
Go, F., 1987, 'Towards a new century', *Canadian Hotel and Restaurant*, Aug.: pp. 8–18.
Guiltinan, J. P., 1987, 'The price bundling of services: a normative framework', *Journal of Marketing*, Apr.: pp. 74–85.
Levine, D., 1988, 'Rewarding repeaters', *Restaurant Business*, Aug. 10: pp. 120–2.
Long, D. A., 1988, 'Long-term promotions', *Restaurant Business*, March 1: p. 74.
Main, B., 1988, 'Do-it-yourself market research', *Restaurant Business*, Jan 1: pp. 64–71.
McClelland, B., 1986, 'Direct mail', *Canadian Hotel and Restaurant*, March: pp. 32–7.
McClelland, B., 1987, 'Tie-in promotions', *Canadian Hotel and Restaurant*, Feb.: pp. 25–7.

McClelland, B., 1987, 'Sports promotions', *Canadian Hotel and Restaurant*, March: pp. 28–34.

McClelland, B., 1987, 'Outrageous vs. tasteless', *Canadian Hotel and Restaurant*, Apr.: pp. 37–9.

McClelland, B., 1987, 'Bringing your customers back', *Canadian Hotel and Restaurant*, May: pp. 47–8.

Niepold, C., 1986, 'Menu size debate: large vs. small', *NRA News*, Feb.: pp. 29–32.

Papa, A., 1986, 'Restaurant design: finding the right look', *NRA News*, Jan.: pp. 12–25.

Riell, H., 1988, 'Business barometer: the hard facts shaping our industry', *Restaurant Business*, Jan. 20: p. 2.

Ryan, N. R., 1989, 'Under the silver dome', *Restaurants and Institutions*, Jan. 9: pp. 146–9.

Toft, M., 1986, 'Market research', *Canadian Hotel and Restaurant*, May: pp. 42–3.

Weinstein, J., 1987, 'New rules for playing old games', *Restaurants and Institutions*, March 18: pp. 22–3.

12 Developments within the catering equipment industry in Great Britain

M. Storey and C.G. Smith

Background

One of Britain's leading catering equipment manufacturers recently sponsored a programme of research at the University of Surrey in order to widen understanding and knowledge of the industry. The main direction of the research was to conduct a comprehensive overview of the catering equipment market. As there was a dearth of available and usable statistics covering the industry, original data on various aspects of the market had to be gathered through a series of postal and personal interview surveys. These, combined with a thorough review of relevant literature, yielded a vast amount of information about the equipment market. This chapter seeks to focus attention on the market developments most likely to occur in the future, especially in terms of demand patterns for major kitchen appliances and emerging technologies.

Introduction

For the purposes of the survey, the commercial catering equipment industry in Great Britain was taken to include all those concerns involved in the production, selling and after-sales service of machinery and equipment intended for the storage, preparation, cooking and service of meals provided by the catering industry. The industry is extremely diverse in terms of products and participating companies.

The research project concentrated upon prime cooking appliances, which were taken to be all those items of equipment which used heat-transfer techniques to transform the raw food materials into the finished products. The study also focused on the market's main indigenous and foreign equipment manufacturers, distributors and caterers.

As will become apparent, the sub-divisions within these various market elements played a vital role in the understanding of the market, most notably within the catering industry. The main sub-divisions in the catering industry were (1) the commercial or profit sector and (2) the non-commercial or subsidized sector.

Role of the catering industry

The development of the catering equipment industry is inextricably linked to the continued prosperity of the catering industry. Indicators of sales, turnover and profit levels suggest that, barring an unforeseen equipment catastrophe, the future for the catering industry is one of expansion (*British Business*, 1987, 1988; UB Brands, 1987; *Caterer and Hotelkeeper*, 1987). This confirms its position as a major contributor to the British economy.

The growth rate within the catering industry has not been universal, however. The commercial division has expanded at the expense of parts of the non-commercial division (MSI, 1987). But even in areas which seem to be contracting, like the health sector, other events, such as the lifting of Crown Immunity (that is, protection from prosecution of Health and Hygiene infringements for Government establishments), have stimulated an interest in new equipment. These are positive signals to the equipment industry. Nevertheless, the catering industry remains a difficult market to serve, as it is overwhelmingly composed of small, geographically dispersed businesses with limited capital for expenditure on new equipment. While this situation is likely to persist in the short term, official statistics (such as those shown in Table 12.1) indicate that turnover levels are rising and levels of concentration are increasing.

Table 12.1 *Percentage breakdown of turnover levels in the catering industry*

Turnover £'000s	20–50	51–100	101–250	251–500	501–1000	Over 1000
1985	40.0	34.3	20.2	3.8	1.0	0.7
1987	34.3	34.1	24.4	4.9	1.4	0.9

Source: British Statistics Office, 1985 and 1987.

The changing catering equipment industry

As a corollary with the growth of the catering industry, the equipment industry has experienced a moderate increase in sales during this decade (Euromonitor, 1987). However, the growth in sales of cooking appliances was far less than in other sectors of the industry, as can be seen in Table 12.2.

Of the many changes affecting the industry, the most marked has been the success of foreign firms in capturing a growing proportion of cooking equipment sales (an estimate of the position in 1986 is given in Table 12.3) and the activity of these firms in acquiring traditional British companies. One indicator of their success is the ever-widening trade gap in favour of imports, which has been particularly marked in recent years (HM Customs and Excise, 1985,

Table 12.2 *Value of the catering equipment market, 1981 to 1986*

£ million	1981	1982	1983	1984	1985	1986
Cooking	38.0	41.5	44.5	48.0	52.5	54.5
Food preparation	13.8	13.5	13.1	12.2	12.0	13.5
Refrigeration	10.5	10.7	14.0	17.0	20.0	22.0
Servery	18.0	18.5	21.0	24.5	27.0	29.5
Dishwasher	10.5	11.5	12.5	14.0	15.5	17.5
Waste disposal	1.7	1.8	1.9	1.8	2.0	2.0
Fabrication	20.0	20.0	24.0	29.0	31.0	31.0
Total	112.5	117.5	131.0	146.5	160.0	170.0

Source: Euromonitor, 1987.

Table 12.3 *Import penetration as a percentage of catering equipment sales, 1986*

Equipment item	Percentage
Microwave oven	90.0
Fryer	30.0
Steamer	30.0
Convection oven	25.0
Boiling pan	20.0
Range	20.0
Back bar equipment	15.0
Bratt pan	15.0
Grill	0.0
Others	50.0

Source: Euromonitor, 1987.

1986; City Data Services, 1987). It is possible that with the harmonization of technical standards throughout the European Community and the lowering of tariff barriers in 1992, British manufacturers may concentrate their efforts on exporting to Europe and help delay this trend.

The changing demands of the customer and the realization that imported goods are restricting the equipment industry's market opportunities are forcing the industry to pay greater attention to equipment design and marketing strategies. In the future, companies will have to heighten their awareness and recognize that users' demands centre on several key factors: the level of technology of a product, its efficiency and the availability of after-sales services. The increasing financial resources arising from the rationalization within the equipment industry should enable British manufacturers to address the challenges of research and the higher expectation levels of the customer.

The historical pattern of demand for cooking appliances

The rapid rate of change in the structure of the equipment industry resulted from a complex set of economic, demographic, industrial and market factors. But it was market factors and questions about the ways in which these factors would affect demand patterns that formed the focus of the Surrey research project.

Historical purchasing patterns form a sound reference point for demand extrapolations. A survey across the sectors of the catering industry provided a distinct picture of the catering industry's stock of equipment and thereby an indication of the cooking appliances that would form the basis of future needs. The research discovered that the six most common items of equipment in a standard catering kitchen were a range, fryer, grill, dishwasher, microwave, oven and convection oven. Also, where there was an option, there was a probability of 0.6 that the appliances would be fuelled by gas in preference to electricity. This was a pattern that was remarkably constant over time.

Of the stock of equipment, 54% was under six years old but a further 20% was retained beyond the normally accepted life span for equipment of ten years. These age profiles revealed that certain items of equipment had markedly increased their share of the stock over recent years and could begin to challenge the historical pattern of demand. These were bratt pans, griddles, char grills, combination ovens, microwave ovens and regeneration ovens (see Table 12.4).

Table 12.4 *Age profiles of equipment items*

	New–2 years	2–5 years	5–10 years	10–15 years	15–20 years	Over 20 years
Industry average	26.1	27.9	26.8	11.0	6.3	.0
Bratt pans	29.5	33.8	24.3	7.9	4.3	–
Griddles	31.8	30.6	28.7	3.6	4.9	0.4
Char grills	32.0	30.9	13.2	4.2	19.7	–
Combination ovens	48.4	18.3	20.6	12.7	–	–
Microwave ovens	39.3	42.6	17.5	0.6	–	–
Regeneration ovens	56.7	27.3	8.0	8.0	–	–

Market factors affecting the future pattern of demand

While the age profiles obtained from the survey data provided some indication of changes in the pattern of demand, a wider examination of current trends in the market was necessary to assess the changing needs of both the consumer and the caterer.

The influence of the consumer

The last decade has witnessed a shift in the public's attitude towards food which has given rise to a new set of expectations (Frank and Wheelcock, 1988). As the new health consciousness spreads amongst the public, caterers will have to look for alternatives to traditional fat-based cooking methods. They will also be forced to invest more heavily in rapid cooking ovens, with accurate temperature and time controls to ensure product quality and freshness. The standard kitchen, as described earlier, could begin to look very different as the balance between the main items of equipment alters. But, in light of the continued proliferation of fast-food outlets, it is perhaps somewhat premature to predict an imminent collapse of the demand for fryers and associated equipment. A gradual shift in emphasis is more likely (Keynote, 1987(a)).

The changing needs of the caterer

The main impetus for change in the catering industry during recent years has been fierce competition for the extra business created by the rise in demand. This has caused many businesses to thoroughly review their methods of operation and has encouraged the widespread adoption of a systematic approach to planning. Consequently, full costs are now taken into consideration, elevating the status of equipment in the operational equation and leading to greater professionalism in the purchasing of appliances. The result has been that equipment is being used to reduce wastage from the peaks of demand, to improve quality and to save on the expensive and increasingly scarce resource of labour.

The effect on the equipment manufacturer

Changes taking place in both consumer attitudes and the operation of the catering industry will place increasing pressure on manufacturers to develop alternative appliances and refine existing designs. This will necessitate a stronger financial and staffing commitment to research and development and a continuing awareness of market trends.

Although manufacturers have reacted to the changes taking place in the catering industry, they have at the same time had to take into account other factors within their business environment. Rising costs have caused many manufacturers to move away from direct selling and to restrict their product ranges. To satisfy the customer's demand for a full range of equipment, some manufacturers have formed into groups or have used the services of distributors. Greater competition has forced them to approach marketing more aggressively and to review their methods of production. At the same time, the speed of technological change has necessitated flexible R&D and production departments that can achieve economies of scale while encouraging investment in plant and machinery. On the whole, there now seems to be a greater awareness amongst British manufacturers of the need to keep abreast of market developments and to assess and meet the requirements of the end user more objectively.

Technological factors affecting the future pattern of demand

Until this decade, little research was done into the basic principles of cooking. Perhaps the most relevant aspect for equipment designers is heat transfer to and through the food, and its effects, including protein denaturation, water release and meat tenderization. Only recently has an adequate scientific understanding of heat transfer materialized through the work of organizations like the Swedish Food Institute and the US Army Research and Development Command (Andersson, 1986). Several pieces of new equipment have resulted from their work and some ideas have been adapted from the food processing industry, where continuous and standardized production is required.

Significant technological advances

Five main areas of technological change are likely to have an impact on the market for prime cooking appliances. They are, in order of immediate potential, combination ovens, electronic controls, halogen heating, induction heating and heat foils.

Combination cookers are not a completely new technology, but more an adaptation of existing technologies. They combine the function of one or more appliances in the same unit, with the processes being used independently or in conjunction with one another. The operational modes can include convection, steam, microwave and infra-red heating. Hence they afford the operator the advantages of each method of cooking but without the disadvantages. In addition to this flexibility of use, they save on floor space.

In any cooking process, the two critical variables are temperature and time and their precise control has an important bearing on both the efficiency of the process and the quality of the end product. Electronic controls are more accurate than electro-mechanical controls, and much more versatile. They can be used to trigger temperature alarms, find faults, initiate non-use cut-offs, lift fryer baskets and set cooking cycles as well as control time, temperature and humidity. Some can accommodate multiple products and different start times and achieve elasticity of time by compensating for factors such as the opening of the oven door. Their use is particularly appropriate in cook-chill and *sous vide* systems, where precision of control is vital. Although there were problems with their initial application—the greasy, hot and humid environment of the kitchen proved to be very hostile—these difficulties have now been overcome.

Electronic controls and computers are an integral component of the more sophisticated cooking appliances and kitchens.

Both **halogen** and **induction heating** technologies have been incorporated into ranges. They provide large energy savings and reduce the amount of heat passing into the working environment. Units can be incorporated into a flat surface for easy cleaning. Their disadvantages are that their initial purchase price can be high and they are still more expensive to run than gas ranges. In addition, only ferrous pans can be used with induction ranges.

Heat foils are another innovation, and trials which have attached this type of element directly beneath the cooking plate on a griddle or fryer have indicated that they have potential. The main advantage of heat foils is that they eliminate hot spots.

Acceptance of the new technologies by the market

Horton's comments on the importance of the new equipment to the catering industry must be heartening for the manufactuerers.

Capital expenditure on technically advanced equipment can be a major factor in assisting caterers to achieve their overall objectives of providing quality food with good service within sound financial parameters (Horton, 1986).

Pine, however, warns that expenditure on new equipment can be obviated by a lack of investment in training and supervision of the staff (Pine, 1987). But the possibilities of improvements in quality and consistency combined with savings on labour costs are arousing interest in all sectors of the industry. The survey revealed that generally the caterer's reaction to new technologies was positive. The main reasons caterers cited for their interest were hopes of cutting costs, improving their standards of service and upgrading hygiene. Negative responses could be attributed to a lack of capital, inherent conservatism and ignorance of the options. The success of the new technologies will undoubtedly depend on a combination of marketing campaigns, economic feasibility and positive results—how far the equipment goes in solving their main operational difficulties.

Final appraisal of the equipment market

The market factors affecting the growth and development of the catering equipment market are many and varied. Some factors affect the equipment industry directly, while others have an indirect influence by causing changes in the operational practices of the catering industry.

As noted above, the catering industry is diverse and fragmented. Its task is to provide meals and snacks that are not always the primary activity of the businesses concerned. As the agro-food system has industrialized, the catering industry's contribution to the country's economy has grown to the point where it is now the fourth largest industry, in terms of the total number of businesses, and a major employer with an annual turnover of more than £20 billion. Despite the emergence of chain operators and the frequency of take-overs, the industry still exhibits a low level of concentration, with only a tiny percentage of businesses achieving a turnover of above £0.5 million (British Statistics Office, 1985, 1987).

One of the main forces of change within the catering industry is the shifting attitudes and demographic characteristics of the consumer. As a result there has been a growing awareness of the dietary implications of different food types and methods of culinary preparation. This knowledge among consumers will influence the equipment needs of caterers, perhaps more markedly in the non-commercial division, where healthy eating campaigns seem to be most active.

It is widely accepted that the catering industry will continue to grow until the end of this century. As some 80% of meals are taken at home and only 10% of consumer expenditure is devoted to eating out—there remains considerable scope for expansion (Keynote, 1987(b)). The result will be a strengthening of the demand for catering equipment. However, the sales task will not be an easy one due to the continued fragmentation of the catering industry.

According to the findings of the Surrey research project, on average, a catering-kitchen is most likely to contain a range, a fryer, a grill, a dishwasher, a microwave oven and a convection oven. It would seem that in the immediate future this pattern is likely to continue despite a predicted move away from boiling, range-top and frying techniques to steaming and cooking in combination ovens. The growing proportion of bratt pans, griddles, char grills, combination ovens, microwave ovens, pizza ovens, regeneration ovens and pressureless steamers in the equipment stock of the catering industry during the last five years would suggest that in the longer term the pattern is changing. For the immediate future, however, advances in steam oven and combination technology are likely to have the greatest impact. If the economics of induction, halogen and heat-foil technology prove to be attractive, they are areas for likely expansion in the longer term. All of these developments will undoubtedly be aided by the application of electronic controls. However, the main increase in the volume of equipment sales will come from the sales of dishwashers and steamers, with bratt pans, griddles, char grills, combination ovens, microwave ovens, pizza ovens and regeneration ovens making an increasingly important contribution.

As the systematic style of managing a catering operation gains a wider acceptance, the true cost implications of the investment in catering equipment will lead to a more professional approach to purchasing. The main issues will be the spreading of production over time to combat peaks in demand; the standardization of the product so quality can be maintained; and the possibility of introducing savings on labour and space.

Although smaller than the catering industry which it serves, the equipment

Table 12.5 *Company shares of the cooking equipment market in 1986*[1]

Company	Percentage share
Falcon Catering Equipment	23.0
Stott Benham	21.0
Jackson Catering Equipment	9.0
Moorwood Vulcan	8.0
Bartlett	8.0
Others	31.0

[1] Figures exclude microwave ovens.
Source: Euromonitor, 1987.

manufacturing industry is also fragmented, though its cooking appliance sales remain dominated by a few large firms, as illustrated in Table 12.5. A combination of economic pressures and increased foreign interest in the British market have precipitated a number of changes in the structure and operation of the equipment manufacturing industry. These include ownership changes and the emergence of major groupings of companies which should facilitate the attainment of economies of scale and higher profit levels. During recent years, distributors have increased their share of equipment sales, especially to the sectors of the catering industry not characterized by centralized control (PRS plc, 1986). To perpetuate this trend—to continue to meet the demands of the emerging chain operators in the catering industry and to claim a greater proportion of the non-commercial division's business—distributors will have to grow in size and capability.

The foreign equipment manufacturers are obviously offering the catering industry an attractive product at an acceptable price. Although they played a minor role in the market in the early 1970s, today they probably account for more than half of sales. Their success is often attributed to the technological superiority of their appliances over indigenously produced equipment. There are now signs that the domestic manufacturers have increased their research and development budgets and that they are actively involved in developing the new technologies of halogen and induction heating. One of the constraints placed on the R&D budgets of British manufacturers in the past was the limited size of the domestic market. With the harmonization of technical and safety standards throughout the European Economic Community, British manufacturers will, in theory, have the same cross-border market opportunities as their European competitors.

References

Andersson, Y., 1986, 'Food preparation in the foodservice business—fundamental and applied work done at SIK-the Swedish Food Institute', *Journal of Foodservice Systems*, 4, pp. 69–79.

British Business, 1987, 'Distributive and service trades—results of 1985 inquiries', *British Business*, 25(1), 26(4): pp. 31–5.

British Business, 1988, 'Trends at a glance', *British Business*, 28(12): pp. 32–3.

British Statistics Office, 1985, *PA1003*, HMSO, London.

British Statistics Office, 1987, *PA1003*, HMSO, London.

Caterer and Hotelkeeper, 1987, 'Caterer and hotelkeeper business survey—1987', *Caterer and Hotelkeeper*, 178 (3490).

City Data Services, 1987, *Returns of Imports/Exports*, City Data Services, London.

Euromonitor, 1987, *Catering Equipment in the UK*, Euromonitor Publications, London.

Frank, J., Wheelcock, V., 1988, 'International trends in food consumption', *British Food Journal*, 90(1): pp. 22–9.

HM Customs and Excise, 1985, 1986, *Returns of Imports/Exports*, HMSO, London.

Horton, A., 1986, 'Man, machine, method', *HCIMA Reference Book*, 1986/87, pp. 321–3.

Keynote, 1987(a), *Keynote Report—Fast-food Outlets*, Keynote, London.

Keynote, 1987(b), *Market Review UK Catering Market*, Keynote, London.

MSI, 1987, *MSI Database: Catering: UK*, Marketing Strategies for Industry (UK) Ltd., Mitcham.

Pine, R., 1987, 'Catering technology—some issues for effective utilization', MPhil. thesis, Huddersfield Polytechnic.

PRS plc, 1986, *Recent Developments and Projected Changes in the UK Equipment Market*, British Gas plc.

UB Brands, 1987, *Catering Research Report 1987*, United Buscuits (UK) Ltd., Isleworth.

13 Hygiene and hazard analysis in food service

J. Sheppard, M. Kipps and J. Thomson

The problems

The catering or foodservice industry in the United Kingdom, like other sectors comprising the food chain, has had its share of hygiene problems. Over the years numerous commentators have documented its failings and called for stricter controls. Many of these calls have, unfortunately, gone unheeded. Neither the industry nor the Government has rushed to rectify these short-comings. This legacy of inaction is now reflected in a rising tide of food-borne illness. The public debate over the unprecedented rise in food poisoning over the last two or three years has again rekindled the hygiene question within the industry. Just as the food-poisoning outbreak at Stanley Royd Hospital in the North of England eventually led to the abolition of Crown Immunity (where particular public sectors of the industry, such as hospitals and prisons, were immune from prosecution for contravening hygiene laws), so too the 'food scares' of the late 1980s are forging a new hygiene consciousness, reflected in the Food Safety Bill introduced to Parliament in the Autumn of 1989 (DHSS, 1986). The industry's traditional complacency is being undermined and old attitudes are slowly changing.

Paradoxically, just as the need for stricter hygiene standards in food handling is beginning to be more fully appreciated, the conventional wisdom about hygiene is changing. The industry is no longer being exhorted to comply with some fixed, unchanging definition of hygiene. On the contrary, the increased incidence of food-borne illness is seen as a sign that traditional hygiene measures are no longer adequate to control modern-day hazards. A new flexible approach to controlling food hazards, rather than a set of rigidly applied rules, will best reflect these changing realities. The apparent failure of these traditional approaches represents an unparalleled opportunity for those who have advocated the implementation of Hazard Analysis Critical Control Points procedures (HACCP). Improved quality control is, say HACCP's

Note: Julie Sheppard joined the Department of Management Studies in Tourism and Hotel Industries, University of Surrey in 1989 to carry out research into HACCP applications in the UK catering industry. The research was supervised by Michael Kipps and James Thomson. They are grateful to British Gas plc for the provision of funds, and for the help provided by John Barnes and Jack Roberts, Research and Technology Division, Watson House Research Station, Peterborough Road, London SW6 3HN.

proponents, the only way to hold these unprecedented hazards effectively in check.

The rising incidence of food poisoning

The 1980s have seen an exceptional rise in the number of reported food-poisoning cases. Throughout the decade there has been an almost continuous annual increase, averaging approximately 10% per annum. This compares with an average of only 4% for the previous decade. But even this high figure of 10% conceals spectacular increases in the most recent years. According to figures supplied by the Communicable Disease Surveillance Centre (CDSC), formal notifications increased by more than two and one-half times between 1980 and 1988, and by 23% and 38% in the last two years respectively (see Table 13.1) (Social Services Committee, 1989).

Most of this dramatic increase is attributable to the rising incidence of salmonella, accounting for 90% of all cases. Between 1981 and 1987 salmonella isolations doubled from 10,251 to 20,532 (Agriculture Committee, 1989). Of all the salmonella serotypes, one, *S. enteritidis*, increased sixfold between 1981 and October 1988. According to evidence presented to an inquiry on salmonella in eggs, this one serotype now accounts for just over half of all formal notifications in England and Wales—nearly two-thirds of all salmonellas. *S. enteritidis* phage type 4 (PT4), the serotype associated with eggs, accounted for 4% of all salmonella isolates in 1981, but for 24% by 1987.

Table 13.1 *Food poisoning: annual corrected notifications and incidents reported by laboratories, England and Wales from 1980*

| Year | Notifications[1] | | |
	Formal	Other	Total
1980	10318		
1981	9936		
1982	9964	4289	14253
1983	12273	5462	17735
1984	13247	7455	20702
1985	13143	6099	19242
1986	16502	7446	23948
1987	20363	8968	29331
1988	28189	13007	41196

[1] Includes confirmed and suspected cases.

Source: Figures supplied by Communicable Disease Surveillance Centre and Reproduced in *Social Services Committee Report* (1989).

The most likely cause of this rise in salmonella food poisoning is the extensive contamination of commonly eaten foods. Many raw foods are already contaminated with salmonella before they reach their final destination. It is well known, for example, that poultry are frequently contaminated with salmonella, and are therefore an important source of infection in humans. Several surveys undertaken since 1979 suggest that 60% of chickens are likely to be contaminated with salmonella, and that since 1980 *S. enteritidis* PT4 is the most commonly found serotype (Agriculture Committee, 1989). Although poultry meat is an obvious source of infection, its significance has been somewhat eclipsed by problems with eggs. In 1987 only six outbreaks were associated with eggs. By 1988, however, they had become the most commonly identified source of infection (Agriculture Committee, 1989).

Salmonellosis is by far the most important cause of food poisoning, but other organisms are also implicated. Incidents due to *Clostridium perfringens* are significant, as well as *Bacillus cereus* and *Staphylococcus aureus*, although to a much lesser extent. Recent evidence suggests that all of these are declining in importance historically (CDSC, 1988).

The problem of interpreting official data is especially acute in relation to food poisoning. Food-poisoning figures are notoriously unreliable. It is now widely accepted that the actual incidence of infection is much greater than the number of officially recorded cases. To be able to obtain a realistic assessment of the problem, official figures must be multiplied by a factor of disputed magnitude. This gives rise to varying estimates depending on the assumed multiplier.

Some dispute that the incidence of food poisoning is actually increasing and point to better reporting and improved laboratory procedure to explain the apparent rise in the number of cases. Recent developments, in terms of increased public awareness and better laboratory techniques, will undoubtedly have had some effect on reporting. As a result, the actual prevalence of infection is probably more accurately reflected in official statistics than before. It cannot be assumed, however, that the continued and upward trend is simply a reflection of improved reporting. On the contrary, according to Donald Acherson, the Chief Medical Officer, 'no-one that I know would be prepared to accept the view that the majority of this increase is due to better reporting. There is undoubtedly a problem which is appearing in larger numbers' (Social Services Committee, 1989).

Food poisoning and the catering industry

There is strong statistical evidence that the incidence of food poisoning caused by caterers is greater than that in any other sector of the food industry. According to official figures, the catering industry is responsible for nearly 70% of all general outbreaks (CDSC, 1988). It would be easy to view this evidence as yet another indictment of the industry's inferior hygiene standards. Yet these unfavourable comparisons must be treated with some caution. The complicating factor, yet again, is one of statistical validity.

Catering is a very diffuse and diverse industry. It is one of the few remaining industries where production and consumption invariably occur on the same premises. Unlike, say, the food-processing industry, its markets are highly concentrated in particular localities. As a result, when a local caterer causes a food-poisoning incident it tends to affect victims in the immediate area within a relatively short period of time. The effects of a catering-induced outbreak are, therefore, highly visible, immediate and localized. This is particularly evident when an outbreak occurs in an institutional context such as a hospital or a school (see Table 13.2). In these situations the outbreak is likely to be more severe due to the vulnerability of the client group, and also its source more obviously apparent. Hence it is possible that such outbreaks are disproportionally represented in the statistics.

There is also an increased awareness of how sectors other than catering are contributing to the recent rise in food poisoning. The massive increase in the numbers of sporadic cases reported to CDSC has led public health officials to speculate that they are, in fact, *undetected outbreaks* caused by foods incorrectly stored by large retail chains. Prolonged storage and national distribution of foods are now thought to mask the underlying source of large numbers of apparently unrelated cases. Again, this factor should be taken into account when assessing the validity of statistical comparisons. Outbreaks attributed to sectors other than catering may be significantly under-reported for reasons already discussed. Conversely, the number of outbreaks linked officially to catering establishments may, in fact, be a much more accurate reflection of their true incidence.

Questioning the conventional wisdom about the industry's burden of responsibility should not, of course, provide any comfort concerning hygiene standards in the average catering establishment. On the contrary, any food-

Table 13.2 *Food poisoning outbreaks by type of establishment, 1986–1987*

	1986	1987
Private houses	326	324
Restaurants and receptions	71	92
Hospitals	33	26
Institutions	19	13
Schools	8	3
Shops	4	13
Canteens	9	4
Farms	2	0

Source: Figures from CDSC (personal communication, 1989).

poisoning incident caused by a professional caterer is one too many. The number of incidents caused by caterers is on the increase. According to the Public Health Laboratory Service, one of the factors contributing to the growth of salmonella food poisoning is the growth of eating out, 'so that an incident that once would have been confined to a family may now involve many people' (Agriculture Committee, 1989).

Information on the number of meals eaten outside the home, in hotels and restaurants or as snacks, is recorded by the National Food Survey. It shows that the number of meals eaten outside the home rose from 2.23 per person per week in 1985 to 2.54 in 1987 (MAFF, 1988). If food poisoning continues on its present upward trend, caterers will be increasingly implicated in outbreaks.

The diversity of the industry, however, means that such generalizations can be misleading. According to Table 13.2 some sectors of the industry appear to bear a larger responsibility for food poisoning than others. Restaurants, for example, are twice as likely to be implicated than hospitals. Similarly, schools are much less likely to be involved in an outbreak than hospitals. Again, it is difficult to assess what significance the published figures have for the relative standards of food handling between different types of establishments. Outbreaks in large institutions such as schools and hospitals are, for example, much more likely to be recorded than those occurring in small restaurants and take-aways.

The impact of food-borne illness

Past discussions about food poisoning tended to assume an identity of interest between the consumer and the industry. But what appears as an unacceptably high frequency of infection on public health grounds may, nevertheless, appear much less unacceptable in commercial terms. The costs of food poisoning, particularly those borne by the producer, is a crucial issue. And yet despite its importance, very little work has been undertaken to calculate the real costs of food poisoning. Most attempts have tended to concentrate on the costs borne by the community—in terms of treating victims and investigating the outbreak—rather than those directly borne by the business causing the incident. Consequently it has always been difficult to conduct a full-blown cost-benefit analysis of different preventive measures. Without knowing what the costs are to caterers it is impossible to determine the likely benefits resulting from improved food handling and reduced disease incidence.

Calculating the costs to businesses can, of course, be problematic. Costs may be direct or indirect, tangible or intangible. When outbreaks are caused by food manufacturers the costs are likely to be direct and tangible. The costs of product recalls, in-house surveillance and losses in production are usually quantifiable. Even indirect costs such as a fall in quoted share price can be measured. But costs to the catering industry are likely to be indirect and less tangible. Factors such as *loss of reputation* or *lost business* are much more difficult to calculate. For a small business the likely financial losses are even more in-determinate. Given the volatility of the catering market, almost 10% of catering establishments go out of business every year, even without the aggravating circumstances of an outbreak. The diversity of the industry also means that even if these calculations could be made, they would have little relevance to operations in the 'non-profit' sector or to organizations with a largely *captive* clientele.

In the UK it must be assumed that the major costs of food poisoning borne by caterers are due to lost business. This may not always apply in other countries. In the USA, for example, a higher proportion of costs are incurred due to litigation on behalf of victims. The possibility of legal suits and settle-ments out of court also has a direct influence on insurance premiums which have, of course, to be added to the total cost of doing business in that country. In the UK litigation is still unusual. Legal redress is not, however, unknown.

Large catering organizations, comprising a chain of national outlets, are increasingly relying on a carefully controlled branded image to market their foodservices. The branded chain is designed to appeal to particular market segments through instant recognition on an increasingly competitive high street. A strong brand identity also strengthens the parent company's presence in the national market, and gives it considerable leverage at local level. The most notable example of this trend is McDonalds, but it is by no means confined to the fast-food sector. These types of branded chain are especially vulnerable to the economic impact of food poisoning. Although there is no research to substantiate the conclusion, it is reasonable to assume that an incident affecting one outlet could also affect consumer's perceptions of other outlets in the same chain. If the branding exercise has been successful, this association should be automatic. Given this, the economic argument might prove to be more persuasive in this sector than in many others.

New microbiological hazards

One of the most disturbing features of the recent escalation in food poisoning has been the increased prevalence of 'new' microbiological hazards which have not hitherto attracted much serious attention. *Listeria monocytogenes*, *Yersinia enterocolitica* and *campylobacter* have been added to the list of bacterial hazards. Of the three, listeria has excited the most media attention, with successive surveys revealing an unacceptably high incidence in a wide variety of foods. In fact, the presence of listeria in some foods, notably some varieties of imported soft cheeses and pre-cooked chicken dishes, prompted official Department of Health action. On 10 February 1989 the Chief Medical Officer issued a state-ment to the public on listeria. The advice contained specific warnings to pregnant women and those with impaired immune systems to avoid eating cer-tain types of soft cheeses and to make sure that cook-chilled meals and ready-to-eat poultry were adequately reheated before being eaten. The potential dangers to the public from listeria had, however, been recognized almost a year earlier (WHO, 1988(a)).

Listeria monocytogenes

An informal working group on food-borne listeriosis convened by the World Health Organization drew up recommendations for the control of listeria at the beginning of 1988. It concluded that since listeria was a widely occurring environmental microbe, the critical issue was not how to prevent its presence, 'but to control its survival and growth in order to minimize amounts in food' (WHO, 1988(a)). According to the group, 'it appears impossible, at present, to ensure supplies of food which are completely free from listeria'. Its lists four major food commodities as likely vehicles of infection: milk, and dairy products; meat, especially raw meat products; vegetables and salads; and sea-foods. As a result, the group felt unable to recommend withdrawing contami-nated food from sale except where foods in sealed packages were already contaminated or had been identified as causing human cases of listeriosis. Instead, they urged public health authorities to 'make every effort, together with the food industry, to reduce listeria contamination as far as possible, and eliminate it where feasible'. They also recommended that control procedures should be carried out at all stages of the food chain—again emphasizing the need for a systematic approach like HACCP.

There are three main reasons why health professionals are becoming more concerned about listeria. First, its incidence appears to be increasing. This is reflected in the increased detection of listeria during the course of routine microbiological surveillance and in a dramatic leap in the reported number of human cases of listeriosis. Second, the severity of the illness, listeriosis, is itself a cause of great concern. Although the disease is still comparatively rare, unlike salmonella it has a high mortality rate. Lastly, unlike other food-borne pathogens, listeria is able to multiply at temperatures previously assumed to be 'safe', for example, below 10 °C.

Surveys conducted throughout 1987 and 1988 in England and Wales revealed the presence of listeria in a wide variety of raw, fermented, cooked, chilled or frozen foods bought in retail outlets. Towards the end of 1988 and the beginning of 1989, further studies were undertaken by the PHLS Food Hygiene Laboratory to determine the incidence of listeria in cooked poultry and chilled meals (PHLS, 1989). The results are shown in Table 13.3. Of the foods tested, only soft cheeses yielded the organism in large numbers, i.e. >10,000 per gram. Soft cheese has also been implicated in two large outbreaks in other countries (WHO, 1988(a)). The high level of contamination may, in the words of the PHLS, be 'due to methods by which soft cheeses are made, including the maturation process, and to the long shelf-life which gives the opportunity for listeria to multiply' (PHLS, 1989).

The trend in reported cases of listeriosis in England and Wales has climbed

Table 13.3 *Listeria in retail foods in England and Wales, 1987–1988*

Food	Percentage of samples positive for *L. monocytogenes*
Raw chicken	60
Soft cheeses	10
Prepacked salads	7
Cook-chill food	24
Salami and continental sausage	16
Cooked, cured or smoked meat	7
Cooked prawns, shrimps and cockles	0
Raw pork sausages	52

Source: Microbiology Digest (PHLS, 1989).

steadily since 1967. Numbers increased from 25 in 1967 to a total of 291 by 1988. This increase has been particularly marked in recent years, some of which may be due to improved diagnosis and reporting. It is still likely, however, that these figures are a gross under-estimation of the real incidence of the disease. Listeriosis is not yet a notifiable disease like salmonella, and because it is still relatively uncommon it is less likely to be accurately diagnosed. Some estimates put the real incidence closer to 800 to 900 cases annually with nearly 200 fatalities. Although there is disagreement about its prevalence, no one disputes its severity. In humans listeria can cause a feverish 'flu-like' illness, septicaemia and meningitis. In pregnant women listeriosis can result in abortion, stillbirth or neo-natal illness. Although unlikely to cause serious disease in healthy adults, in susceptible hosts such as the immuno-suppressed, the elderly and neonates it has a high fatality rate. Analysis of confirmed cases reveals a rate of 30% if abortions are included. This compares with an estimated 0.4% fatality rate associated with all types of salmonella.

Listeria has the unusual property of being able to multiply, albeit slowly, at low temperatures. One cause of the increase in listeriosis is thought to be the increased use of prolonged refrigerated storage during manufacture and distribution. Refrigeration is thought to act as a selective pressure by allowing listeria to grow while simultaneously inhibiting the growth of other competing pathogens. According to most sources, listeria is not particularly heat-resistant and is killed by pasteurization (PHLS, 1989). There are some reports, however, that organisms which appear at first to have been killed by pasteurization may in some cases be able to recover at 4 °C. It is the growth of these heat-damaged organisms which may eventually cause infection. The infective dose, however, has yet to be determined.

Listeria also has unique implications for the catering industry. Increasingly, different sectors of the industry are beginning to use techniques incorporating extended-refrigerated storage such as cook-chill. Cook-chill can be found in almost every sector of the industry, but has grown rapidly in institutions such as hospitals, which feed precisely those groups most susceptible to listeriosis. This has led to a wholesale re-examination of the safety of these methods, especially when used to feed vulnerable people. Consequently, a number of surveys have investigated the incidence of listeria in foods produced by cook-chill units (PHLS, 1989; Bristol City Council, 1989). Some results are presented in Table 13.4.

Table 13.4 *Public health laboratory surveys on the incidence of listeria in cook-chilled meals from catering units, 1988–1989*

	No. of samples	Lm detected in 25 gms (%)
Nationwide survey		
Main course items	627	10 (2)
Desserts	73	0
Bristol survey		
Main course items	20	1 (5)

Source: Surveys, in order of appearance: PHLS, 1989; Bristol City Council, 1989.

Although these findings might allay some fears about the use of cook-chill within the catering industry, they also challenge current thinking. The assumption that the catering industry has uniquely poor hygiene standards is again, on this evidence, questionable. On the contrary, the problem of listeria appears to be confined exclusively to every sector but catering!

This has important practical implications for the future control of incoming ingredients. Until recently, caterers were persuaded to buy-in precisely because it was thought that outside manufacturers were able to provide food of a higher microbiological standard. This was especially the case with poultry products. Some hospital units, in fact, do not even allow raw poultry onto their premises, preferring to buy-in cooked poultry items. This is done to minimize the risk of introducing contaminated material into production kitchens. It was assumed that outside suppliers were better equipped to handle these high-risk items. According to recent evidence, this assumption about the superior hygiene capability of suppliers appears to be unwarranted. It also highlights the importance of increased vigilance over the standards of bought-in materials and the need to continually monitor and vet suppliers.

Yersinia enterocolitica

Whereas listeria has attracted the most media attention in the last two years, another organism with similar growth properties has also been increasing. *Yersinia enterocolitica* is another 'low-temperature pathogen' which is increasingly recognized as a cause of gastro-intestinal illness. Laboratory reports to the CDSC rose from only one in 1975 to 411 in 1985 (Galbraith *et al*., 1987). Most of these reported cases were sporadic, although two small outbreaks in residential schools were reported, one of which was possibly food-borne. Yersinia has been isolated from a wide variety of foods, but nearly all the serotypes identified are not those associated with human infection (Gilbert, 1987). Like listeria, the organism is capable of growth at refrigeration temperatures. Prolonged storage of food under refrigeration enables a few contaminating organisms to grow sufficiently to produce infection and illness. Fortunately, the organism does not appear to be as virulent or to produce such severe effects in humans as listeria, which probably explains why it has attracted so little public attention.

Campylobacter

Reports of campylobacter infection now exceed those due to salmonella. In England and Wales the number of confirmed cases rose from 1,349 in 1977 to 28,714 in 1988 (Gilbert, 1987; Social Services Committee, 1989). Campylobacter can be found in water, unpasteurized milk and poultry. The organism is usually responsible for sporadic cases of illness and rarely causes outbreaks. One particular serotype, *c. jejuni*, is now a leading cause of gastroenteritis in children. According to evidence presented by the Chief Medical Officer to the Social Services Committee, 'much sporadic human campylobacter is probably attributable to cross-contamination from poultry and to eating under-cooked chicken' (Social Services Committee, 1989). He concedes in the next sentence, however, that more information on sources of contamination is urgently needed to help devise appropriate methods of control.

Conclusion

The rising tide of food-borne illness, both from traditional and 'new' micro-organisms, gives the debate about food hygiene fresh impetus. Although care must be exercised when interpreting the various statistics available, food poisoning looks set to continue rising. The recent reports have highlighted the degree to which the environment is already contaminated by pathogenic micro-organisms. Whereas, in one sense, this shifts attention to sources of contamination further back down the food chain, it has also more clearly defined caterers' responsibility for food safety.

The traditional aproaches to food hygiene have manifestly failed to stem the rising tide of food-borne disease. Some would argue that this is because the *traditional approach* has never been applied, or indeed, effectively enforced. Others are more radical in their criticisms, arguing that traditional hygiene management is no longer adequate to meet the challenge of new circumstances. Instead, an entirely new approach is now required. But what precisely is the *traditional approach*, and what, if any, are its shortcomings? This and other issues are now discussed.

Traditional responses to food safety

The adequacy of traditional approaches to hygiene is increasingly being questioned. It is recognized that new foodstuffs and new technologies have introduced additional hazards into the food chain, necessitating a completely new approach to food safety. Concern over the apparent lack of success with previous hygiene measures, combined with the need to reduce their cost, means that the climate is much more favourable to approaches such as HACCP.

Education and training

The purpose of education and training programmes is to educate food handlers about the causes of microbial contamination and the factors which affect their survival and growth. There is widespread agreement that food hygiene training is probably the most cost-effective method of reducing food-borne illness. Yet, many sectors of the catering industry rely heavily on large numbers of unskilled, and often untrained employees. The Hotel and Catering Training Board estimates that less than 15% of catering employees have any kind of formal catering qualification, and even fewer receive any formal food hygiene instruction, either at school or on the job (HCTB, 1983).

Structural conditions within the industry are not conducive to a systematic or consistent approach to training. High turnover and poor staff morale can effectively undermine even the most determined training initiatives. In addition, research has demonstrated that the most highly trained staff are also those most likely to switch employers, thereby providing employers with further disincentives to train staff. There are, consequently, many employees handling food within the industry who lack even an elementary understanding of hygiene. Some know little more than the customers they are serving about how to prevent food poisoning.

According to recent research, the general awareness of food-borne hazards amongst consumers is, at best, incomplete. Recently, the Ministry of Agriculture (MAFF) decided to investigate how much the general public understood about food-borne illness and how to prevent it. They conducted a survey and published its findings (MAFF, 1988). It revealed that the public had little general understanding of the exact mechanisms of food poisoning. Less than a third, for example, understood that keeping food at room temperature, or allowing cooked food to come into contact with uncooked foods, is a likely cause of food poisoning. And although most people had heard of salmonella, they tended to be rather hazy as to 'whether these organisms should be destroyed, and if so, how this could be done'. These gaps in understanding are disturbing, especially if they are shared by catering staff.

It is easy to see why training is thought to be all-important. Instructing food handlers on the basic mechanisms of food poisoning is bound to help to eradicate poor hygiene—or so it is commonly assumed. But training, no matter how crucial, is only one part of the solution. Training can help to dispel ignorance. But is ignorance the major problem? The problem of changing peoples' behaviour is rather more complex (WHO, 1988(b)). Many incidents of food-borne disease are due not solely to ignorance of the facts, but to a failure to apply already well-known principles. The real challenge for hygiene education is to persuade employees to translate what they know into practice. But before any persuasive powers are even brought to bear on the problem, educators and trainers have to understand why people behave as they do. Employees invariably have good reasons for their behaviour, even when this involves practices known to affect food safety. Educational initiatives are much more likely to be successful in changing behaviour if they take account of employee motivations and actively explore the resistances, barriers and constraints on change. Effective education must be based, according to the World Health Organization, 'on knowledge and understanding of the prevailing beliefs and practices, the cultural values attached to these practices, and the social and economic roles they fulfil' (WHO, 1988(b)).

Undesirable practices, often deeply rooted in the culture of the kitchen, are not easily overturned, even by the most imaginative training programme. Training is not, unfortunately a magical fix for the hygiene problem. Poor food handling is not simply a product of ignorance, but is sometimes a perfectly rational response to prevailing circumstances. Indicating why a certain practice is unhygienic will have little effect if the circumstances in which it is rooted remain unchanged. Moreover, unless prevailing circumstances are conducive to changed behaviour, training may not merely be ineffective, but actually counter-productive. Advocating behavioural change without providing the material wherewithal will merely induce cynicism, and probably explains why training on its own is so often unsuccessful.

This has important implications for training initiatives in the future. Much of the training advocated is based on an inappropriate and discredited educational strategy. It assumes that training involves the unproblematic transfer of knowledge from experts to food handlers, which, in turn, is automatically translated into desirable behaviour. Many years of expensive health education programmes throughout the developed and developing world prove that this is invariably not the case (WHO, 1988(b)). Unless the various agencies charged with training adopt a much more sophisticated approach to the issue of behavioural change, future efforts will have only limited value. A new radical approach to training and promotion will be examined in more detail later.

Microbiological sampling

Sensitive to criticism of inadequate safety controls, some large caterers have increasingly emulated their counterparts in the food manufacturing sector. Traditionally, food processors have undertaken extensive end-product sampling to ensure the safety of batches before releasing them for sale to the public. In some cases foods are examined for specific pathogens or toxins, such as salmonellae or staphylococcal enterotoxins, or more often for organisms which indicate the presence of pathogens or spoilage organisms. Given the recent spate of food poisoning, caterers are now beginning to look to end-product sampling as a means of insurance. This trend is particularly evident in large production units using cook-chill or cook-freeze, where sampling is used to *prove* the unit's capability.

The use of end-product sampling has limited applications for general use within the catering industry. In most catering operations food is prepared and consumed on the same day. By the time any pathogens are detected in a specific food it will certainly have been eaten by some unsuspecting customer. For the vast majority of operations, sampling can never exercise a preventive function. But even where the gap between production and consumption is longer and the accuracy and speed of analyses are continually improving, the relevance of sampling will always be limited (Sprenger, 1988).

As a method of controlling safety within catering establishments, sampling is always retrospective. As one writer states:

microbiological standards are only a measure of the hygiene at the time of food production and cannot be seen as a guarantee that the consumer cannot acquire food poisoning, nor should it be used to convey the impression that products are free from all risk (Sandys and Wilkinson, 1988).

Moreover, because micro-organisms are unevenly distributed in food, the probability of detecting contaminated samples from a batch is extremely small. The probability of accepting a batch in which 50% of the sample units contain salmonella is 0.5, which, as one writer points out, could be achieved by tossing a coin (Sheard, 1986). When the frequency of contamination falls significantly below that figure, the probability of detecting defective samples falls correspondingly; unless, of course, the number of samples taken from each batch is increased. Increasing the number of samples analysed may increase confidence in the sampling procedure, but it is prohibitively expensive.

Microbiological results offer no information about why a particular food product has failed to meet required bacterial standards. This is because the number and type of bacteria in a finished product may reflect several different factors:

(i)   initial bacterial loading on the raw product;
(ii) hygiene standards during storage, manufacture or preparation;
(iii) type of food, preservatives used and processing;
(iv) type and quality of packaging;
(v)   time and temperature history of product.

When a positive sample is detected it is crucial that the point of failure is identified to prevent similar results in the future (Sprenger, 1988).

The value of microbiological sampling is limited to a number of clearly defined circumstances. Sampling may be useful in determining the effectiveness of cleaning and disinfection; the effectiveness of processing; to ascertain whether handling techniques are satisfactory or to indicate trends in product quality. In these instances bacteriological monitoring is used to assess the effectiveness of in-process procedures rather than to confirm the safety of the end-product. Despite warnings about the limited use of bacteriological sampling and its prohibitive cost, the trend towards extensive sampling continues. It is a trend which is disturbing some experts. One writer argues that sampling can often prevent any serious attempts to get to grips with the industry's real hygiene problems:

Instead of paying attention to the real problems in food hygiene, people were vainly looking for microbiological indicators for unhygienic situations. In addition the use of these techniques did not contribute to an understanding of food hygiene, but, on the contrary, it strengthened illusory feelings of safety (Beckers, 1988).

The writer concludes that unless these limitations are fully appreciated, the increased use of microbiological techniques in catering will do little to improve hygiene or protect the safety of the consumer.

These inherent dangers have not altered the indiscriminate use or popularity of microbiology. In part, this is due to a genuine misunderstanding about its legitimate role in food safety. But there are other reasons. Over recent years there has been increased pressure on managers to *prove* the safety of their operations. Hard scientific data, however spurious in relation to safety, satisfy a legitimate demand for reassurance. Reams of sampling results, couched in suitably technical language, are precisely the tangible evidence required by those outside the organization. The activities of commercial laboratories have also fuelled the popularity of extensive sampling. With many previously public laboratories now having to be self-financing, laboratories are adopting much more aggressive marketing techniques. In their eagerness to obtain extra business, the appropriateness and relevance of sampling is sometimes overlooked.

Control and inspection of premises

Governments have traditionally relied on regulatory controls and inspections to maintain certain standards of safety in food operations. The Food Act 1984 is the main statutory instrument for controlling food safety in England and Wales, and is enforced at local level by environmental health officers. The Food Hygiene (General) Regulations 1970 are, however, probably more important when considering hygiene standards in the majority of food premises. The main aim of the Regulations is to 'secure a standard of construction and of equipment in food premises . . . and of conduct of food handlers to ensure the protection of foodstuffs against contamination' (Hobbs and Robert, 1989). They set down standards relating to premises, washing and sanitary facilities, equipment, food handlers and working practices. The Regulations have, in effect, dictated the framework for food hygiene since their inception.

The very existence of statutory requirements has not always had a positive effect on hygiene standards. Very often compliance with the legislation has been viewed as an end in itself. In fact, it outlines minimum standards below which no caterer should fall, and which, in practice, should be exceeded. The requirements have also tended to shift the focus of responsibility for managing hygiene from inside the organization, where it properly belongs, to outside enforcement officers (Mathews, 1986). When hygiene is defined exclusively in terms of compliance, the role of the local environmental health officer is greatly circumscribed. This shortcoming was first highlighted at the public inquiry into the Stanley Royd food-poisoning outbreak. Here, the official report made a clear distinction between the minimal requirements to ensure compliance with the law and those working practices, which, while not in themselves legal offences, are nevertheless likely to lead to food poisoning (Mathews, 1986).

The weaknesses of the Food Hygiene Regulations are widely acknowledged throughout the environmental health community. Over the years they have been subjected to a number of criticisms. First, the Regulations, having been formulated in 1970, are hopelessly outmoded. Since the early 1970s new processes and new microbiological hazards have emerged which the Regulations could not have foreseen. Second, the Regulations give undue emphasis to relatively unimportant factors while ignoring more crucial matters. They are overly concerned with maintaining standards of construction and equipment in food premises at the expense of hygienic work practices—despite the fact that the most commonly recurring faults in food-poisoning outbreaks relate to failures of operation rather than flaws in surroundings (Roberts, 1984). Third, the Regulations contain many exemptions. This means that in circumstances where compliance might be beneficial, the Regulations cannot actually be applied. Lastly, the requirements are very general and specify no clearly defined standards. Vague terms such as 'satisfactory', 'adequate', 'acceptable' and 'suitable' are frequently used, leaving the question of compliance to the discretion of the individual inspector. This produces inconsistencies when applying the law, undermining the credibility of the enforcement officer and bringing the law into general disrepute.

Conclusion

The implication is that the *traditional approach* to food hygiene has left an un-fortunate legacy. It is responsible for propounding powerful fallacies about hygiene which will not be easily dislodged, among which is the assumption that a clean kitchen is automatically a hygienic kitchen. As an inquiry report so succinctly states:

it should be remembered that, just as it is possible to avoid food poisoning in a bad kitchen, it is possible for it to arise from faulty hygiene in the most suitable premises (DHSS, 1986).

Nevertheless, there is a tendency to use the terms 'clean' and 'hygienic' synonymously—to equate visible cleanliness with microbiological safety. This myth has been sustained by cleaning companies whose marketing activities have re-enforced the connection for obvious commercial ends. In the popular imagination, hygiene and cleaning are one and the same thing. The notion is also perpetuated in most forms of hygiene training and by official documents which misleadingly refer to *clean food*.

Traditional approaches have resulted in a powerful and insidious 'common-sense' about food hygiene which actively obscures the real causes of food poisoning. These approaches, in that sense, are less effective than they might be, and on some occasions, may actually be counter-productive. By directing attention and resources towards practices which have no direct relationship with preventing food poisoning, they engender a false sense of security while leaving the operation exposed to real hazards. Anyone wishing to adopt a new and more effective approach to hygiene must, unfortunately, first dispel these illusions.

HACCP: a new approach to quality control

The apparent failure of traditional approaches to food hygiene has led to an increased interest in more systematic and cost-effective methods of control. The HACCP approach is currently being promoted as one such method. The World Health Organization (WHO) has advocated its implementation throughout the food chain as a way of controlling food-borne disease in both developing and developed countries. The Department of Health has recom-mended its use in relation to cook-chill and cook-freeze catering methods and the National Health Service Training Board is now actively investigating its effectiveness for controlling hospital foodservices.

The HACCP approach, however, is not new. It was developed first by the Pillsbury Company in association with NASA to control microbiological hazards in the manufacture of food for the United States Manned Space programme in the early 1970s. Since that time, it has also been applied successfully to other branches of food manufacture, especially in canning low-acid foods, where strict standards of control are required. Whereas its origins are indisputably in the food manufacturing sector, it may also be applied to the control of foodservices.

HACCP and the Food and Drugs Administration (FDA)

In the USA, HACCP was adopted by the FDA as part of its national inspection programme. There, the FDA, which held nation-wide responsibility for inspecting food manufacturing plants, wished to institute a national programme of inspection to replace the rather *ad hoc* measures which had hitherto existed. HACCP was intended to provide the agency with a uniform and consistent approach to inspections across the entire country. Joseph Hile, then the FDA's executive director for regional operations, described it as a cost-effective means of inspecting an industry where safety problems were known to exist (Hile, 1974). The idea was to start off with a series of in-depth inspections to determine critical control points in the process, and then to use these key indicators to direct limited inspections:

While we view the technique as an investigational tool, it is of significant value to the firms for their own use as well. It encourages a firm to analyze its own process from a systems viewpoint. Plant management can identify and correct potential trouble spots, and it can verify the adequacy of the internal quality-control system or develop one if none exists (Hile, 1974).

By applying HACCP to its inspections programme, the FDA made a deliberate decision to inspect the control of processes rather than the operation itself. The inspector determined the capability of the processor's own quality-control system, and in so doing shifted responsibility for day-to-day safety from the agency onto the organization and its management:

Our approach is designed to give the FDA insight into how the firm is running 365 days a year, particularly when an inspector is not there. It is designed to identify the potential problems associated with the product rather precisely, and it provides a clear definition of what needs to be done to correct objectionable conditions and procedures (Hile, 1974).

This approach, claimed Hile, was beneficial both for the FDA and the consumer because it prevented the production and distribution of hazardous food products, thereby avoiding possible recalls at a later date.

Basic principles of HACCP

HACCP has been variously described as 'preventive quality control' (Sheard, 1986); 'a management control system' (Coates, 1986); and an 'investigational tool' (Hile, 1974). However described, it represents a significant break with traditional approaches to controlling microbiological hazards. Increasingly, HACCP is being suggested as a method of assuring quality in an industry which is renowned for its variable and inconsistent end-products. In this sense HACCP is viewed as one step towards 'total quality management'.

Whatever its present-day meaning, originally HACCP was concerned solely with the control of microbiological hazards. The two components of its title—Hazard Analysis and Critical Control Points—offer some clues as to its provenance. The aim of the system is to identify potential hazards in the production process and to eliminate them where possible. Where eliminating those hazards is not practicable, the aim is to control them within acceptable parameters.

Hazard analysis

'Hazard analysis' is now an accepted part of the hygiene vocabulary, but its meaning with HACCP is very precise. It is, according to one writer, 'a rational, logical process of estimating the risk associated with processing and marketing a given food product' (Bauman, 1974). A 'hazard analysis' estimates risks in producing, processing or preparing foods by assessing all possible hazards and the likelihood of them occurring (Bryan, 1981). Here, the terms *hazard* and *risk* also have a specific meaning. *Hazard* refers to 'the potential to cause harm' (Kilsby, 1988). *Risk*, on the other hand, is the likelihood of that potential actually being realized. The aim of 'hazard analysis' is to assess the likelihood, given certain processing operations, of a theoretical hazard becoming an actual risk.

Identifying hazards requires both microbiological knowledge and a detailed understanding of all the processes to which a given food will be subjected. There are many different organisms which can cause food-borne illness, and all have different growth characteristics. Because of this it is important to consider the types of organism likely to be present in raw materials or to be introduced during handling, and how they will be affected by each processing or handling stage. An analysis is undertaken for each individual product in order to reflect the many different foods and environmental conditions in which pathogens are able to survive and grow. The hazards identified are, therefore, specific to a given food product and unique to those processing requirements.

The use of certain food ingredients is known to pose a risk. From previous epidemiological evidence, some foods, such as poultry, for example, are strongly associated with food-borne disease. Consequently, ingredients can be categorized according to their hazard potential. The objective is to identify those products which comprise ingredients with a known risk of contamination. These may include:

1. ingredients which are assumed to be a potential source of contamination;
2. intermediate ingredients which have not undergone any treatment which could destroy any pathogens present;
3. ingredients with a composition which will support the growth of pathogens.

This categorization also helps to identify which products can safely be excluded from a detailed hazard analysis. Only those comprising ingredients with a known hazard potential require detailed investigation.

Armed with information about the conditions which sustain the survival and growth of harmful micro-organisms, scientists can then examine the production process to determine where potential hazards could occur. Conducting a hazard analysis should provide a complete picture of how specific food products are actually produced. This, in itself, is a potentially radical undertaking. It is concerned only with how food is actually produced as opposed to assumptions about how it is produced, or even how stated policy says it should be produced. Obtaining a full picture of what actually happens may mean long and detailed observation.

Hazards can arize at all stages during production—in raw materials, in processing and in post-processing. The aim of the investigation is to reveal:

1. **employee practices** which could lead to, or fail to prevent cross-contamination;
2. **time-temperature combinations** which may permit the survival and subsequent growth of pathogens, or fail to destroy sufficient numbers during reheating;
3. **procedures** which might contaminate foods after reheating;
4. **environmental conditions** which might permit the survival and transfer of pathogens from the surrounding environment (Bryan, 1981).

Generally speaking, the hazards identified will correspond to faults specified by one or more of the above categories.

Although the analysis is specific to both product and operation, it is still possible to identify general hazards associated with, say, a certain type of operation or a particular production method. So, for example, several writers have identified a number of potentially hazardous operations found within most catering establishments (Bryan, 1981; Munce, 1984). These are: procuring and receiving raw materials; storage; thawing; handling and preparing raw foods; cooking; handling cooked products; hot holding; cooling; reheating; serving; cleaning and maintenance; and personal hygiene. If not properly controlled, hazards may arise during any of these processes or events. Hazard analysis can also identify general hazards associated with certain production methods such as cook-chill or cook-freeze. This may provide useful guidance prior to conducting a more detailed analysis of an individual operation. Despite these more general applications, hazard analysis is still, first and foremost, a *bespoke* rather than an *off-the-peg* approach.

Critical control points

Hazard analysis is an interesting and educative exercise in itself. But the information gained from the investigation is only useful if it is translated into action to remove or control the hazards which it has identified. Too often the analysis is treated as an end in itself, rather than as a means to prevent hazards arising in the future. Alternatively, all the identified hazards are controlled indiscriminately, irrespective of how or whether they will affect the safety of the final product (Sheard, 1986). In the first case, too little is done; in the second, too much. Both stem from a failure to appreciate what is and what is not critical to food safety. The concept of a *critical control point* aims to help organizations differentiate between the two and direct their efforts where they will have most effect.

A critical control point is a location, a practice, a procedure or a process which, if not controlled, could result in an unacceptable safety risk (see Figure 13.1). The term 'critical control point' draws attention to the fact not all hazards are equally critical to the safety of the end-product. *Safety* is itself a relative term, so clear standards have to be specified in advance to provide a benchmark against which the effectiveness of controls can be evaluated. In contrast to traditional hygiene approaches, HACCP is both highly selective and prescriptive.

It may not be necessary, or even desirable, to control every hazard identified. Determining which hazards must be tightly controlled, and how that control is to be exercised and monitored, is the key to an effective safety system. But deciding which hazards are to be controlled depends on a number of factors. The severity of a hazard and its likely frequency are important considerations. *Clostridium botulinum* is a more severe hazard than *Clostriudium perfringens*. Similarly, *Listeria monocytogenes* is a greater hazard to patients in a maternity ward than to the customers of a workplace canteen. Consideration of where the hazard occurs in the sequence of operations is also relevant. Controlling the possibility of contamination *before* cooking might be judged less significant than *after* cooking. The reason for such discrimination is largely pragmatic. In most organizations resources are limited, and therefore, it is desirable to keep the number of critical control points to a minimum—confined to risks judged to be truly significant (Sheard, 1986). With these considerations in mind, critical control points can be ranked in terms of importance, with resources and effort directed accordingly (Kilsby, 1988).

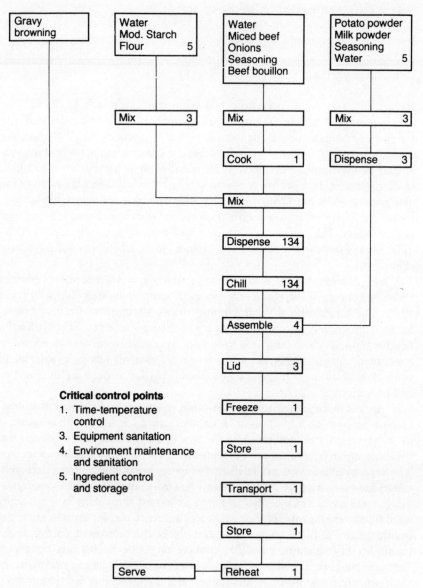

Figure 13.1 *A process flow diagram for cottage pie (cook-freeze system) indicating critical control points.*
Source: After Sheard (1986).

Monitoring and control

Having determined which hazards are critical to the safety of the product, effective measures must be devised to control them. Past experience highlights a number of control measures critical to many foodservice operations. These include:

1. time/temperature control;
2. personnel sanitation;
3. equipment sanitation;
4. environmental maintenance and sanitation;
5. ingredient control and storage.

Once it has been decided how a particular hazard is to be controlled, it is important to set a limit or standard against which that control can be monitored.

Whereas it is theoretically possible to set quantitative microbiological limits for control points, in practice, these are far too cumbersome and expensive to monitor on a large scale. They also provide only retrospective information about whether a particular hazard has been effectively contained. Consequently, when setting appropriate standards or limits, practical considerations are paramount:

Appropriate standards will be of a nature and level which will successfully limit contamination, survival or proliferation of pathogens at critical control points and be capable of being checked by *some test, measurement or observation with sufficient frequency to allow management to know whether control is being maintained*. The nature of the critical control points used and the standards set will have to depend, to some extent, on the resources and expertise available (Sheard, unpublished, our emphasis).

Here again, pragmatism is the order of the day. Standards are appropriate only if they are capable of being routinely monitored, usually by simple observation or measurement. So, for example, objective quantitative standards for time-temperature combinations are relatively simple for employees to monitor at regular intervals.

One advantage of the HACCP approach is that when setting acceptable limits and standards for critical control points, employees, and especially managers, are forced, often for the first time, to consider why certain routine hygiene measures are performed. Actions which are performed routinely can quickly degenerate into unthinking rituals. HACCP provides the opportunity for employees to ask why a certain practice takes place, or whether it is done at the appropriate times and to a standard which will achieve its stated objective. Take, for example, routine hand-washing. HACCP provides a timely reminder that the ultimate aim is to limit the contamination of the food from personnel at critical stages in the process. Saying this does not underestimate the importance of hand-washing routines. On the contrary, it highlights the reasons why it is important at particular points in the process. Similarly, it draws attention to the importance of establishing standards for hand-washing which will prevent significant contamination of food, or re-contamination of the hands after washing, or cross-contamination between foods.

Being able to monitor that a processing or handling procedure at an established critical control point is properly carried out is crucially important. For there to be confidence in the safety of the end-product, evidence that controls have been correctly executed is required. Unless this requirement is met, no manager can ever guarantee that the system of controls implemented will prevent contaminated food reaching the customer. **Food safety is thus controlled indirectly by means of a series of tests and measurements at a number of critical control points.**

These tests and measurements can range from careful temperature monitoring to straightforward visual observation. It is equally important that the results of these observations are recorded. Records provide tangible evidence that measurements have actually been undertaken. The results can also be used retrospectively to investigate any recurring deviations. Unexpected results are investigated to determine whether any process or procedure requires modification. This feedback mechanism is an important feature, since it allows the system to be continually up-dated and tailored to suit changing circumstances. HACCP is, in this sense, not a system, but a process which is continually evolving over time.

From past experience, the most reliable means of ensuring that controls are understood and executed is through the extensive use of documentation. A detailed written specification for each product or group of products lays down ingredients, formulation, production methods, critical control points, acceptable limits, control methods and instructions for monitoring. This information is then made available to all relevant personnel and acts as a technical manual which can be continuously referred to throughout the production process. These specifications are, in effect, rules governing all aspects of production and handling. Once HACCP is in place, adhering to it is simply a matter of following these rules and knowing what to do when the system breaks down.

HACCP and the management of quality

HACCP was originally developed as an alternative and more effective means of assuring food safety. Of necessity, then, it attached critical importance to control of microbiological hazards rather than the sensory or nutritional condition of food. Recently, however, the industry is placing much greater emphasis on those attributes which affect customer acceptability. The customer's perception of quality is now seen as a key to profitability (Lockwood, 1989; Jones, 1983). But arriving at a clear definition of *quality*, incorporating customers' needs and preferences, is not always easy.

Traditionally, quality has often been confused with excellence or even the absence of complaints (Sheard, 1986). Generally speaking, it refers to sensory attributes such as flavour, appearance and temperature. The commonly accepted way of controlling these attributes is through critical tasting. Tasting the final product is thought to be an effective means of maintaining the quality of food served to customers. The problem, of course, is that this measurement of quality lacks any reliability or validity as a form of control.

Conventional definitions of quality tend to be production oriented. But there is an increasing realization of the need for a marketing orientation. Defining quality can only be done by constant reference back to what the customer wants and also what he/she is prepared to pay. Lockwood (1989) argues that a more appropriate definition is the one adopted by the British Standards Institute which stresses the 'product or service's ability to satisfy the customers' needs'. Within an increasingly segmented consumer market, the management of quality becomes a more differentiated exercise since each segment has its own specific quality requirements. It is no longer a mere technical matter. It becomes a sociological or behavioural one, where the operator must consider 'the customers' attitudes, preferences and perceptions to be able to provide *quality*' (Lockwood, 1989).

Some see HACCP performing a broad function in quality management, extending control of quality beyond solely *back-room* activities to all aspects of customer service (Jones, 1983; Wyckoff, 1984). The rationale for this extended role is, as Wyckoff points out, the realization that 'a product or service of high quality is the result of a total system of quality throughout every aspect of the firm'. This is particulary true in the hospitality industry, where the customers' perceptions of quality involve a mix of tangible and intangible elements such as food and beverage, service and atmosphere (Jones, 1983). According to Jones, 'extending the critical points model, it is possible to encompass the service aspect of the "product" and suggest assessment determinants and revision procedures for the atmosphere element'. Both physical and service attributes can, in principle, therefore, be the subject of the same quality procedures of specification, documentation and control.

It can be seen that the original HACCP concept has developed and broadened beyond its pre-occupation with hygiene to encompass every aspect of management. It is increasingly being seen as the basis of total quality management—an alternative system of controlling both the tangible and the notoriously intangible elements of the catering business.

The application of HACCP to the catering industry

Systems catering

Catering is one of the few remaining industries where production, or cooking, and consumption, or service, occur relatively contemporaneously and on the same premises (Gabriel, 1988). Throughout its history, catering has struggled with the logistical problems this situation has created. One of the biggest is how to produce large amounts of food for serving at a particular time. Traditionally, in order to bring together all the components of a meal simultaneously, the industry has resorted to the much-discredited practice of warm-holding. Food is prepared in advance and held warm until required for service. The adverse effects of warm-holding have been well documented (Glew, 1985). Holding food at warm temperatures creates ideal conditions for bacterial growth and adversely affects nutritional and organoleptic quality. Unfortunately, it remains a widespread and persistent practice. But increasingly the catering industry is attempting to resolve its central logistical problem by the use of new catering methods. There is a growing realization that some form of cooling after cooking is preferable to holding food hot.

Refrigeration is now seen as a crucial link in bringing together all the components of a meal simultaneously without the disadvantages of warm holding. The use of specialized refrigeration technology has allowed another intermediate stage to be interposed between production and service, providing a convenient time buffer between the kitchen and the customer. This intermediate holding stage aims to alleviate the problems inherent in conventional catering, relieving the traditional stresses and strains on the production process.

The introduction of this extra stage between cooking and service has spawned a number of new catering techniques. The use of refrigeration extends the normal *life* of food, freeing the kitchen from the immediate demands and pressures of customer service. Cold storage, whether at chill or freeze temperatures, severs the link between cooking and service so that production is no longer fixed at a particular place or to particular times. Instead of concentrating on feeding customers, the focus shifts to 'feeding' a controlled, predictable demand. Increasingly, caterers are combining these techniques with large-scale centralized systems in which food is prepared, cooked and perserved prior to service (North, 1988). Utilizing these principles, cook-chill and cook-freeze catering are already in widespread use. More recently, vacuum and modified-atmosphere packaging is being used to extend shelf life even further (Sheppard, 1988(b)).

Cook-freeze, cook-chill and *sous vide* are all examples of what is now known as *systems catering*. The defining characteristics of the *systems* approach represent a decisive break with traditional forms of catering. Although these methods share many features with conventional catering skills and techniques, the scale of production, the introduction of refrigeration and reheating technologies, the rationalization of shift work and the distancing of the central production unit from the customer make them radically different. It has been said that, in many respects, they represent a new *industrialized* form of catering, involving disciplines and techniques more commonly found in food manufacturing than traditional catering (Gabriel, 1988).

The applicability of HACCP to 'systems' catering

As the name suggests, systems catering involves a more systemized approach to catering. The very fact that production can be separated in time and location from service means that the traditional pressures on the kitchen are suddenly removed. Production no longer has to be geared to the unpredictable demands of consumers, but can be spread more evenly throughout the day. Cooking becomes operations-led rather than customer-driven. Opportunities for proper production planning and scheduling increases eliminating the need for peaks and troughs in activity and rationalizing the use of both labour and equipment (Sheppard, 1987).

The buffer provided by refrigeration and vacuum packaging also liberates production from the place of service. Very often these new methods are combined with centralized production in large 'kitchens' capable of supplying several end-units. Centralized production imitates the conditions of industrial production. The larger volumes of food to be handled merit the use of large-scale specialized equipment. Consequently, larger batches of food receive standard treatment in automatic or semi-automatic cookers. Food produced within a central production 'kitchen' is, therefore, much more likely to be of a consistent and uniform quality. This is re-enforced by the greater ease of supervision and control when production is concentrated under one roof.

Systems catering enhances managerial control. Cook-chill, in fact, has often been described as a *management catering system*. The combination of refrigeration technologies and centralized production facilitate work methods and forms of organization which increase opportunities for management prerogative. HACCP, too, is strongly associated with the managerial ethos and has been referred to as a *management control system*. While the conditions required to implement it effectively simply do not exist within the vast majority of catering operations, they do pertain in systems catering. A more systemized approach to production is also highly conducive to an increasingly systemized approach to hygiene management. There is a strong conceptual symmetry between systems catering and HACCP, and in theory, at least, they provide powerful re-enforcement for each other.

While systems catering is an obvious candidate for the HACCP approach, it appears that its need is less pressing here than in other sectors of the catering industry. There is, for example, no evidence that any cook-freeze or cook-chill system operating in this country has ever been responsible for an outbreak of food poisoning. In this sense, systems catering does not appear to present a particular risk. On the contrary, if selective measures are to be concentrated where they will be most effective, effort should be directed towards those types of catering outlets already known to cause food poisoning. Paradoxically, these would tend to include precisely the types of operations where HACCP would be most difficult to apply. The prospect is, therefore, that HACCP will be adopted in operations where it is easiest to apply but where the risk of food poisoning is small, and less likely to be applied in those operations which the risk is greatest. If this is the case, its contribution to reducing food-borne illness will be extremely limited.

However, is the absence of any reported outbreaks associated with cook-freeze or cook-chill foods reliable grounds for discounting risk? The absence of such reports is adduced to *prove* that these systems are not inherently more hazardous than conventional catering. However, this line of reasoning is extremely dubious. Although initially plausible, it ignores the distinction between *hazard* and *risk*. The term *hazard* refers to 'the potential to cause harm', whereas *risk* denotes 'the likelihood of that potential being realized' (Kilsby, 1985). Consequently, cook-chill can be evaluated in terms of its inherent potential to cause harm, as opposed to how frequently it is implicated in actual outbreaks.

Any statistical comparison of food-poisoning rates in cook-chill establishments with other forms of catering is, in any event, spurious. There are approximately 340,000 catering premises in the UK, of which cook-chill accounts for no more than 300. Given that the total number of premises are responsible for 177 confirmed outbreaks, 'any sample of 300 would have the statistical probability of causing an outbreak of 1:0.16 in any given year. In other words, the chance of an outbreak attributable to cook-chill is less than one in every six years' (North, 1988). Given that the majority of units have been in operation for less than that period, it is premature to assume anything about the systems' safety. Similarly, central production would produce a very different pattern of food poisoning. It would, for example, tend to reduce the frequency of outbreaks overall but increase their severity, when they did occur, due to the large numbers of meals produced at each site.

The hazards of new catering systems

Rather than relying on the past safety record of these systems, a hazard analysis would provide a much more valid and rational assessment of the risks they might pose in the future. An analysis of each one—cook-freeze, cook-chill and *sous vide*—would reveal general hazard characteristics. At each processing stage it would be possible to identify both common hazards and those which are specific to any one particular production system.

When assessing the risk inputs associated with different production systems, certain inputs will be shared. Potentially hazardous ingredients such as poultry are in common use throughout the catering industry and have to be viewed as a general hazard. Certain other pathogenic organisms are selective in their habitats. *Sous vide* and cook-chill are now known to provide precisely the conditions required for the survival and growth of certain micro-organisms. Anaerobic bacteria such as *clostridia* may survive and multiply within *sous vide* packs when they are stored for prolonged periods. Refrigerated storage also provides an hospitable environment for the so-called 'low-temperature pathogens' such as listeria. This must be considered where these systems are used to feed groups with a known susceptibility to food-borne illness, such as the elderly, the very young, pregnant women or the sick.

Coincidentally, the major stages of production identified in Table 13.5 are also stages at which possible hazards could arise. Table 13.6 identifies the potential hazards and their associated control points. At this level of generality, the risk assessment is relatively crude. The analysis gets considerably more complex when specific foods are introduced or when other processes or materials in the same area or using the same equipment are also taken into account.

Technical obstacles to HACCP

There are many obvious and immediate differences between food production in a large manufacturing plant and in a large production kitchen. Some of these

Table 13.5 *Main stages of production in conventional, cook-chill, cook-freeze and* sous vide *catering systems*

Conventional	Cook-chill	Cook-freeze	Sous vide
Procurement	Procurement	Procurement	Procurement
Preparation	Preparation	Preparation	Preparation
			Vacuum packing
Cooking	Cooking	Cooking	Cooking
Warm-holding			
	Chilling	Freezing	Chilling
	& chilled	& frozen	& chilled
	storage	storage	storage
		Thawing	
Portioning,	Portioning	Portioning	
assembly	& assembly	& assembly	
& distribution			
	Cold-holding	Cold-holding	Cold-holding
	& distribution	& distribution	& distribution
	Re-heating	Re-heating	Re-heating
			Portioning
			& assembly
SERVICE	SERVICE	SERVICE	SERVICE

Table 13.6 *Risk inputs and relevant control points*

	Possible hazard	Control points
Procurement	Contamination	Ingredient control and storage
Preparation sanitation	Contamination	Personnel and equipment
	Survival and growth of pathogens	Time-temperature exposure
Vacuum packing	Contamination	Personnel and equipment sanitation
	Growth of pathogens	Packaging atmosphere and integrity
Cooking	Survival of pathogens	Time-temperature exposure
Warm-holding	Contamination	Personnel and equipment sanitation
	Growth of pathogens	Time-temperature exposure
Chilling and chilled storage	Contamination	Personnel and equipment sanitation
	Growth of pathogens	Time-temperature exposure
Freezing and frozen storage	Contamination	Personnel and equipment sanitation
	Growth of pathogens	Time-temperature exposure
Portioning and assembly	Contamination	Personnel and equipment sanitation
	Growth of pathogens	Time-temperature exposure
Thawing	Contamination	Personnel and equipment sanitation
	Growth of pathogens	Time-temperature exposure
Cold-holding and distribution	Contamination	Personnel and equipment sanitation
	Growth of pathogens	Time-temperature exposure
Service	Contamination	Personnel and equipment sanitation
	Survival and growth of pathogens	Time-temperature exposure

differences are crucial to understanding why applying HACCP to the food-services industry is likely to be more difficult and complex. The following features, common to the industry, represent problems which must be overcome if any effective quality-control system is to be achieved:

1. Complex food-handling systems involving a multiplicity of different products, many employees and intermediate handling;
2. A lack of standardized methods;
3. Lack of systematic production planning;

4. Mainly batch rather than continuous operations;
5. Frequent mis-matching of equipment capacity.

Paradoxically because of these complications, one writer claims that there must be 'a much more thorough and extensive use of the HACCP concept than there would be in the normal food processing plant' (Snyder, 1986).

Complex food-handling systems

In many ways catering involves a much more complex food-handling system than the conventional large-volume food production plant. A kitchen menu is likely to have far more items than a comparable manufacturing plant (Sheard, 1986). In addition, the normal steps in producing food will nearly always be more extensive, including recipe formulation, specifying ingredients, ordering from suppliers, receiving, inspecting, storing, pre-preparing, cleaning, cutting, and weighing; preparing, cooking and blending, staging, holding, plating or packaging, serving, disposing of leftovers, cooling, recycling (Snyder, 1986). In a kitchen, unlike a processing plant, incoming ingredients are likely to be in different stages of preparation, ranging from raw right through to cooked. Some will require extensive treatment; others will simply be held and then amalgamated with other meal components before being served. Because of this, there can be no simple linear workflow. All ingredients, whatever their stage of preparation, will eventually have to be integrated into one single production flow (North, 1989). At most stages of the operation, food and food handlers will be in constant contact, thereby increasing the possibility of contamination. Attempting to control this complex flow of ingredients, processes and people is a formidable challenge, and one which is rarely seen in the average manufacturing plant.

Lack of standardized methods

Standardized methods are a crucial component of the HACCP approach. Critical controls are identified and then implemented on the basis of standardized procedures applicable to different batches of food, from one day to another. While the use of standard recipes is becoming more widespread within the catering industry, standard and consistent procedures are still uncommon. Even in large production kitchens, there is considerable scope for improvisation. As long as food is produced in the quantities and at the time required, how it is produced is often left to the discretion of employees (Sheard, 1986).

Lack of production planning

Proper production planning is rare within conventional catering. This is because the kitchen is demand-led rather than production driven. Cooking to demand makes proper planning very difficult. Although some forecasting of demand takes place so that the kitchen is in a reasonable state of readiness, this is far from being a precise science, and in practice, the kitchen will occasionally be forced to cope with unforeseen surges of demand. Very often, only when these conventional time pressures are removed, as in the case of cook-chill or cook-freeze, is it possible to even contemplate proper production planning.

Batch production

Unlike most manufacturing plants, where food is produced continuously by machines, food is still produced in batches within the catering industry. Batch production is intrinsically more difficult to control. Food must be transferred from one piece of equipment to another, creating both opportunities for contamination and delays between different stages of production. The identification of discrete batches of food for monitoring purposes is also problematic. Defining what constitutes *a batch* is less significant than being able to differentiate it as a discrete entity during processing. Effective monitoring at critical control points requires that the results, whether illustrating time-temperature exposure or pH, can be related directly to a particular batch. Defining a batch will always be an arbitrary decision, based on what is deemed to be a convenient unit of measurement. Ever mindful of the practicalities, Sheard defines a batch as 'that quantity which undergoes the major heat step in one piece of equipment at one time' (Sheard, unpublished).

Mismatching of equipment capacity

Proper production planning and scheduling is made considerably more difficult when equipment of different capacities is used. With most catering operations, kitchen equipment has been acquired over the years, with little thought given to matching the capacity of one piece to another. Consequently, small-scale equipment is often used in mass-production settings. This leads to delays during processing. Batches from cooking equipment, for example, may be too large to be processed by the next piece of equipment and may have to be held over until there is sufficient capacity available. This produces additional control problems and complicates production scheduling.

Despite these technical difficulties, HACCP offers considerable advantages over traditional methods of quality control. These are not, however, the only or even the most significant problems to be overcome. The preoccupation with the technical substance of HACCP has tended to obscure its other role—that of transforming the organization and culture of what is still an essentially craft-based industry. Consequently, the enormity of its effects and the changes which it requires have been underestimated. These considerations are especially relevant when attempting to understand why HACCP is not already in widespread use.

The craft of catering

In traditional catering, cooks and chefs have always had latitude over how they produce food. The lack of any detailed planning in most kitchens often results in an undue reliance on employee initiative and leaves considerable scope for improvisation. This has given rise to a tradition of *ad hoc* methods and work practices. This highly individual and *ad hoc* approach is responsible for the industry's highly variable results. If HACCP is to be successfully applied, production and service methods must be standardized. Any deviation from standardized methods and practices *may* invalidate the HACCP model, and *ad hoc* decisions, at whatever level, are likely to undermine the reliability of the system.

Sheard (1986) points out that if, for example, frozen chicken carcasses were used instead of chilled carcasses, this would require the extra unplanned operation of thawing. A consequence of this might be that the cooking operation failed to pasteurize the product because its starting temperature was much lower than expected. Employee discretion is, then, the enemy of systematic control.

But the sociological consequences of standardization have not yet been adequately considered. According to Wyckoff, 'some managers and customers feel that the loss of the personal touch is too severe a penalty to pay for productivity gains through "production-line" approaches' (Wyckoff, 1984). He warns of the danger of distorting services to allow the application of standard methods. McDonalds, for example, designed their services standard just so that production methods could be applied. While the approach has proved very successful in commercial terms, its preoccupation with producing a consistent and reliable mass product is not to everyone's taste.

Standardization, critics argue, can be a synonym for *blandification* (Gabriel, 1988; Wyckoff, 1984). It can give rise to a rather rigid approach to service, where customer needs are subordinated to the operator's given package. Henry Ford unwittingly summarized the problem in his famous dictum, 'you can have any colour you like as long as it's black'. Rather than underpinning 'quality', standardization is sometimes seen as diametrically opposed to it.

Another problem is that the types of production concepts applied have often been steeped in *Scientific Management*, a philosophy which has many unfortunate connotations for those working within the industry. A hazard analysis is, in effect, a form of applied work study. Invariably it has been associated with a managerial ethos which seeks to control the work process partly by limiting and directing the activities of employees.

Although HACCP declares an interest in the process rather than the worker, changes to the process inevitably affect the degree of worker autonomy and discretion. Sheard (1986) explicitly acknowledges this implication. When discussing the role of written production specifications, he argues that they should become the focus for staff training so that the 'operation of the food safety control becomes an integral part of the job. The responsibility carried by operatives is increased but the scope for improvisation and discretion is reduced'. Although this aspect of HACCP has not yet been fully explored, it is clearly relevant to any discussion concerning its future acceptance within the industry. Employee resistance may be an important factor in determining whether or not HACCP succeeds. Consequently, it needs to be considered when any education and training plan is being devised.

Conclusion

Catering, even in its most industrialized forms, is essentially a craft industry. Standardized work methods, detailed production planning and continuous operation are the exception rather than the norm. These technical conditions are much less conducive to the application of preventive quality control than those, say, in the average food manufacturing plant. Moreover, technical factors are not the only, or even the most important considerations. The social organization of catering, its culture and its practices are hardly in keeping with an *industrialized* approach. Traditional attitudes to hygiene, the craft training of chefs and the 'partie system' act as a stubborn bulwark against any rationalizing change.

The transfer of HACCP to the catering industry has far-reaching implications, not only for hygiene but also for the way the industry is structured. Not only would that scale of change be painful, some doubt its desirability. In manufacturing industries where excessive fragmentation and labour de-skilling has already taken place, the uncritical use of Scientific Management is now under serious scrutiny. It would be ironic if these lessons went unheeded in one of the last outposts of craft production.

References

Agriculture Committee, 1989, *Salmonella in Eggs*, Vols. 1 and 2, HMSO, London.
Bauman, H. E., 1974, 'The HACCP concept and microbiological hazard categories', *Food Technology*, 28(9): pp. 30, 32, 34, 74.
Beckers, H. J., 1988, 'Microbiology and food hygiene in mass catering', *Catering & Health*, 1(1): pp. 3–5.
Bristol City Council, 1989, *Report on Listeria and Pre-cooked Chilled Foods*, January 11, Bristol.
Bryan, F. L., 1981, 'Hazard analysis of food service operations', *Food Technology*, 35(2): pp. 78–87.
Coates, G. B., 1986, *HACCP and Safety/Quality Assurance in Food Manufacture*, Society of Food Hygiene Technology, Hertfordshire.
Campden Food Preservation Research Association, 1987, *Symposium on Microbiological and Environmental Health Problems Relevant to the Food and Catering Industries*, January 19–21, Chipping Campden.
Campden Food Preservation Research Association, 1987, *Guidelines to the establishment of Hazard Analysis Critical Control Point*, Chipping Campden.
Committee on Medical Aspects, 1970, *Report on the Use of Pre-cooked Frozen Food*, HMSO.
Communicable Disease Report, 1988, *Foodborne Disease Surveillance in England and Wales: 1985*, 88/08, 26 February, Communicable Disease Surveillance Centre.
Cowell, D., 1984, *The Marketing of Services*, Heinemann Publishing, Oxford.
Department of Health, 1989, *Chilled and Frozen: Guidelines on Cook-Chill and Cook-Freeze Catering Systems*, HMSO, London.

DHSS, 1986, *The Report of the Committee of Inquiry into an Outbreak of Food Poisoning at Stanley Royd Hospital*, Cmnd 9716, HMSO, London.

Fine, S. H., 1981, *The Marketing of Ideas and Social Issues*, Praeger Division, Holt, Rinehart and Winston, New York.

Gabriel, Y., 1988, *Working Lives in Catering*, Routledge and Kegan Paul, London.

Galbraith, N. S. *et al.*, 1987, 'The changing pattern of foodborne disease in England and Wales', *Public Health*, Vol. 2, 101, pp. 319–28.

Gilbert, R. J., 1983, 'Hazards of modern foodstuffs', *Proceedings of the 14th Annual Symposium: Infection Control Nurses Association*, Lancaster, pp. 29–31.

Gilbert, R. J., 1985, 'Food poisoning problems', *Chilled Foods*, Campden Food Preservation Research Association, Chipping Campden, pp. 173–80.

Gilbert, R. J., 1987, 'Foodborne infections and intoxications: recent problems and new organisms', *Symposium on Microbiological and Environmental Health Problems Relevant to the Food and Catering Industries*, Campden Food Preservation Research Association, Chipping Campden, 19–21 January, pp. 1–22.

Gilbert, R. J. *et al.*, 1989, 'Listeria monocytogenes and chilled foods', *Lancet*, 18 February.

Glew, G., 1985, *The Effect of Catering Techniques on the Nutritional Value of Food*, Catering Research Unit, Huddersfield Polytechnic.

Hile, J. P., 1974, 'HACCP—a new approach to FDA inspections', *Food Product Development*, Vol. 8, part 1, pp. 50–2.

Hobbs, B. C., Robert, D., 1989, *Food Poisoning and Food Hygiene*, fifth edition, Edward Arnold, London.

HCTB, 1983, *Manpower Changes in the Hotel and Catering Industry*, Hotel and Catering Training Board, London.

Jones, P., 1983, 'The restaurant: a place for the quality control and product maintenance', *International Journal of Hospitality Management*, Vol. 2, No. 2, pp. 93–100.

Kerr, K. *et al.*, 1988, 'Listeria in cook-chill food', *Lancet*, ii, 2 July, pp. 37–9.

Kilsby, D. C., 1985, 'Risk analysis for microbiological safety of chill stable foods', in CFPRA, Chipping Campden, pp. 115–17.

Lewis, A., Light, N., 1988, 'A survey of cook-chill catering in the United Kingdom and the need for the extension of product shelf life', *Food Science and Technology Today*, 2(3): pp. 214–17.

Lockwood, A., 1989, 'Quality management in hotels', in Witt, S. F., Moutinho, L. (eds), *Tourism, Marketing and Management Handbook*, Prentice Hall, Hemel Hempstead.

MAFF, 1988, *Food Hygiene: Report on a Consumer Survey*, HMSO, London.

Mathews, R., 1986, 'The inspection of NHS hospitals and other premises subject to Crown immunity', *Environmental Health*, 94(9): pp. 225–30.

Munce, B. A., 1984, 'Hazard analysis critical control points and the food service industry', *Food Technology in Australia*, 36(5): pp. 214–22.

Munce, B. A., 1985, 'Microbiological data as a management tool in menu design', *Proceedings of an International Symposium on Safe Food in Airline Catering*, LSG Lufthansa Service, 13–14 February, Frankfurt.

Nightingale, M., 1985, 'The hospitality industry: defining quality for a quality assurance programme—a study of perceptions', *Service Industries Journal*, 5(1): pp. 9–22.

North, R. A. E., 1988, *The Chill Manual*, Parts I and II, Highfield Publications, Wakefield.

PHLS, 1989, 'Listeriosis update', *PHLS Microbiology Digest*, Public Health Laboratory Service, London.

Pisharoti, K. A., 1975, *Guide to the Integration of Health Education in Environmental Health Programmes*, World Health Organization, Geneva.

Roberts, D., 1984, 'Good food handling: the final line of defense against foodborne salmonella infection', *Proceedings of the International Symposium on Salmonella*, 19–20 June, New Orleans.

Roberts, D. *et al*., 1989, 'Economic impact of a nationwide outbreak of salmonellosis: cost-benefit of early intervention', *British Medical Journal*, Vol. 298, 6 May: pp. 1227–30.

Sheard, M. A., 1986, *HACCP and Microbiological Quality Assurance in Catering*, Society of Food Hygiene Technology, Hertfordshire.

Sheppard, J., 1987, *The Big Chill: A Report into the Implications of Cook-chill Catering for the Public Sector*, London Food Commission, London.

Sheppard, J., 1988(a), 'Food poisoning: the chicken comes home to roost', *Food Adulteration Handbook*, Unwin Hyman, London, pp. 234–70.

Sheppard, J., 1988(b), *The Sous Vide Handbook*, Convotherm, October, London.

Simonsen, B. *et al*., 1987, 'Prevention and control of food-borne salmonellosis through application of HACCP', *International Journal of Food Microbiology*, 4, pp. 227–47.

Skroder, P., 1988, 'Hygiene: an economic factor in catering', *Catering and Health*, 1(1): pp. 7–10.

Social Services Committee, 1989, *Food Poisoning: Listeria and Listeriosis*, HMSO, London.

Sockett, P., Stanwell-Smith, R., 1986, 'Cost analysis of use of health-care services by sporadic cases and family outbreaks of salmonella typhimurium and campylobacter infection', *Proceedings 2nd World Congress of Foodborne Infections and Intoxications*, Vol. 11, Berlin, pp. 1036–9.

Snyder, O. P., 1986, 'Applying the hazard analysis and critical control points system in food service and foodborne illness prevention', *Journal of Foodservice Systems*, 4, pp. 125–31.

Sprenger, R. A., 1988, *Hygiene for Management*, third edition, Highfield Publications, Wakefield.

Todd, E. C. D., 1985, 'Economic loss from foodborne disease and non-illness related recalls because of mishandling by food processors', *Journal of Food Protection*, 48, pp. 621–33.

WHO, 1984, *Report of the Working Group on Health Aspects of Catering*, World Health Organization, Geneva.

WHO, 1988(a), Press release on foodborne listeriosis, WHO/8, 19 February, World Health Organization, Geneva.

WHO, 1988(b), *Health Education in Food Safety*, World Health Organization, Geneva.

Wyckoff, D. D., 1984, 'New tools for achieving service quality', *Cornell HRA Quarterly*, November, pp. 77–91.

14 Technological aspects of commercial food service

M. R. Nowlis

Introduction

Restaurant managers of the 1960s could barely have imagined the impact of coming technology on their industry. Microwave ovens, electronic cash registers and irradiation processes that prolong the shelf life of fruits and vegetables for several weeks were beyond the imagination of most foodservice managers. Yet two decades later, these technological advances have significantly altered the business of selling prepared food and beverage items to a rapidly expanding consumer market. Many of the most significant developments in the restaurant industry have resulted from the need to accommodate the faster-paced and more independent life style of a young generation with high levels of disposable income. These evolutionary social and economic trends are manifested in the increasing number of working women, a growing concern for health and nutrition, changing marriage and divorce patterns, longer commuting distances between home and work and an emerging middle class in many Third World countries.

More than any other sector of the foodservice industry, American-style fast-food chains have established vast research and development departments to create new equipment, systems and menu items in an attempt to better satisfy customers' ever-changing demands. Engineers, psychologists and food scientists work together to design the means to provide cleaner facilities, friendlier service, tastier products, quicker food delivery and a greater variety of product offerings. Less apparent to the consumer are the research departments' efforts to optimize operational efficiency and maximize check average without negatively affecting customer counts. For example, in an effort to increase seating turnover during peak periods, significant attention has been devoted to the design of chairs which become subconsciously uncomfortable after a carefully determined period of time. One company has had a cash register custom built to display a 'would you like something to drink?' message on a screen to the cashier if he attempts to total an order without including a beverage. Furthermore, fast-food marketing managers have shown great regard for the science of 'psycho-economics', which attempts to evaluate the psychological aspects of product pricing. In a study sponsored by Purdue University (USA), Kreul found that several low-check restaurant companies use pricing models which assist in demand forecasting based upon the psychological effects on consumers of price length, the numerical value of first and terminal digits, menu price spread and the size and frequency of price increases (Kreul, 1982).

Other marketing efforts have assumed a more tangible form. Videotex, an instrument recently introduced in the United States and Canada, serves as a computerized video restaurant guide. Placed in high traffic areas such as airports, hotel lobbies, shopping malls and office buildings, Videotex assists consumers in locating restaurants with a desired set of criteria (Johnson, 1984). For example, by following a friendly enquiry procedure, a user can locate an inexpensive steak house serving alcoholic beverages, having a non-smoking area, accepting American Express cards and located within three kilometres of the terminal. Videotex is capable of displaying an entire page of a menu with elaborate colour graphics. To encourage use by frequent travellers, video terminals located in transportation hubs are being linked with other cities. In the near future, Videotex will be available in private homes via microcomputers (Johnson, 1984).

Just as the foodservice manager of the 1960s could not predict the sweeping developments which would drastically alter his work environment, it is difficult for his current counterpart to anticipate the effects of technological progress on the restaurant industry in the 1990s. However, it is clear that advances in the areas of robotics, genetic engineering and integrated-circuit microchip design will be major factors in determining the composition of foods served, the design of equipment used to prepare them and the way foods are paid and accounted for.

Labour input: man or machine?

One area that is likely to be the focus of considerable research is labour reduction. Restaurateurs in the industrialized countries are finding their traditional labour pool smaller and more costly. Stricter laws regulating foreign workers and an upward shift in the age structure of the workforce are strangling the supply of reasonably priced workers who, until now, have served as the human foundation of the foodservice industry. This problem has been accentuated by the rapid rise in minimum wages and social taxes as well as the passage of parental-leave laws in many countries. The On Premise Institute, a Burbank, California market research firm, estimates that the American fast-food industry is 250,000 workers short of the six million needed to keep it running smoothly (Sims, 1988).

Some countries are trying novel solutions. Singapore, for example, recently decided to raise the retirement age by five years (Anon, 1988(a)). However, these can only be considered stopgap measures. Foodservice executives will increasingly seek technological means to reduce the human input for a standard product unit.

France's largest hotel company, Accor, has installed in several of its hotels an electronic machine which allows guests to check in, pay and check out without human intervention (Luttman, 1988). Whether such a mechanism is a desirable instrument for the 'hospitality' industry is debatable. What is certain is that as airline seats, hotel rooms and restaurant meals are increasingly viewed as commodities by budget-conscious consumers, such labour saving devices will become more common. As the most labour-intensive division of the travel/lodging industry, the foodservice sector has the most to gain from automation (Palmer, 1983).

Food processors such as those manufactured by Hobart, Robot Coupe and Cuisinart, unknown 20 years ago, are standard equipment in most of today's commercial kitchens, where they chop, mix and purée in a few minutes ingredients that formerly took several hours by hand. Likewise, modern deep fryers use microchips to control and correct oil temperature, remove fry baskets after specified cooking times and automatically filter oil (Anon, 1989(a)). Similar microchips have been used to create a programmable microprocessor that controls a completely automatic dishwashing machine. By use of pneumatic prehension, the machine loads, rinses, washes, dries and unloads dishes without human assistance. Furthermore, it sorts the dishes by size and type, stacks them to a predetermined height and delivers them by means of a conveyor to heated and refrigerated units in the food production area (Anon, 1986(b)).

Arby's restaurants in the midwestern United States have installed a conveyor belt system called Vittleveyor that carries food vertically and horizontally. With as much as 50% of fast-food business coming from drive-through customers, this food delivery system allows restaurants to provide customers with multiple drive-through lanes (Sims, 1988). After placing the order at a drive-through microphone, the customer proceeds to a stall, places payment in a capsule and sends it into the restaurant. An employee then sends the order and change back to the guest by way of Vittleveyor.

Pepsico, which owns Kentucky Fried Chicken, Pizza Hut and Taco Bell, is currently test-marketing a computerized beverage dispenser which delivers a five-deciliter (sixteen-ounce) drink to guests in fifteen seconds. A cashier enters each order on a cash register, which sends a message to the dispenser to drop a cup and fill it with ice and the appropriate beverage. The drink is then automatically capped and delivered to the guest by means of a conveyor (Sims, 1988).

Modern industrial microwave ovens bear little resemblance to their household counterparts. Originally used by fast-food operations to rapidly thaw and cook convenience foods, current models with sophisticated features are being used to temper, proof, pasteurize and dry various alimentary products (Sicot, 1987). When combined with conventional heating systems such as steam injection and forced air convection, microwave ovens can increase energy efficiency up to 300%. Furthermore, they use less space and are easier to clean and maintain than traditional ovens (Sicot, 1988). The Raytheon Corporation has introduced a proof-and-bake microwave oven which operates in three steps.

Beginning with a microwave defrost cycle, followed by a proof step involving humidity and microwave energy, the process finishes with a hot air/microwave cycle. This system reduces the proofing and baking time of breads and rolls from one hour to less than 30 minutes. Due to its ability to brown meat items, the unit also shows promise for use in roasting (Swientek, 1987). Similar models can be used with most types of metals, including aluminium and have capacities up to 50 litres (45 quarts) (Anon, 1988(b)).

Humanless restaurants

Although unmanned fast-food restaurants may sound like a futuristic illusion, existing technology would allow the development of such an operation today (Mathieu, 1987). Multimedia machines, incorporating sound and full-motion video, could serve as animated menus that actively merchandize various offerings. Equipped with touch-screen terminals, customers could select desired menu items from the top part of the screen with condiments and toppings listed below (Pollack, 1988). In the foreseeable future, electronic voice interpreters could take orders and eliminate the need for manual data entry. Mechanical talking devices such as those currently used in elevators, cars and dishwashers could repeat the order and attempt to upsell and add on extras (Anon, 1988(c)).

Payment could be handled by money-changing machines which are able to distinguish between various denominations of paper currency. More likely is the increased use of smart credit and charge cards equipped with their own microchip and electronic direct debit, which immediately transfers funds from the customer's bank account to the restaurant's (Rappay, no date). This latter form of payment is already being used in some restaurants in England (Trollope, 1985).

State-of-the-art robotics have achieved a level of sophistication that makes feasible the complete *à la minute* preparation of menu items from a stored frozen state to a presentable hot meal without human assistance (Palmer, 1983). For several years, nonservo robots, also known as point-to-point or pick-and-place robots, dominated industrial applications (Condon, 1983). Although they are programmable and multifunctional, this generation of robots has greater application to continuous-line food processing than to à la carte restaurant production. Point-to-point automation lacks the flexibility and *intelligence* to accommodate the numerous variations that a single food order might require. For example, it would be difficult for a nonservo robot to process a custom order, such as a medium-rare hamburger with extra mustard and no tomato and a cola with extra ice. As the giant fast-food chains stress customized orders—such as Wendy's 256 variations of its basic hamburger and Burger King's advertising slogan, 'Have it your way'—the use of pick-and-place robots seems limited.

More recently, as microchips have become increasingly powerful and less expensive, servo robots have been employed more frequently and now outnumber their first-generation predecessors two to one. Servo robots contain apparatus that capacitate the manipulator and gripper to alter their direction in mid-air. This means their movements can follow a non-linear path (London, 1983).

Two procedures are used to program servo robots. The plug-in method requires users to communicate information by way of a data terminal. In the second method, known as walk-through, the programmer physically leads the robot's manipulator through the various movements. The robot registers the passage and repeats the sequence upon a later command. Once programmed, servo robots are able to find more efficient ways of completing their tasks and improve upon their own motions. In the near future, new chips that will be able to store information in three dimensions, in place of the two-dimensional ones being used today, will greatly enhance the power and flexibility of these machines (Bylinsky, 1988).

Servo robots could be adapted with relative ease to the production process of a typical fast-food restaurant. Equipped with capacitators, tentacles, thermometers and mechanical *eyes*, robots can actually improve upon the standardization which has been key to the success of the large fast-food chains. By determining the exact thickness of a steak, hamburger or piece of chicken and ascertaining the precise temperature of the griddle or fryer, a robot could calculate, to the second, the optimum cooking time. It could then transfer the item to a garnishing station where it would be dressed with the desired condiments and accompaniments. Wendy's 256 hamburger variations would pose no problem for such a machine; modern computers can consider and process 256,000 combinations in less than a second. The product could then be plated or wrapped and delivered to the appropriate location for service.

The applications of robotic food production are not limited to the hamburgers, fried chicken and pizza of fast-food operations. Robots could easily apply microwave and vacuum cooking methods to heat previously prepared, complex menu items. Contrary to public perception, microwave ovens have existed in some of the world's most famous kitchens for many years. More overtly, many of France's celebrated culinary heroes, including Michel Troisgros, Gaston Lenôtre, Michel Olivier and Marc Meneau, have enthusiastically embraced vacuum cooking, a method in which airtight plastic pouches of prepared food are heated by steam, hot water or microwave (Anon, 1988(d)). Roger Yaseen, president of the *Chaîne des Rôtisseurs*, an international gastronomic society, says of vacuum cooking: 'The results are outstanding, absolute perfection' (Fabricant, 1985). Although initial preparation in a commissary would probably involve human input, complete dishes could be vacuum packed and shipped directly to units or flash frozen and stored for future use. Even nonservo robots could then heat and plate food to order.

Presumably high check-average restaurants would still have to employ dining room service personnel. Robots may be faster and more efficient than humans, but they have not yet learned to smile and warmly converse with customers.

The use of robots in foodservice establishments is not an unrealistic fantasy. There are approximately 200,000 robots currently being used for diverse industrial applications (Perrin, 1988) and the simpler models can be purchased for as little as US$5,000. The Sony Corporation, one of numerous companies selling robotic automation systems, had sales of $50 million in the US in 1988. By 1991, they expect that figure to rise to $100 million (Anon, 1988(e)).

These robots are not just acting as assemblers and welders in factories. They are replacing draftsmen in engineering firms and will soon be programming computers. They are smart and can consistently beat human champions at chess, checkers and backgammon (Perrin, 1986). Walking robots that can negotiate staircases and obstacles have existed for some time. Current research is focusing on providing these machines with sight by use of lasers, ultra-sound and infrared light. Furthermore, some advanced robots have been equipped with tactile sensors which provide a sense of feel by using extremely small and dense microchips as touch sensors (Anon, 1988(f)). It is clear that the state of the art in robotics is beyond the level necessary to completely automate a typical fast-food restaurant.

The primary impediment to greater automation, in the foodservice industry is the high cost of development. Yet for a large chain organization, the decision not to invest in automation research may be more expensive. A typical fast-food unit disburses in excess of 25% of its revenue on labour-related expenses. The average hourly wage of restaurant workers is three times what it was 20 years ago, while the cost per hour to operate and pay for an assembly-line robot has remained about the same (Condon, 1983).

Consider the McDonalds Corporation, with more than 10,500 units, each employing 40 to 80 people. With most robots replacing three to five human workers, some elementary mathematics provide an idea of the potential cost savings. McDonalds would need only to invest a diminutive portion of its US$16 billion in annual revenue to develop an entirely automated outlet.

This chapter will not attempt to address the numerous social issues created by technological advancement. The foodservice industry is one of the world's largest employers. It provides millions of jobs, many of which require little or no formal skills. Rapid, widespread automation of the restaurant industry would displace enormous numbers of workers who might have difficulty obtaining other employment. Although the new technology described here would most likely be phased in over an extended time period, the author believes that foodservice executives have a moral obligation to find just solutions to whatever unemployment problems may be created by automation.

Raw product manipulation

Scientific advancement will not be limited to menu item production. Progress in the areas of agriculture, aquaculture and primary food processing will have an immense impact on the variety, composition and availability of the products served in restaurants. For example, food costs will be cut significantly by the development of crops which 'fix' their own nitrogen or are perennial.

Supplies of grain-fed, farm-raised fish and shellfish will largely eliminate cyclical gluts and fluctuating prices in the seafood market. A significant proportion of the salmon, trout, catfish, lobster, crayfish, clams, oysters and mussels in foodservice establishments today are commercially raised. Furthermore, the technology used to produce *surimi*, a crab substitute, will be applied to develop other shellfish-like products, notably, a scallop alternative (la Bigne, 1988(a)).

Soy products such as tofu (coagulated soy milk) will become increasingly popular as the result of a growing world-wide interest in nutrition and in Asian cuisines (la Bigne, 1988(b)). Analogues produced from texturized wheat, peanut and cottonseed will be indistinguishable from meat.

Animal hybrids such as beefalo will provide high-protein, low-fat meat that cooks 30% faster than beef and costs 25 to 40% less (Moraczewski, 1975). Researchers at the National Autonomous University of Mexico have bred super-productive mini cows that give four times as much milk per kilo as a normal cow. Standing 70 centimetres (27 inches) tall and weighing 135 kilos (300 pounds) when full-grown, ten of these bovine can survive on just 1.2 hectares (three acres) of grazing land (Orme, 1987).

Veterinary biotechnology has made great strides in developing genetically engineered vaccines which will largely eliminate diseases among domestic animals. By deciphering the interactions of the animal's own healing substances and the underlying causes of disease, researchers have been able to develop novel drugs and methods of treatment. These breakthroughs will result in lower prices and more stable supplies of meat and dairy stuffs.

A trend towards health-oriented life styles and consumption behaviour has led food scientists to develop numerous calorie-free and low-cholesterol food products. For example, a no-calorie, no-nutrient flour substitute called *fluffy cellulose* has recently been developed by the United States Department of Agriculture. Made from wheat bran, corn bran or citrus pulp, this tasteless, odourless fibre can be used to produce low-calorie cakes, breads or other flour-based products. Although the technology to produce fluffy cellulose has existed for years, recent consumer interest in high-fibre/low-calorie diets prompted its development (Hollie, 1987).

Left-handed sugars derived from plantains, seaweed, algae and sugar beets will largely replace conventional sweetners. L-sugars are not substitutes but real sugars which cannot be metabolized and thus do not provide calories nor contribute to tooth decay (Flax, 1985).

Proctor and Gamble researchers have developed a similar non-metabolizable fat that could be used to produce butter, salad oil or shortening. Made from sucrose polyester and called *olestra* by P&G, it passes through the body without entering the bloodstream and consequently, leaves no cholesterol deposits (Bock, 1987).

Rosemary Farms, a Santa Maria, California egg producer, has recently begun production of a low-cholesterol egg. The California Department of Food and Agriculture has confirmed that the egg, which is produced by feeding hens a special diet, contains only 125 milligrams of cholesterol. This represents less than 45% of the cholesterol level of a normal egg (Anon, 1988(g)). Although they currently cost 30% more than regular eggs (Sheraton, 1988), prices are expected to drop as production increases.

In addition to the manipulation of raw nutrients to produce new products, fresh foods will increasingly be treated by irradiation and other processes to arrest germination and diminish their perishability (la Bigne, 1987). In spite of its troubling name, irradiation has been declared safe by many health author-ities. By bathing foods with X and gamma rays, irradiation stops potatoes and onions from sprouting and retards the ripening of fruit while leaving a minute amount of residual radiation in the treated food (Anon, 1985). Some proponents claim that by killing bacteria in meat, poultry and fish, irradiation actually renders food healthier by reducing the possibility of salmonella infec-tion, which is responsible for 70% of all food poisoning (Trollope, 1986). In Japan, 30,000 tons of irradiated food will be sold this year.

The future

Some futurologists foresee the maturation and eventual decline of the tradi-tional restaurant industry. They point to the increasing sales of vitamin tablets and microwavable convenience foods in arguing that the accelerating pace of contemporary life places a priority on food as *fuel* over food for enjoyment (Floriot, 1988). Indeed, a Japanese company has introduced a sixteen-gram edible paper bar that contains all of the necessary calories and nutrients of a complete repast. The credit-card-size *meal* is billed as '100% natural' and is available in fourteen flavours, including beef, salmon, apple, coffee and chocolate. Originally called 'film food' and subsequently upgraded to the more elegant French 'papier', it has proved so popular that sales are limited to three per customer. The company expects to be selling almost a million units a month in the near future.

More importantly, the rate of population growth—a critical factor in the expansion of the foodservice industry—is currently less than 1% in many industrialized countries and is expected to decline further (Lee, 1987). Micro-wave ovens, which reduce meal preparation time to a matter of a few minutes, are currently installed in 65% of households in the United States, Canada and Japan (Sicot, 1988). The Pillsbury Corporation predicts that by 1990, this figure will rise to 90% in North America. Other kitchen technology, such as dishwashers and Teflon, are making home meal preparation simpler and less time-consuming (Lee, 1987).

But perhaps the strongest factor countering the trend towards eating out is television and, more recently, VCRs. These home-enertainment centres provide good reasons not to go out and will increasingly compete for con-sumers' leisure time.

In spite of such pessimistic observations, the foodservice industry in most countries is strong and shows great promise for the future. Total restaurant sales in the US have grown at 10% per year for the last ten years and at an average of 9% per annum for the last 25. Of the $500 billion spent on food in the United States this year, more than 40% will be spent on meals eaten away from home (National Restaurant Association, 1987). Statistics show that by the year 2000, Americans may be spending more money on meals consumed in foodservice establishments than on those eaten at home.

Regardless of major concerns about the economy and labour regulations, the restaurant industry outpaces others by a wide margin in return on equity, sales growth and earnings per share. During the October 1987 stock market crash, restaurant industry stocks fared significantly better than the Dow Jones Industrial Average and the S&P 500 (Anon, 1988(h)).

Opportunities in the 1990s will abound, most notably in the off-premises/take-out market and in the continued subdivision of health care facilities. Nutritioneering and breakfast will play key roles in retaurant firms' overall strategies. Convenience stores and fast-food firms will continue to develop joint units, and hotels, particularly economy and all-suite properties, will further define their guests' food needs and develop concepts to meet them.

However, competition will increase and product life cycles will be shortened by the intensive development of specific markets and submarkets. Ease of product duplication will reduce barriers to market penetration. Restaurant patrons will exhibit pluralistic consumption behaviour, 'inhaling' their lunch at a fast-food unit and leisurely spending the evening at an expensive up-scale restaurant. In free market economies, the large restaurant chains will increase their dominance through superior marketing and operational expertise (Hart et al., 1984). Creativity, quality, standardization, value and cost control will be the key words of the 1990s.

The coming decade will offer great opportunities in the restaurant industry, but many of the criteria for success will involve technological solutions to operational problems. For the commercial foodservice sector, the technological revolution is only beginning.

References

Anon. 1985, 'Traitement ionisant des aliments', *Les Cahiers du Comité Permanent de al Restauration Collective*, October 1985, pp. L, LI.

Anon. 1986a, 'A byte in the kitchen', *Caterer & Hotelkeeper*, 7 August 1986(a), pp. 58–9.

Anon. 1986b, 'Avant-première: le lave-vaisselle pneumatique', *Neo-Restauration Hôtellerie Collectivités*, September 1986(b).

Anon. 1987, *National Restaurant Association Pocket Factbook*, 1987, p. 1.

Anon. 1988a, 'Singapore concerned about a chronic labour shortage and an ageing population', *International Herald Tribune*, Paris, 15 September 1988(a), p. 5.

Anon. 1988b, 'Des appareils multi-fonctions', *Revue Technique des Hôtels et Restaurants*, March 1988(b).

Anon. 1988c, 'Machines that talk fail to sell in US', *International Herald Tribune*, Paris, 14 September, 1988(c), p. 3.

Anon. 1988d, 'Technologie nouvelle pour nouvelles mentalités', *Néo-Restauration*, February 1988(d), p. 66.

Anon. 1988e, 'Sony sells robotics in the US', *International Herald Tribune*, Paris, 9 September 1988(e), p. 12.

Anon. 1988f, 'Teaching robots touch and tininess', *The Economist*, 15 October 1988(f), pp. 121–4.

Anon. 1988g, 'A lower-cholesterol egg', *International Herald Tribune*, Paris, 21 October, 1988(g).

Anon. 1988h, '1988 annual forecast', *Restaurant & Institutions*, 8 January 1988(h), p. 45.

Ghislaine Le Petit-de la Bigne, 1987, 'Qui a peur de l'ionisation?', *Revue Technique des Hôtels et Restaurants*, October 1987, pp. 49–54.

Ghislaine Le Petit-de la Bigne, 1988a, 'La pâte à tout faire', *Revue Technique des Hôtels et Restaurants: Supplément Produits & Boissons*, April 1988(a), pp. 3–6.

Ghislaine Le Petit-de la Bigne, 1988b, 'Un produit venu d'ailleurs', *Revue Technique des Hôtels et Restaurants: Supplément Produits & Boissons*, March 1988(b), pp. 2–3.

Bock, G., 1987, 'Will fake fat yield plump profits?', *Time*, 25 May, p. 41.

Bylinsky, G., 1988, 'Technology in the year 2000', *Fortune*, 18 July, p. 94.

Condon, M., 1983, 'Straight talk about robots', *Training and Development Journal*, November, p. 16.

Fabricant, F., 1985, 'Plastic pouches gain cachet', *New York Times*, 1 May, p. 21.

Flax, S., 1985, 'It's sugar, all right, but it's not fattening', *Fortune*, 9 December.

Floriot, J.-L., 1988, 'Tradition gastronomique et innovation', Fondation Brillat-Savarin, Belley, France, 23 September.

Hart, C. W., Casserly, G., Lawless, M., 1984, 'The product life cycle: how useful?', *Cornell HRA Quarterly*, November, p. 62.

Hollie, P. G., 1987, 'Piece-of-cake dieting', *New York Times*, 18 January.

Johnson, S. C., 1984, 'Dining out with computers', *Restaurant Hospitality*, pp. 150–4.

Kreul, L. M., 1982, 'Magic numbers: Psychological aspects of menu pricing', *The Cornell HRA Quarterly*, pp. 70–5.

Luttman, J.-C., 1988, 'Formule 1', Institut de Management Hôtelier International, Cergy-Pontoise, France, 8 January.

Mathieu, A., 1987, 'Restauration automatique aux Pays-Bas, ca marche', *Néo-Restauration*, pp. 99–102.

Moraczewski, B., 1975, 'Is there home on your range for beefalo?', *Big Farmer*, January.

Orme, W. A. Jr., 1987, 'Mexico's designer cows: only the moo is the same', *International Herald Tribune*, Paris, 5 June, p. 1.

Palmer, J., 1983, 'Automatic food service: the meal of the future?', *The Cornell HRA Quarterly*, May, pp. 63–70.

Perrin, N., 1986, 'Do we really want robots to do all our dirty work?', *International Herald Tribune*, Paris, 18 September, p. 7.

Pollack, A., 1988, 'Industry asks what is next?', *International Herald Tribune*, Paris, 14 October 1988, p. 15.

Rappay, O., (undated), 'La monnaie révolutionnaire', *Gastronomie & Tourisme*, p. 57.

Sheraton, M., 1988, 'Something to cluck about', *Time*, 21 November.

Sicot, D., 1987, 'Micro-ondes, les minutes comptent', *Néo-Restauration*, pp. 90, 92, 95.

Sicot, D., 1988, 'Micro-ondes, une demande tous azimuts', *Néo-Restauration*, pp. 89, 90, 94.

Sims, C., 1988, 'Robots to make fast food chains still faster', *The New York Times*, 24 August, p. D5.

Swientek, R. J., 1987, 'Industrial microwave applications accelerate in food industry', *Food Processing*, pp. 136–9.

Trollope, K., 1985, 'Will cashless payment catch on in restaurants?', *Caterer & Hotelkeeper*, 7 November, p. 19.

Trollope, K., 1986, 'Irradiation fears', *Caterer & Hotelkeeper*, 17 April, p. 19.